HONKY-TONKS

HONKY-TONKS

★ Guide to ★ *Country Dancin' and Romancin'* ★

Eileen Sisk

HarperCollins*West*
An Imprint of HarperCollins*Publishers*

FIRST EDITION

Library of Congress Cataloging-in-Publication Data:
Sisk, Eileen.
Honky-tonks : guide to country dancin' and romancin' / Eileen Sisk. – 1st ed.
p. cm.
ISBN 0-06-258609-2
1. Country dance–West (U.S.) 2. Country dance–West (U.S.)–Directories.
I. Title.
GV1624.W35S47 1995 95-19873
793.3'4–dc20 CIP

95 96 97 98 99 ❖ RRD(H) 10 9 8 7 6 5 4 3 2 1

For Jeff and Doug, my legacies

and

For honky-tonk hearts everywhere

Contents

Preface

DRIVING UP to the Ken Lance Sports Arena and Dance Pavilion just outside of Ada, Oklahoma, I couldn't help but notice the trees. Their thick trunks twisted and turned until they reached the point where they branched out into long, lithe limbs whose leaves provided shade for grazing livestock. These trees, I thought, possessed great character and strength, and I wondered what kind they were. Having grown up in the godforsaken desert of Nevada, I have never professed to know much about trees, and, having been a journalist most of my adult life, I have never been afraid to ask a basic question. So I inquired.

"Oh, those. Those are just old oaks," Ken said, with the air of someone who has taken them for granted all his life. They were there when Ken bought the place and will likely be there long after he moves on.

I encountered other oak trees in my honky-tonk travels, but it wasn't until I saw the massive one in front of the Broken Spoke in Austin, Texas, that I realized that the oak, long a symbol of strength and longevity, could easily symbolize the cowboy honky-tonks I was profiling for this book. Like the oaks, the honky-tonks have great character and have withstood the test of time. Like the gnarled trunks, these honky-tonks may not be much to look at, but they are firmly rooted in tradition. They are secure in knowing they serve a vital purpose and that if not for them their fancier offshoots would not exist.

Oaks do more than supply imagery, however. Most notably they have provided the wood for many a dance-hall floor. They also have lent their name to some establishments, such as the Post Oak Ranch in Houston and Austin. And for clubs like Ken Lance's and the Broken Spoke, they are there for whatever reason–to shade, to landscape, or maybe just to inspire.

Trees aside, I discovered other common threads while researching this book. In addition to several dirt parking lots and the requisite cowboys, "guitars, Cadillacs, and hillbilly music" that Dwight Yoakam sings about, I found that many honky-tonk owners are singers and songwriters who love country music and have always dreamed of having their own venue. Honky-tonk owners also love horses and many raise thoroughbreds. Growth is another thing honky-tonks have in common: Walls are knocked out and clubs expand every which way to accommodate the ever-growing number of honky-tonkers.

PREFACE

As in life, the only constant in the honky-tonk business is change. In writing this book I wanted to document the history and the mystery surrounding some of the older honky-tonks before they vanished altogether or became yet another "Disco Gone Dallas." I also wanted to provide a comprehensive directory of Country Clubs, even though they are difficult to track, for other natural-born honky-tonkers. You see, living in the East has brought out the West in me. Simply by pulling on a pair of boots I can return to my western roots. On any given weekend I can be found hanging out at any number of honky-tonks, listening to country music and dancing away my frustrations. In a sense I am able to go "home" without having to leave the area. These Country Clubs have provided me respite from the subway-rat race and the rampant careerism of the gray-flanneled minions. Come Monday, I am better able to face third-world traffic patterns and life in the concrete jungle. I know I am not alone. It is the age of the suburban cowboy, and thousands of people like me are finding that there is no greater stress reliever than a good old boot-stomping honky-tonk where they can hoot, holler, and sweat bullets while dancing to the best of the West.

In 1990 I wrote an essay for the "Outlook" section of the *Washington Post* called "Squares Dance: Why We're a Country Capital" that explored the country music and dance phenomenon in the Washington area; then-President Bush wrote an accompanying piece about what country music meant to him. Since those articles ran, membership in this informal Country Club has grown beyond everyone's expectations–and not just in the nation's capital. Consider that the number of adults who listen to country music has almost tripled in a decade to forty-two percent of the U.S. population. At this writing, more than sixty-seven million Americans tune in weekly to one of the nation's 2,600 country radio stations, which rank first in fifty-seven of the top one hundred radio markets, according to the Country Music Association (CMA). And these stations draw the most listeners in urban areas, specifically New York City, Los Angeles, Chicago, and San Francisco, in that order. The country phenomenon is also growing overseas. Country Music Television signed up 8.4 million subscribers when it went international in 1992, Voice of America broadcasts a weekly country music program to forty-seven countries, and Tokyo has a twenty-four-hour-a-day country radio station with satellite transmission to Southeast Asia.

Conventional wisdom tells us that what goes up, must come down, however. So does this mean the current love of country will wane? Music, like life, is cyclical, but as long as both are around there will be country songs. Standard country anthems such as Merle Haggard's "Silver Wings" and the two-step will prevail in spite of catchy novelty tunes like Billy Ray Cyrus's "Achy Breaky Heart" and its namesake line dance. To me, what some folks call a country craze is not so much a fad as it is a trend, driven by people who are listening and dancing to more meaningful music in their search for a more meaningful lifestyle.

Country music is a thread that is woven throughout the fabric of these honky-tonks, our lives, and our nation. The lyrics tell our stories, both good and bad, something we all can relate to. It is not just about drinking, counting flowers on the wall, or cheating hearts, but about happiness, love, faithfulness, values, and so on. In the 1940s, country music was referred to as the white man's blues because it told the trials and tribulations of an American people so well. The music has evolved over the years, most recently from a traditional retreat in the 1980s to a social-consciousness raising in the 1990s. Songs now tackle such serious subjects as abuse, alcoholism, and AIDS. No matter. It is still about life and the human experience. The virtual unintelligibility of heavy metal and rap music may be another reason folks convert to country. Liberty Records president Jimmy Bowen told *Time* magazine, "Thank God for rap. Every morning when they play that stuff people come running to us." Proponents say this trend will only gain momentum as country cable and radio stations penetrate more markets. Forecasters contend that popular culture in the next century will continue to be influenced by western themes. So settle in folks, it looks as if the cowboy way is in for the long haul.

Over the years the honky-tonk, like country music, has changed. Its television image has come a long way from the rough and rowdy Longbranch Saloon in *Gunsmoke* to the crowded dance floor of the Nashville Network's White Horse Cafe on *Club Dance*. There is less fighting and drinking and more dancing and romancing, although all are essential elements of any cowboy bar worth its jukebox.

So whenever I travel, I search out the local honky-tonks, keeping notes on each one and the people I meet. Much of the information for Part One of this book was gathered from 1989 to 1994. Most of the information for Parts Two and Three was gathered between 1989 and 1995. I made three trips between 1991 and 1993, stopping in Arizona, Colorado, New Mexico, Oklahoma, and Texas. In the summer of 1994, I returned to those states and eight others as well. In the course of six weeks I hand-delivered many of the more than five hundred surveys circulated for this project, tuned in to the rhythm of the road–driving more than eight thousand miles and averaging 1,350 miles a week–and retired one pair of boots. I took one last trip to Texas in December 1994. Along the way I was chauffeur, dancer, honky-tonker, photographer, and reporter. I talked to people at gas stations, stores, and laundromats about their favorite honky-tonks. I also asked dancers, relatives, and friends for their recommendations. Anyone in boots, jeans, or a cowboy hat was fair game. I interviewed club owners, musicians, bartenders, and patrons. And I danced with as many people–women included–as possible so I could paint a realistic word portrait of each club. Because, you see, honky-tonking is highly subjective. What appeals to me may not appeal to someone else. I sought to represent the interests of everyone; so the clubs range from the very traditional to the one that spawned the country disco trend.

Even though I have lived in the East since 1980, I have never lost the candor endemic to westerners. So in writing my perceptions and impressions, I may offend some honky-tonks while seemingly glorifying others, but know that no harm is intended and that I do not profess to know it all. Hopefully you will come away a little more enlightened and entertained after reading *Honky-Tonks.* Feel free to form your own opinions by visiting these clubs yourself. If you aren't already, you may find yourself hooked on country.

To make this book work best for you:

- ⋆ Part One is a honky-tonk primer of sorts, in which you can learn almost everything you need to know to survive in a cowboy bar. It provides the background and basics for honky-tonking, and should save you many an embarrassing moment if you are new to the scene.
- ⋆ Part Two profiles twenty-nine clubs in sixteen states that have demonstrated longevity. The clubs featured here are among those that best deserve the "Honky-Tonk Seal of Approval" for keeping it country. The chapters are organized alphabetically by state and by club. Directions and tips on dress code, dance dynamics, and music format follow each address and phone number. Hours are also provided, but like cover charges they do change, often without warning.
- ⋆ Part Three is designed to be a user-friendly directory of close to a thousand clubs in all fifty states and the District of Columbia. It is alphabetized by state, city, and honky-tonk, and should serve as an indispensable guide to any boot-scooting traveler. There may be more information on some clubs than others, depending on which ones received, completed, and returned my survey. In any event, there should be more than enough to choose from that most venerable of all American institutions, the honky-tonk.

Eileen Sisk
Bena, Virginia
January 10, 1995

Acknowledgments

ONE PERSON could never be solely responsible for a book that covers as much ground as this one does. I am indebted to many, but for brevity's sake will mention those who especially made a difference. The following have my deepest gratitude for the following reasons:

God for the West.

Cowboys, just because.

Texas for the smoothest two-steppers on Earth.

My agent, Denise Stinson, and Harper editor Shirley Christine for believing in me and this book. Also, Harper editors Beth Weber for seeing things through, and Lisa Zuniga Carlsen for a Texan's touch.

Sam Mellar for mailing my boots and sticking by me.

All my children, Jeffrey Tetreault for loading hundreds of honky-tonk entries into the database, Douglas Tetreault for making copies and keeping my office clean, BrieAnn Mellar for highlighting honky-tonk names, and Kendra Mellar for doing more than her share of the chores.

My colleagues at the *Washington Post* who helped chart my course over the years, especially Jeff Frank for being a "bridesmaid" and seeing yet another essay to book form; Jodie Allen, Kitty Chism, Janet Duckworth, Linda Halsey, and Audrey Wennblom for running my stories; Carl Kramer for stepping in where my dad left off; Mason McAllister and Lisa McAllister (no relation) for no special reason except they are the best; Carol Guzy for shooting for the first proposal; Mark Finkenstaedt for the prints and making me look good; Joel Garreau, Kent Jenkins, Frank Johnston, and Bob Reeder for their kindred spirits; Dennis Slazer for "The Dance"; and Billy Mills for calling me "Nevada" and never letting me forget who I am.

The honky-tonks–too many to mention–and the people behind them, especially Lois Adair, L. C. Agnew, Mike Amburn, Bill Bachand, Arkey Blue, Dan Burris, Jim Butler, Blake Dowen, Vince Dudenhofer, Roger Dudley, Rhonda Gore-Scott, Herb Graham, Mikal Hardin, Ken Lance, Susan Lewis, Hank and Sherry Moore, Mary Jane Nalley, Jason Palumbo, Fred Reiser, Bob Rustigian, Bruce Ruth, Trudy Walters, James and Annetta White, Martin Zanzucchi, Betty Zeller, and Tadeus Zubricki. Extraspecial recognition goes to Johnny Lemmons of Graham Brothers for going a two-step above the rest and to Pam Minick for being the coolest cowgirl ever.

The makers of the music–both great and small–especially Bob Bice, Arkey Blue, Pete and Jennifer Cowett, Alvin Crow, Bill Johnson, Chris LeDoux, Dennis Lord, Christian Miller, Gilford Sisk, Chad Watson, and Michelle Wright.

The country dance family for sharing tips and places to dance, especially Mark Benjes, Sophie Hamilton, Laurie Kral, Johanna Lynch, Dick and Geneva Matteis, Wally Quinn, Bill Ray, Tom Scherer, Rhonda Shotts, Stacy Sweat, Lloyd Thompson, Ron and Sally Threlfall, "Skip" Wilson, and June Woodall.

My Nashville contingent, John-Paul Daniel, Cynthia Dodson, Lynn Schults, and Jeff Walker.

Those who made a difference on the dance floor, especially Scott Beaty, Bobby Burrell, Steve Charles, Joe Dickens, "Doc" Frank Nuanes, Jim Horton, Johnny Lemmons, Michael Naughton, Tom Scherer, Bobby Schleif, and Evan Williams.

All those whose paths crossed mine, especially the Washington state trooper who didn't give me a ticket and tried to find me a room in the inn when there was none; "Red" for taking me where no others could go; June Roberts for her wisdom; Scott Beaty for sheltering me from the storm; Greg Friend for the fading flower; Carl Johnson for fixing my laptop on the airplane; all the Chambers of Commerce for the maps; Mary Ellen Duerr, Mitch Henley, and Dave Loose for the honky-tonk tips; Paul Holper for the prayer; Whitley Dresser and Sue Spencer for helping out along the way; Janet Scharfstein and Jay Posklensky for the film; Rick Antony, Ken Ellsworth, Paul Gero, Glenn Miller, and Terry Welling for shooting; Rick Antony and Shirley Aaen for the film and honky-tonk tips; Gene Chandler for his "spiritual" knowledge; my mother and stepfather, Susan and Carl Shellenbarger, for their love, mailing my boots, taking photos, rounding up logos, stuffing envelopes, and overall moral support.

Everyone who provided gas, food or lodging for me along the way, especially Sam Mellar, Scott Beaty, Bob Bice, Shirley Christine, Josh Friedman, Greg Friend, Joe and Kevin Haag, Loriann and David Hoffmann, Paul Holper, Johnny Lemmons, Lee Marmon, Pam Minick, B. J. Monroe, Mary Jane Nalley, Joan Remington, Carl and Susan Shellenbarger, Tom Scherer, Harriet and Fred Shipman, Hank and Kristen Sisk, Ralph and Diane Sisk, Brenda and Bobby Stephens, Robin Webb, and Roland, the Cajun "chef."

And Sam Mellar, just because.

Introduction

Welcome to the Country Club

A FEW YEARS AGO, after a night of boot-scooting, a handful of us diehards was eating home fries and eggs-over-easy at a Denny's in a suburb of Washington, D.C. There was a lull in the conversation until a recent divorcé announced quite matter-of-factly that all he ever wanted to be was "poor white trash." Having made his fortune early in life allows this fortysomething to pursue guilty pleasures like hanging out in honky-tonks; wearing short-sleeved, snap-button shirts; and dancing his boots off. I was taken aback by his comment. What was this White Trash Envy? I thought. Why did this man, who seemingly had it all, aspire to be what I had spent my life trying to escape? I wondered if there were others who felt the same way. I began asking people like him–successful, educated, well-to-do–why they traded white-collar days for blue-collar nights. Why, I wanted to know, did these upper-middle-class folks yearn for membership in the Country Club?

I discovered this Redneck Renaissance has as much to do with lifestyle as it does with dancing and music. Call it the "City Slicker Syndrome." Cowboys are viewed as people who eschew the material for the less tangible things in life; they believe in hard work, family, loyalty, and love. They symbolize all that is strong, honest, and good about this country.

This cowboy mystique is so deeply ingrained in our heritage that other countries still view the United States as being a cowboy culture. There has been much debate about what a cowboy is and isn't. One school of thought argues that only working cowboys on ranches are real cowboys, while rodeo cowboys are mere athletes. In this book, however, "cowboy" is used in a generic sense and the only differentiation is between working and rodeo cowboys vs. disco and drugstore cowboys.

As rancher and cowboy Don Brown of Livermore, California, says, "Being a real cowboy has a lot to do with how you were raised, values and such." But as long as you acquire the values at some point, membership in the Country Club is not exclusive. It accepts people of all ages, races, and walks of life. There are few entrance requirements, just a dress code and a code by which to live. Here there is no generation gap (where else but in a honky-tonk can you find twentysomethings dancing with ninetysomethings and thinking nothing of it?) and people are generally color blind, except, perhaps, some of the good old boys. We have a common bond, the love of country; and the music is the message. It permeates every aspect of our lives. As Dennis Lord, who cowrote "Country Club," the song that made Travis Tritt famous, says, "The music is my passion, whether I am writing songs or practicing law . . . and as a lifetime member [of the Country Club], I alternate between navy blue suits and blue jeans with a sports coat. Either way though, it's with a pair of boots–always with boots."

For starters, I come from a long line of white trash (which I say in a most affectionate sense). In fact, my family holds a charter membership in the Country Club–and we have more than paid our membership dues. My life has been like many a country song. I come from a large family of small means. I have worked hard and loved hard, and have experienced the happiness and fulfillment that comes from knowing that I have always given my best. I also have felt my share of loss, loneliness, and pain. So much so that a musician friend of mine once joked that he was going to write a song and call it: "Life Ain't Easy for a Girl Named Eileen." No, it hasn't been easy, but it's been one heck of a ride.

My father, Hugh Albert Sisk, was a true "Okie from Muskogee," as the Merle Haggard song says. His biggest dream in life was to own a pickup truck–a dream he did not realize until late in life. Dad was as much a cowboy as anyone back then. A slight man, he used to wear his spurs backward so no one would mess with him, which earned him a reputation and a nickname–Hugh Buck. Nicknames are big in the Country Club. For example, I have a shirttail aunt we call BoPeep, and my brother, Gilford–a sometime bull rider, sometime country singer–has held a lifelong passion for Hank Williams Sr. that prompted him to nickname his only son after the singer. My nephew's real name is John Henry, but he is and always has been "Hank" to everyone who knows him.

I was born in Henderson, Nevada, the eighth in a family of ten children, just a couple of months before Hank Williams died. We didn't have much. My dad, who had picked up the electrical trade, was out of work off and on. Eventually we homesteaded land outside of town and built a house that we lived in while it was still under construction. We came to add on a lean-to porch to house the old woodstove on which my mother cooked Sunday breakfasts and holiday dinners. Poke salad, mustard and beet greens, fried green tomatoes, okra, and pinto beans were staples of our diet. We raised our own chickens. There were two kinds of salad dressing: mayonnaise or a mixture of ketchup and mayonnaise, my father's favorite. The only cheese I ever knew existed was Velveeta. I wore hand-me-downs and my mother sewed most all my other clothes. We had fences made of chicken wire, a broken-down truck, and piles of "stuff" in our yard. "Stuff" can be defined only as a collection of things or parts, working or nonworking, that somehow got where it was but nobody knows when or how. Oh, and you could never throw any of it out because you never knew when you might need it.

The western way of life was ingrained in me at an early age. Every year us kids dressed up like cowboys or Indians to watch the kick-off parade of Helldorado Days on Fremont Street in Las Vegas; then we'd head over to the old Cashman Field to watch the rodeo at night. It was a necessary extravagance for us, and Helldorado only came around once a year.

We had a black-and-white television on which we watched a lot of westerns. There were John Wayne and Randolph Scott movies and TV shows like *The 20-Mule Team Borax Show, The Rifleman, The Virginian, Rawhide, Maverick, Paladin, Gunsmoke, Bonanza,* and more. On Saturday nights we watched *Hee Haw,* not *The Lawrence Welk Show.*

Like his father before him, my father taught me the work ethic when I was no more than four. He'd take me out in his old green Chevy to scavenge construction sites for pieces of copper wire that we would take home, burn off the insulation, and then sell as scrap. While we worked, his car radio provided a steady soundtrack of Hank Williams Sr., Hank Thompson, Lefty Frizzell, Marty Robbins, Tammy Wynette, Loretta Lynn, and others. If we had an especially good day, he would buy me an "orange sody" and then give me a shiny new silver dollar to keep.

Every Saturday, our day of worship, hymns sung by Tennessee Ernie Ford were the only music in our house from sunup to sundown. My second oldest brother, Tom, noted that my father "always had a mess of kids around him." Although my dad was a man of few words, we knew he cared about us and that we were valued. Dad also felt it was important for his second bunch of kids to know the first bunch. There was no such thing as "half" brothers or sisters, only whole. He made sure we were all connected. So on many Saturday afternoons we'd go to visit Tom, who boarded our horse, Tex, and who raised Appaloosas on the other side of town. On the half-hour drive to Tom's we'd go past the Silver Dollar, which I would stare at from the car window. My mother told me it used to be called the Saddle Club, and I longed to know what it was like inside–a thought I never dared share with my strict, religious parents. More than thirty years would pass before I would be able to find out what went on behind that old honky-tonk's heavy wooden doors.

I have two-stepped my way in and out of scores of honky-tonks, witnessing firsthand how people conduct their social rituals. Call me the Margaret Mead of honky-tonks. In this microcosm of society there exists a hierarchy of sorts, as well as regional differences in dance, dress, and demeanor. There is also a feeling of family among the regulars, and honky-tonks are "home" for many. At Arkey Blue's Silver Dollar, manager Sharon Cabiness says, "We don't have customers, just friends and family." And finally, there is an unspoken code of rules that can get a bit confusing for someone new to honky-tonking. Hopefully this guide will clarify things for the uninitiated.

With time, members of the Country Club appear to develop a spiritual fervor for the music and dancing that makes it seem more like a religion than just another passing fancy. It is no accident that Nashville's Ryman Auditorium, original home of the Grand Ole Opry, is called the "Mother Church." Country dancer Jake Willingham, a retired courier for NBC, says it best: "We are disciples of the two-step; our only commandment being: Thou shalt not disco." There is something comforting about knowing that no matter where we are or where we are headed, honky-tonks and country music will be there for us–something soothing and familiar in a high-speed, high-tech era. As the legendary Johnny Cash once said, "Country music will never make a comeback because it will never be gone." It not only speaks to us, but it is also easy on the ears, has a beat, and you can dance to it–the old-fashioned way, a man and a woman, together. Thus the music has sparked a wildfire interest in country dance and a renewed interest in the honky-tonk, which, like it or not, is American culture at its best–and sometimes its worst.

PART ONE

Background and Basics

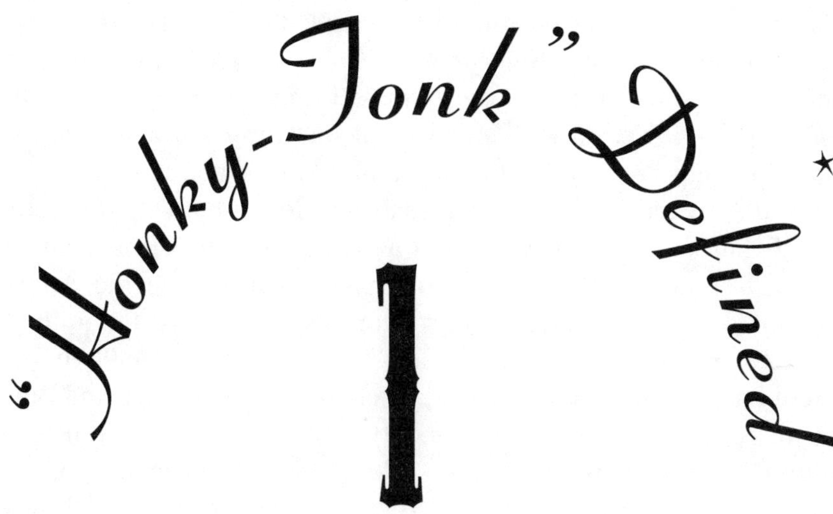

1 "Honky-Tonk" Defined

Through the years there have been countless references to honky-tonks in newspapers, magazines, books, and songs. American literary icons Carl Sandburg, William Faulkner, John Steinbeck, and the like have documented honky-tonks in the written word, while Ernest Tubb, Hank Williams Sr., Dwight Yoakam, and others have immortalized them in song. These days the word honky-tonk has become quite commonplace, but have you ever wondered about where it came from or what it means? Ask anyone. Everybody seems to have a different idea of what constitutes a honky-tonk. Longtime saloongoers do seem to agree on one thing, however: A cowboy bar does not a honky-tonk make, and a honky-tonk is more than just a building. These places are about survival, freedom of choice, a sense of belonging, letting loose, and, yes, looking for love.

As the ranks of would-be cowboys have swelled in recent years, so has the number of would-be cowboy honky-tonks. They now come in all shapes and sizes, and finding one is much easier than defining one. They all have this in common, however: Every night's a party and you never know who is going to show up. These days a truly Traditional honky-tonk is about as scarce as a real cowboy on the American cultural landscape; although both still exist, they are increasingly harder to find because they are constantly being reinvented.

In the past, "honky-tonk" conjured up images of a ramshackle watering hole out in the middle of nowhere. Nowadays honky-tonks can be found in Shopping Center, USA. Outside, pickup trucks and 4-by-4s line the asphalt where horses once might have stood; inside, it's a trip back to a simpler place and time, an escape from today's high-tech, high-anxiety world. In the 1990s you're more likely to find a gleaming parquet floor sprinkled with dance wax, a DJ, and an air-filtration system than you are well-worn hardwood covered with sawdust, a jukebox full of twangy songs, and air blue with smoke. Times have changed, and, like many words in the English language, "honky-tonk" has changed with the times. Dictionary writers have little space to wax eloquent, so where they leave off, this book begins.

So what exactly is a honky-tonk?

Today, and for the purposes of this book, "honky-tonk" is used almost exclusively as a catchall for clubs that feature either live or recorded country music and dancing. But let's examine the word's roots. The first known published reference to a honky-tonk was printed on Tuesday, February 27, 1894, in the *Daily Ardmoreite* in the Chickasaw Nation of Indian Territory. The front-page news item stated: "The honk-a-tonk last night was well attended by ball heads, bachelors and leading citizens. Most of them are inclined to kick themselves this morning for being sold." And Noah Webster's first dictionary (published in 1828) had no honky-tonk entry, so it is safe to assume that the word is less than two hundred years old. The *Oxford English Dictionary,* considered the mother of all dictionaries, calls "honky-tonk" a colloquialism, and cites its U.S. origins, whereas Webster's *New Collegiate Dictionary* flat-out states: "Origin unknown." When it comes to defining the word, both reference books offer the usual cop-out. By standard definition a honky-tonk is a dive, a joint, a roadhouse, a saloon, a bar, a house of ill-repute, a cheap dance hall–all of the above. That's the easy answer, but it sells these places short. A honky-tonk is about too many things to be neatly defined. "Honky-tonk" is one of those amorphous words that defies categorization. Think about it. It simply refuses to be pigeonholed. It even seems to have a western mentality; it bucks authority.

Honky-tonks are as much a product of what happens inside them as they are about the people who frequent them. Ken Lance, proprietor of the Ken Lance Sports Arena and Dance Pavilion outside Ada, Oklahoma, says: "You can't be a pessimist and come to one of these places." He's right. Honky-tonkers, more often than not, are eternal optimists who are seeking a little pleasure to ease their personal pain. Some of these folks may be "looking for love in all the wrong places," as the song contends, but the way they see it, they're going to keep trying until they get it right. And things might get a little rough and rowdy once in a while, but that's just part of what gives a real cowboy bar backbone. Note the caliber of honky-tonkers in Ardmore back in 1894. It appears that they were upstanding citizens, which dispels the notion that honky-tonks have always been the domain of lowlifes and losers. But why did these pillars of the community want "to kick themselves" the next morning? Any good honky-tonker will already know the answer to that, but we cannot know for sure because that is all that was written on the subject. It is also interesting that this first documented "honk-a-tonk" was in what is now Oklahoma, and not Texas, which is commonly believed to have been the birthplace of the cowboy honky-tonk as we know it. Somewhere along the way, however, the reputation of "honky-tonk" went downhill from what was reported in Ardmore. The *Facts on File Encyclopedia of Word and Phrase Origins* states that a jazz musician testified in reference to an early honky-tonk that "it was nothing for a man to be drug out of them dead." Then there is a telling passage from *The Deputy Sheriff* (1930), written by Clarence E. Mulford, creator of Hopalong Cassidy: "This place ain't no damn honkatonk, stranger. . . . Folks get throwed outa here sometimes."

The *Oxford English Dictionary*, which lists just about every known early reference to a honky-tonk, says a honky-tonk also can be the musical interpretation of a train journey, a twelve-bar blues. When you think about it, what is traditional country music if not train songs and the white man's blues? Just as country music had jazz and blues roots, so did honky-tonks. Note that the early honky-tonks and the songs about them were jazz- and blues-oriented, but it was not until 1936, when Al Dexter (a.k.a. Albert Poindexter) released "Honky Tonk Blues," that the term officially reached the domain of country music.

As a part of speech, "honky-tonk" is first and foremost a noun from which another noun can be made, i.e., "honky-tonker," someone who frequents a honky-tonk. The word also can become either an adjective ("honky-tonk nights") or an intransitive verb ("Chad was no good at honky-tonking; he couldn't hold his liquor."). There are also many theories–some so far-fetched they merit being ignored–about the morphology of "honky-tonk." Vanderbilt University professor Cecilia Tichi, author of *High Lonesome: The American Culture of Country Music,* purports that honky-tonk actually means "white shack." Tichi told me she came to that conclusion based on blacks' references to whites as "honkies," and the term for delta cotton pickers' shacks, "tonks." Both are derogatory, she says, just as "honky-tonk" conveys a negative image. *A Browser's Dictionary,* however, claims that the natural progression to "honkies" would have been a shortening of "honky-tonkers," a derisive term for white jazz buffs that did not come into play until the 1940s. Another guess, according to *Facts on File,* is that around the turn of the century black meat-packers in Chicago called Hungarian immigrants "hunkies," which probably came out "honkies," and eventually came to be a derogatory term for all whites. But that doesn't explain why the first reference was made in the early 1890s far from the slaughterhouses of Chicago. It basically comes down to this: Which came first–the "honkies" or the "honky-tonks"? Who knows? Who even cares? Still, this debate could make for some serious "holding forth," a favorite activity at many a cowboy bar.

Many club owners are ambivalent about the honky-tonk moniker because of the negative connotations of days gone by, preferring instead to have their establishments characterized as dance halls or country nightclubs. Still others, like the folks at Billy Bob's Texas, a slick country entertainment complex in Fort Worth that is billed as "the world's largest honky-tonk," obviously don't view it as a negative. Owners of clubs that play a mix of recorded Top 40 country and rock tunes generally welcome the honky-tonk label, but cringe when their establishments are called country discos. Then other complications arise. The enterprises or limited partnerships that run these cookie-cutter Country Clubs do not like being referred to as "chains"; they prefer "independently owned."

See what we're up against here? I believe in truth in labeling. For the sake of brevity–and to be as politically correct as possible–I have divided honky-tonks into two broad categories: Traditional and New Breed. Each draws a particular clientele, depending on what the club has to offer. I have broken them down based on some very general observations, which should not be taken so seriously as to prevent anyone from patronizing either type of club.

Traditional	**New Breed**
Rodeo Cowboys	Disco Cowboys
Pickers and Grinners	Competitive Dancers
Partner Dancers	Line Dancers
Older Set	Younger Set

Couples	Singles
Truckers	Computer Programmers
Singles	Couples
Straights	Straights
Gays	Gays

So why include sexual preference on this list? Some gay honky-tonks are out of the closet and prefer being billed as such, so in those cases a distinction will be made. Although rednecks and gays may not seem to mix, just remember this book is about lifestyle, music, and dance–not about people's hang-ups. All Country Clubs cater to everyone regardless of their proclivities, and gay honky-tonks are prevalent in every corner of this country.

There is one type of honky-tonk, however, that will not be addressed in this book because of its mutable and transient nature. I call these "Clubs Without Walls," because there is no permanent structure per se to house the dances, just a honky-tonk attitude. They run the gamut from a street dance held in Kaycee, Wyoming, every Saturday night to dances sponsored on weekends in rented halls by country dance groups. Also, there are clubs that play *banda,* a kind of Mexican hillbilly music, which have caught on quicker than wildfire in California. These *quebradita* dances are held in various halls and warehouses for club members who don cowboy hats and boots. In Los Angeles *quebradita* dancing, which combines elements of country-western polka, lambada, and flamenco, has been credited with keeping Latino youths off the streets and, thus, out of gang activity. Likewise many white youths have turned to country line dancing, which has led some honky-tonks to sponsor teen or family nights. Detractors say the clubs that do this are not pure country, but what can be more country than creating a sense of community among young people?

Music and dance are the main qualifiers I use for distinguishing Traditional from New Breed clubs. A Traditional honky-tonk generally offers live music and little to no line dancing; anything else is New Breed. Veteran honky-tonkers can tell the two apart just by the kind of vehicles in the parking lot. Hell, they can tell by whether or not the parking lot is paved! Neophytes, on the other hand, may need a little more help in telling the difference between the two.

Dancing as a Contact Sport

Most would argue that these days a honky-tonk has to be a little flexible if it wants to stand the test of time, but that isn't necessarily true. As you will discover in Part Two of this guide, some clubs have stayed surprisingly true to tradition while bucking the odds. But it is exceedingly rare to find a truly Traditional honky-tonk. To be considered a bona fide honky-tonk, a club should meet the following standards:

* Longevity.
* A following.
* Cheap eats and cheap beer.
* No cover charge.
* Live country music.
* A jukebox with a country song.
* Something different.
* A story.
* A good brawl now and then.
* No karaoke.
* No line dancing.

This is a pretty tall order to fill, especially in the 1990s, but it can be done. There are a few honky-tonks that would meet all of these qualifications if not for lack of control over the occasional line dancer or the need to charge a cover fee on the weekends.

Unlike the clientele at some of the newer country music clubs, folks who frequent Traditional honky-tonks are not so much driven by the dance as they are by the need to enjoy themselves. They prefer cement or hardwood to parquet and view dancing primarily as a contact sport between a man and a woman. Two-stepping or buckle-shining are the dances of choice. So if you want to line dance, you'd best not step foot through these swinging doors. Instead, head on down the street to one of those new neon cowboy bars. Usually only the very young or the disco cowboys have the gumption to try "Slappin' Leather" here, if they can withstand the steely glares or sharp elbows they're sure to encounter. Nothing raises the hackles of cowboys more than line dancers, whom they refer to as disco, drugstore, or attitude cowboys. I once overheard a honky-tonker at the Longhorn Saloon and Grille in Richmond, Virginia, say: "If God had intended for us to do the same thing at the same time, we all would've been born line dancing." That about sums up the feeling of the folks who frequent Traditional clubs. The way real cowboys see it, line dancing has all the allure of a coed aerobics class in full dress. Sure it's great exercise, but better it be done in a gym, where there's more room and folks can wear fewer clothes.

You'll find more real cowboys per square foot at these clubs than at some of the New Breed clubs because they value a honky-tonk for what it has to offer and not for how it looks. They come in as often as possible, sometimes seven nights a week, to support their favorite "Honky-Tonk Bar Association," as the song goes.

Men here can be a little old-fashioned and they still open doors for a lady, walk her back to her seat after a dance, buy her drinks, and say, "Yes, ma'am," which can be a welcome change to women used to more citified men. You see, folks here usually come from hard-working, blue-collar backgrounds and their mamas taught them some manners. They are down-to-earth, sincere, and have values. Many, save for the obsessive rodeo cowboy, place more stock in raising a family than in nurturing a career.

The truest test of a real honky-tonk, however, is time. A bar in this category must possess a track record; it has to have a past to give it a presence. A true roadhouse has its own intimacy and has seen its share of country-music greats pass through its doors. The many autographed pictures adorning its walls testify to a club's commitment to country music–make that *live* country music. Folks here are Grinners first and Dancers second, which will be explained in Chapter Three. There is a strong conviction among them that the spotlight should shine on the makers of the music rather than on someone who simply chooses it. Real honky-tonkers have an outlaw mentality and don't like to be told what to do or how to do it, especially on the dance floor by some disc jockey. That's akin to telling them how they should feel. They view dancing as a form of self-expression, not as something that has to be perfected or controlled. Besides that, a band provides an energy that just doesn't translate off compact disc. About the only time canned music is acceptable is when the band is on break, and even then it's better to have a jukebox–so honky-tonkers can pick the tunes. Karaoke nights, one of the worst sins a honky-tonk can commit, has the ability to shift a honky-tonk into New Breed status quicker than a rattler's bite unless there are mitigating circumstances.

Each Country Club has a distinct personality; some are sedate while others are rough and tumble. But every real honky-tonk must have a ritual or some claim to fame that gives it a character all its own, which will be explained further in Part Two.

Keeping It All in Line

Line dancing used to be the domain of widows and coyote-ugly women, but that's all changed. Now it seems the majority of country dance enthusiasts is pushing its collective tush. It is considered "cowboy cool" to strut your stuff on the dance floor by freezing a stance, doing the splits, or snapping a turn. Line dancing is viewed by practitioners as great exercise and the perfect nonthreatening singles activity. You're more likely to line dance at a New Breed club, unless that club happens to be deep in the heart of Texas. If you enjoy both partner and line dancing, there is usually a balance of the two at these clubs.

You won't hear any live music at New Breed clubs except for an occasional concert featuring a local or regional band opening for a major label act. Here a disc jockey is the star and calls the shots for dancers, many of whom compete and fancy themselves a cut above their down-home counterparts. The dancer mentality is not too difficult to understand. The more you dance, the better you feel and look. It is an aerobic activity and there is always that challenge to move on to a higher level of proficiency. Therefore many dancers demand a consistent beat or a longer dance-hall version of their favorite country song that the average house band usually doesn't deliver. So they are perfectly happy with a DJ who plays songs from a Top 40 list.

Most chain clubs follow the dance-club formula: Disc jockeys, not bands. They do this because a disc jockey comes cheaper than a band. It is also easier for payroll to deal with one or two dependable people rather than five or six creative types who may possess mercurial personalities and come and go weekly. Says Johnny Lemmons of the Graham Brothers, the largest country nightclub operation in the nation: "You can control a disc jockey, you can't control a band." He adds that many local bands change personnel often, which makes for an inconsistent sound. The bands also develop a following of fans that come and go with them, which makes for an unpredictable club clientele.

The biggest plus of a chain is consistency. If you're a regular at the Phoenix Denim & Diamonds, then you pretty much know what to expect at every other Denim & Diamonds in the Graham Brothers empire. But don't confuse the Graham Brothers' Denim & Diamonds, located mostly in the South and Southwest, with those owned by Graham Gilliam, which are situated throughout California and in Manhattan. Both outfits are based in Texas and run New Breed clubs that employ disc jockeys, but ownership is separate.

The biggest minus of chain clubs is that what is a Country Club one day could be a rap club the next. The bottom line is what counts here, and a chain club is more likely to change formats to stay afloat financially and to keep any investors happy.

Chains have a huge financial advantage over smaller independent clubs. They have state-of-the-art sound systems, top-quality facilities, and large dance floors, all of which attract a high-volume business. They are also able to offer food and drink specials at dirt-cheap prices their competitors cannot match.

These operations are masters of marketing promotions that draw in customers with homemade bikini, tight-fitting jeans, or best-looking cowboy and cowgirl contests.

So there you have it, all you need to do now is get dressed and read up on bar behavior before you get honky-tonking.

It isn't mandatory to dress western in a honky-tonk, but clothes do make the cowboy. One surefire way to tell the genuine article from the drugstore variety is the ranch vs. the raunch dressing. Clothes are pretty much standard-issue cowboy gear in a Traditional Country Club, but in a New Breed club they are of the dress-to-impress category and more flesh is flaunted. Still, when there's a sea of cowboy hats floating around, it can be difficult to tell which is which. A disco cowboy may think that any jeans, boots, or cowboy hat he buys in a department store or boutique will do. Uh-uh. Nope. Real cowboys identify their clothes like livestock–by the brand–

and they invest in garments made by real western outfitters to get the most for their hard-earned money. Most clubs don't care how you dress, as long as you've got clothes on; it's the clientele that cares. And while all types of western wear are worn in all types of clubs, cowboys and cowgirls can get downright critical of outsiders who aren't dressed like them; they like to keep things familiar.

Here are some general "fashion opposites":

City	**Country**
Exotic Skins or Synthetic Boots	Leather Boots
Roach Killers	Ropers
Boot Bracelets	Spurs
Levis	Wranglers
Skirts and Shorts	Rockies
High-Water Jeans	Stacked Jeans
Knock-Offs	Name Brands
Beads and Fringe	Exclusive of decoration
Dance Buckles	Rodeo Buckles
Beepers on Belts	Key Chains on Belts
Bubble Tape in Back Pocket	Skoal in Back Pocket
Charlie 1 Horse Hats	Stetson or Resistol Hats

Common sense dictates that when you're in a metropolitan area you should dress "city" and when in the sticks, dress "country." At least that's what Lisa White, who works at Steppin' Out Western Style in Pauls Valley, Oklahoma, recommends. Of course, the real key to successful dance-floor dressing is knowing what to wear in a particular town or region.

In the Old West you could tell where a cowboy was from by the crease in the crown of his hat or the size of the brim; in the New West you can recognize a Texan, Oklahoman, or Arizonan by their Roper boots and Wrangler jeans. But anything goes in Chicago, New York, or Los Angeles and in tourist-trap towns like Jackson Hole, Wyoming, where people spend big bucks on suede or leather outfits with fancy fringe and beadwork for their cowboy-bar forays. City slickers tend to go overboard on apparel that is flashier than their country counterparts. So much so that Jason Palumbo, who owns the Cowboy Saloon and Dance Hall in Laramie, Wyoming, calls the New Breed clubs "Halloween" because, he says, "it's like people dress up in costumes and pretend they're something they're not." True, but that is part of the escape and part of the fun. As competitive dancer and dance instructor Lloyd Thompson of Washington, D.C., says, the best thing about honky-tonking is that people often check their other lives at the door–"When they're in their boots and hats, they are someone else."

In the Old West a cowboy could blow a whole month's pay at the town haberdashery. Back then clothes were designed with practicality and durability in mind. Just after the Civil War, J. B. Stetson of Philadelphia started producing hats to meet the needs of range riders. A hat was the most essential element in a cowboy's wardrobe: It protected him from searing sun and driving rain, and served other purposes, such as a pail to water his horse or extinguish a campfire. The hat of choice was the Stetson Boss, because it withstood all types of weather. Good boots were the second most important item in a cowboy's wardrobe because the high, stitched shaft protected his legs from snake bites and such. The pointed toe made it easy to slip a boot into a stirrup, while the high, slanted riding heel prevented the boot from slipping through. The heel also helped him gain a foothold on the ground when wrangling a steer. By the 1870s German-born Levi Strauss had made his first pair of riveted jeans from a tough sailcloth called "serge de Nimes" (after the town in France it came from), hence the name "denim." Years later Wrangler developed its cowboy-cut jeans with their longer rise and higher backs to accommodate long hours in the saddle. The large yoke on the back of a cowboy's shirt gave extra protection against the elements, and any fringe, "borrowed" from the Indians, also helped rain run off.

Nowadays western-wear manufacturers still cater to working and rodeo cowboys, but with the upsurge in country dancing they have branched out to include clothing for the serious boot-scooter. Some clothes are made of lighter-weight fabrics in bright colors and bold designs in roomy styles that allow movement and air circulation. Toward the end of this chapter, the essentials of a dance-floor wardrobe will be examined with an eye as to what's hot and what's not on the dance floor.

Meanwhile, it is possible for men and women alike to fit in any country club in any state wearing a basic uniform consisting of:

- ★ Black or brown leather boots with a medium-round toe and a riding heel.
- ★ Matching belt.
- ★ Blue or black denim jeans.
- ★ A white or blue denim long-sleeved shirt.

You can dress these basics up or down by putting on some silver jewelry or sporting a bandanna. If you are just getting into country dancing, or are traveling, these are all the clothes you need. If you already have everything but the boots, just slip on a pair of leather-soled shoes instead until you have finished reading this chapter. Should you plan to get serious about honky-tonking, you will want to shop wisely. Good leather boots will be the most important purchase you make for the dance floor. A cowboy hat, which will cost as much or more than the boots, can always be added later if you choose.

The idea of a basic uniform should not be misconstrued to mean that we need to look like a bunch of pupils at a Catholic school, so don't let the constraints of cowboy dressing keep you from developing your own style. If you're the subdued type, not into bright colors, then to be different you might want to stick a feather in your hat à la the late champion bull rider Lane Frost and let it go at that (just remember, the feather always goes on the left side). Or if you have an overriding desire to flaunt a secure financial status, you can invest in a pair of full-quill ostrich boots and matching belt, a fifty-ply beaver hat, or handcrafted Native American jewelry.

Among honky-tonkers, Pickers are probably best known for making strong personal fashion statements. One night at the Museum Club in Flagstaff, Arizona, two cowboys at the bar were fussing about the apparel of a particular band member with shoulder-length hair (cowboys keep theirs short) who was wearing "heifer boots." Neither one of these guys would be caught dead wearing hair-on boots, but, then again, showpeople can get away with far more than your average Grinner or Dancer. You can blame all this on Brooklyn-born Nudie Cohen, who was the first to dress country stars to excess with his trademark soutache braidwork and rhinestones. He was a struggling tailor in Los Angeles in the early 1940s when he hooked up with singer Tex Williams, who ordered costumes for his band. Tex plugged the tailor's work and it wasn't long before word spread and Nudie was outfitting every major country singer of his day, including another Williams–Hank Sr. After Nudie died in 1984, his protégé, Manuel Cuevas, took up the torch as premier tailor to the country stars, including Hank Williams Jr., Dwight Yoakam, and Marty Stuart. Cuevas works out of Nashville where he joins other custom clothiers such as Riflefire! and bootmakers such as Bo Riddle. (Nudie's legendary Hollywood shop closed its doors in 1994.)

Custom clothes, priced in the thousands, are not affordable to the majority of honky-tonkers and there is no practical reason for a weekend cowboy to invest in them. Affordable western wear is available off the rack in a variety of quality name brands such as Justin, Tony Lama, Stetson, Resistol, Levis, Wrangler, Roper, Rocky Mountain, and Panhandle Slim. Many cowboys opt for Mo'Betta shirts, the kind singer Garth Brooks wears, which average seventy dollars a shirt. Come to think of it, that may be one of the reasons Brooks appeals to so many people: He is one of us. Mo'Betta shirts have signature bold color blocks that stand out in a crowd, which is why Brooks likes them.

Mo'Betta started out as a cottage industry that grew out of rodeo cowboy Maury Tate's desire to have a unique look while competing as a calf roper. Tate, a twentysomething, designed some shirts and had a friend of his mother's sew them. Before he knew it, other rodeo cowboys were literally buying the shirts off his back. The Apache, Oklahoma-based company now sells more than twenty thousand shirts a year. To set honky-tonkers apart from the solids, stripes, and plaids of the world, other western retailers have come up with their own unique offerings. For example, singers Kix Brooks and Ronnie Dunn market shirts with stylized designs of flames and piano keys that cost about half the price of a Mo'Betta and look just as good. Wrangler offers an array of Aztec prints in addition to the ever-popular canvas Brushpoppers.

While cowboys make their fashion statement mainly in the shirts that they wear, cowgirls do it in brightly colored Rockies or Wrangler jeans that match their Justin Ropers. For those of you who don't already know, "Rockies" is the affectionate term for Rocky Mountain jeans, a brand that accommodates a range of womanly figure styles. Rockies are generally smaller in the waist and larger in the seat and thigh, whereas Wranglers tend to be larger in the waist and smaller in the seat and thigh. As honky-tonker Scott Beaty of Las Cruces, New Mexico, points out, "Women basically have two body types, Rockies or Wranglers–the trick is knowing the difference." Of course, some lucky women are capable of wearing both. But if your figure tends to be shaped like an hourglass, opt for Rockies. If you are not as curvy, then choose Wranglers.

Now that you've got the lowdown on basic honky-tonk attire, let's run down each item in a western wardrobe and rate them according to danceability. And remember this: Less is more!

Apache Ties

- ★ DO wear if you perform or for special occasions.

This small strip of cloth goes around a man's neck with a ring instead of a knot keeping it in place. Generally only performers or dance instructors wear these to look western. A cowboy prefers not to have anything constricting his neck. Save them for dressy occasions.

Bandannas

- ★ DO use to mop up sweat.
- ★ DO use as a flash of color.
- ★ DON'T tie around your neck if you are a man.

These are twenty-two-inch-by-twenty-two-inch squares of colorful cotton that serve many purposes on the range, chiefly as a dust mask, neckerchief, handkerchief, and tourniquet. On the dance floor, a colorful bandanna comes in handy to mop up perspiration. Stuff one in a back pocket for a flash of color until you are ready for it or use it as a headband under your hat if you sweat to excess. Usually only women can get away using these as neckerchiefs; men tend to look silly in them.

Belts and Buckles

- ★ DO match belts with boots.
- ★ DON'T wear vinyl belts.
- ★ DO wear belts one and a half inches in width.
- ★ DON'T have your name embossed on the back.
- ★ DO wear rodeo buckles if you have them.
- ★ DON'T wear "turkey platters."
- ★ DO beware of phony buckles.

These strips of leather are used to keep the moon from coming up over the mountain, so to speak, but cowboys and cowgirls wear jeans so tight these days they really aren't necessary. Belts finish a look more than anything else and they come in a variety of materials and colors to effect that purpose. Men generally wear wider belts than women, the norm being about one and a half inches. Women can get away with thick or thin belts, depending on if they're wearing skirts or jeans. Wider belts usually look best with jeans. Inexpensive braided nylon belts are very popular on the dance floor, because they keep you cooler around the midsection. Moderately priced leather belts laced on either edge with stainless steel are also a favorite. Steer clear of vinyl, however, because it will make you sweat. You won't see many belts with names like "Buck" embossed on the back except on old-timers or in the mountains of Tennessee and the backwoods of North Carolina.

Time was when everybody wore a buckle the size of a small turkey platter. Today moderation is the key. Buckles come in all materials, shapes, and sizes. Some people prefer silver buckles handcrafted by Native Americans and inlaid with semiprecious stones. The choice is up to the wearer and is one of the ways you can make a personal fashion statement. The most authentic buckles you'll find in a honky-tonk, however, are the silver ones trimmed with gold that belong to real rodeo cowboys. But even these can be deceiving. For example, at the National Finals Rodeo you can buy a commemorative buckle and later have your name engraved on it. "Buckle Bunnies" (rodeo cowboy groupies) should be aware of this and not fall for every cowboy sporting a buckle. Ever since country dancing came to be the competitive sport that it is, Dancers, too, wear buckles similar to a rodeo cowboy's. Even Pickers have buckles, the most coveted of which goes to the CMA "Entertainer of the Year." Chances are you won't see any of these in your average honky-tonk.

Bola Ties

- ★ DO say "bola" not "bolo."
- ★ DON'T wear these in the country.

These string ties can be worn by either men or women in New Breed clubs. Sometimes you'll see a few in Traditional honky-tonks, but they're usually of the plastic-embedded-scorpion variety. And, yes, it's bola, not bolo. Both words are Spanish in origin, but nobody in their right mind would wear a bolo–a long, single-edged knife–around their neck. Bolas, on the other hand, resemble the weapons they're named for, consisting of stones or iron balls attached to cords that are hurled and used to entangle unsuspecting animals.

Boots and Boot Socks

- ★ DO wear leather boots.
- ★ DON'T buy cheap imitations.
- ★ DON'T wear "roach-killers" or python boots in the country.
- ★ DO wear pointy-toed boots with tapered jeans.
- ★ DON'T wear Ropers with skirts unless they are lace-ups.
- ★ DO wear Ropers with straight-leg jeans.
- ★ DO wear white boots only from Memorial Day to Labor Day.
- ★ DO let boots rest a day between wearings.

Boots are absolutely the most important purchase you'll make for your dance-floor wardrobe. But before we talk boots, let's get one thing straight: Tennis shoes just don't cut it on the dance floor. Neither do deck shoes or any kind of shoes with little ridges on the bottom. These are designed to grip, not slide, which is what you want and need to do when you are country dancing. Even the new Horseshoes, athletic-style shoes designed for riders, don't work. Smooth soles, especially leather ones, are best for ease of movement. Synthetic soles tend to get hot and stick to the dance floor. The same is also true with any synthetic materials used in the construction of a boot–they'll make your feet hot. It may cost a little more to buy all-leather boots, but if you plan to dance a lot, it is well worth the investment.

Boots come in assorted styles and skins, but not all are conducive to honky-tonking. Nothing brands you as a dude quicker than a pair of cheap imitations, roach-killers (very pointy-toed boots), or python boots. Lizard boots are okay in the country, but wear them in clubs, not on the ranch. I don't know why, but it seems that a lot of people get talked into buying python for their first pair by some commission-hungry salesperson. Don't do it. You're best bet is to buy black cowhide boots for your first pair, either Ropers or a medium-round-toed boot with a riding heel, depending on your budget and taste. You'll get a lot more mileage out of them in the long run. And you can wear black in summer, with black, blue, light blue, natural, or white jeans. As you get more into dancing, you may want to expand your boot collection to include other styles and basic colors such as brown, tan, taupe, or navy, in that order. Red is also a versatile color for women. A lot of women wear white boots year-round, not realizing that the same fashion rule for shoes applies to boots, that is: White from Memorial Day to Labor Day. The only exception to this rule is if you live in a hot-weather state; otherwise, wear darker boots in the fall and winter months. A lot of women also like to match their boot color with their jeans, which is fine if you have money to burn. If not, be practical. There really is no need to buy expensive hair-on, inlays, or fringed boots unless you are a performer or competitive dancer and must dress flashy. Just wear them in the city and protect those hair-on boots (and belts) from silverfish.

Cowboys prefer Ropers, a low-heeled, round-toed boot that functions well in the rodeo arena or out on the ranch. These boots are a favorite out West, especially in Arizona, Oklahoma, and Texas, where folks will chide you for wearing anything else. There are two types of Ropers: pull-on and lace-up. The pull-on variety is a short version of an English riding boot, while the lace-up is similar to a paddock boot. Both styles are a versatile addition to city closets as well. Men can wear the pull-ons as a dress boot with a suit, whereas women can wear the lace-ups (minus the detachable kiltie) with tights or leggings and thick socks rolled over the boot top paired with a short skirt.

But when it comes to dancing, medium-round- or pointy-toed boots with riding heels at least one and a half inches high are best because they help you keep up on the balls of your feet, which is the proper way to dance. Boots can cost anywhere from $80 for a leather roper to thousands of dollars for custom-made boots. Full-quill ostrich boots start at around $600, which may sound extravagant, but consider that this highly durable skin will last forever. Lizard boots cost about $260 retail. Your basic black boots with a medium toe and a riding heel should cost no more than $140. If you dance holes in the bottom, then take them to a shoemaker and get them resoled for $25 or $30–it beats buying a brand new pair when the uppers are still in mint condition.

Wear boot socks when trying boots on to ensure a proper fit. These thick-soled socks cushion your feet and are high enough to keep the boots from rubbing on your calves. (Women should scrunch tops of boot socks around their ankles if they wear boots and a skirt so the socks won't show.) If the boots are good quality and fit well–that is usually a half to one whole size smaller than your regular shoe size (boot sizes run bigger) with room for heel slippage–you'll be able to dance all night on the first wearing. Leather "nails" pegged in the instep of a leather sole indicate that the boots are well-constructed.

Boot Bracelets

- DO wear if you can dance.
- DON'T wear if you are a man.
- DO wear only on the left boot.
- DON'T wear one on each boot.
- DON'T wear on Ropers.
- DON'T wear in the country.

A boot bracelet usually indicates that a woman is a force to be reckoned with on the dance floor. A single strand of silver or rhinestone catches the light and adds interest, whereas a leather strap studded with conchos will make you look more like a dominatrix than a dancer. Men should not wear boot bracelets under any circumstances. Bracelets look better on medium-round- or pointy-toed boots than they do on a round-toed Roper. Although a recent guidebook advocates the wearing of boot bracelets on Ropers, do not, and I repeat do not, unless you want to look like a cowgirl nerd. Always wear the bracelet on the left boot, just as the trim always goes on the left side of a cowboy hat. Never wear a bracelet on both boots–this is overkill.

Chaps, Chinks, and Woollies

- ★ DON'T wear these on the dance floor.

"Chaps" (pronounced shaps) originated from the Spanish word *chaperreras,* meaning leather pants, and are protective outerwear worn over jeans when working on the range or rodeoing. "Chinks" are a shorter version of chaps and "woollies" are chaps made of wool from sheep or angora goats. Like spurs, these have absolutely no place in a honky-tonk unless you came straight from the ranch. Bat-wing chaps, in particular, only get in the way on the dance floor. If you simply must wear these to be different, buy a pair of dance chaps, which are straight-legged and fringed on the side–but even these will make you hot.

Dresses and Skirts

- ★ DON'T wear either in the country, save them for the city.
- ★ DO wear dance pants or bike shorts no matter how long the skirt is.
- ★ DON'T let any leg show between a long skirt and a boot, unless it's a granny boot.
- ★ DO let a lot of leg show between a boot and a short skirt.

If you are a woman and want to make a fashion statement by wearing a dress or a skirt, just remember to do so only in the city, at a New Breed club, or in a tourist trap. In the Old West, eastern women who came in on the stagecoach wearing fancy dresses made of silk or satin were viewed as prostitutes. It's not quite the same in the New West, but if you go to a Traditional honky-tonk wearing a skirt or a prairie dress you will be viewed as something else again. Feelings about dresses and skirts on the dance floor are mixed. Women like them because they are cool and allow the air to circulate when they dance. Men like them because they reveal a lot of leg, and then some. In some states nobody likes them on the dance floor because they "get in the way," as one Texas cowboy told me–especially the car-wash type. Let's face it, though, women who haven't missed many meals look better in skirts than in jeans and should wear what flatters their figure. Generally you'll get more use out of coordinating pieces than you will out of a prairie dress. Short skirts are better than long skirts, especially for those who like to swing, and you can wear a pretty garter on your thigh to add interest when you twirl. Lightweight denim, cotton, and rayon are the most suitable for dancewear; suede, leather, wool, and corduroy are simply too hot.

Styles such as circle, broomstick, or tiered skirts are best for twirling. Wear long skirts so they cover the tops of your boots. Skirts look best with boots that have pointed toes or medium-round toes.

Dusters

- ★ DON'T wear on the dance floor.

Dusters are cowboy overcoats, usually canvas. Short or long, they get in the way on the dance floor, so check them when you come in.

Hair

- ★ DO wear the style best suited to your looks.

Real cowboys like their hair short so it won't get tangled up or caught in anything when they're riding or roping. Disco cowboys can pretty much wear their hair however they please. Time was that honky-tonk angels wore BIG hair like Dolly Parton. Not anymore. You're just as likely to see short styles as long. Wear your hair the way it flatters you, but remember hats tend to look better on women with longer hair.

Hats

- ★ DON'T wear backward.
- ★ DON'T wear pushed way back on your forehead.
- ★ DON'T wear a small hat on a big head, and vice versa.
- ★ DO wear straw hats in summer and in hot-weather states.
- ★ DO wear felt hats in winter and in cold-weather states.
- ★ DO store upside down on the crown to protect the brim.
- ★ DON'T take on and off.

The biggest hat mistakes newcomers make are wearing their hats backward (a little bow inside the hatband indicates the back) and wearing their hats pushed back too far. Just because cowboys in the last century pushed their hats back when they honky-tonked doesn't mean you should today. The whole point of dressing like a cowboy is to look cool, not like a hayseed.

There are many fine cowboy hats on the market these days, but the most popular brands on the dance floor are Stetson, Resistol, and Charlie 1 Horse. You won't see too many Charlie 1 Horse hats in the country, though–too fancy. Usually men wear hats more than women do.

Hats should fit snugly, but not too tight, and should be no more than a thumb's width above the ears. The brim also must match the width of the face and be in proportion to your entire body. So if you have a narrow face, wear a narrow brim; and a wide face, a wider brim. Don't wear a small hat if you are a big person, likewise, don't wear a big hat if you are small. If the retailer doesn't steam or shape hats, find someone who does. Many honky-tonks offer this service.

Straw should be worn in warm-weather states and in summer. Felt is for winter and for dress. Straw hats are rated on a star system and felt on an X system, the more stars and X's, the higher the quality. Black is a good starter color because it doesn't show dirt and always looks dressy. Always handle your hat by the crown and set it upside down on the crown so the brim won't become misshapen. And if you check your hat, ask that it be placed upside down on the crown.

For more hat-related issues, read the next chapter.

Jeans

- DO wear them tight.
- DON'T tuck them in your boots if you're a man.
- DO keep them starched and pressed with a sharp crease down the leg.
- DON'T wear high-waters.

A popular bumper sticker says: "Wrangler butts drive me nuts!" These bun- and thigh-hugging jeans are pure perfection if they fit right, which is probably why they are the preferred brand of many a cowboy. But jeans should be a matter of what best suits your body style, be they Levis, Rockies, or Sheplers; just make sure they are 100 percent cotton denim. Generally jeans look better on slim women. You should wear them tight, so buy a size smaller because they'll stretch while wearing. Buy them at least two inches, but no more than six inches–four inches is the norm–longer than your regular inseam so they will "stack" over your boots whether you're in the saddle or sitting with your legs crossed. Never wear jeans tucked inside your boots unless you are a woman, live in the city, or have custom boots that you want to show off. Tapered legs tuck in better than boot cuts. Always use "cheaters," elastic grips that clip onto the bottom like a stirrup, so the jean won't work its way up and bunch over the top like knickers.

Shirts

- ★ DO wear one size larger than you really need.
- ★ DON'T wear sleeveless shirts if you are a man.

The main thing to remember about shirts is to buy them one size larger so they'll be roomy enough to raise your arms and execute turns without the tails coming out of your jeans.

Both men and women can wear long sleeves year-round and short sleeves in summer, but only women should wear sleeveless shirts.

Shorts

- ★ DO wear in New Breed clubs if you are a woman with nice legs.
- ★ DO pair with boots.
- ★ DON'T wear in Traditional clubs even if you have nice legs.
- ★ DON'T wear when riding a horse or mechanical bull.

Shorts serve a dual purpose: Not only do they keep ladies cooler when they're dancing, but they also attract more cowboys. Yes, this is a sexist attitude, and if this bothers you then perhaps you are not cut out to be a honky-tonker. Besides, women look much better in boots paired with shorts than men do. I know of only a handful of clubs that allow males to wear them during hot weather. So, men, if you wear shorts, find some footwear other than boots unless you want to look like a cowboy nerd. The main thing to remember, for men and women both, is to save the shorts for the city. Never wear shorts in the country, no matter how hot it is; wear a sleeveless denim shirt, T-shirt, or tank top to keep cool. Also, don't wear shorts if you plan to mount a horse or mechanical bull unless you want to remember your ride for a few days.

Spurs

- ★ DO wear studs on the outside.
- ★ DO wear in a honky-tonk if you rodeoed that day.
- ★ DON'T wear if you are not a real cowboy.

The unspoken code among cowboys dictates that only those who rodeoed that day should wear spurs in a honky-tonk that night. Disco cowboys often mistakenly wear spurs with the studs on the inside of the leg, unlike rodeo cowboys. Spurs, like chaps, chinks, and woollies, serve absolutely no purpose on the dance floor. These should be worn only when ranching or rodeoing.

Stampede Strings

- DON'T wear in a Traditional honky-tonk.

One of the biggest fashion faux pas a honky-tonk newcomer can make is wearing stampede strings, pieces of braided horsehair that attach with cotter pins through sweatband stitching to keep a hat in place when rodeoing or ranching. Some cowboys also disparagingly refer to horsehair hatbands with tiny dangling braids as stampede strings. Either way, wearing these in a Traditional club will verify your drugstore origins.

Suspenders

- DON'T wear with a belt.

Generally not that many men wear suspenders with their cowboy clothes, but WAH Maker of Yuma, Arizona, markets a line of frontier wear that is made to be worn with them. If you do wear suspenders, do not wear a belt at the same time under any circumstances. Wear either one or the other.

Vests

- DON'T wear if you dance a lot.

Vests add a touch of the West, but will only make you hot if you dance a lot. Wear at your own discretion.

3 Manners ON and OFF the DANCE FLOOR

A honky-tonk is not the same as other nightclubs. The rules are different–especially on the dance floor. But the etiquette addressed in this chapter covers more ground than a Texas dance hall. We're talking basic bar behavior here. Manners, pure and simple. Common courtesy. Three broad categories of people frequent cowboy dance halls–Pickers, Grinners, and Dancers–and each has its own perception of the other and of proper bar behavior. Both Traditional and New Breed clubs have unspoken rules that must be learned and followed. But when such an aggregate group of people congregates in the same place at the same time, no club, no matter how upscale, is immune from some amount of trouble. But one thing is certain, you'll never lack for entertainment, even if you elect to sit on the sidelines and watch. This chapter focuses primarily on the Dancers, because the Pickers and Grinners are usually on stage or sitting back, making or enjoying the music–which they would prefer to do without a bunch of fancy dancers getting in the way.

Pickers

These are the people who make the music happen, from roadies to songwriters to record producers to musicians. Their days are spent setting up, jamming, brainstorming, and rehearsing. They usually don't dance, and some quietly resent those who do.

Grinners

Anyone who loves the music and lives to listen to it falls into this category. Grinners rarely dance, and when they do, it is of the freestyle or buckle-shining variety. They have little tolerance for show-off dancers, especially those who block their view of the stage.

Dancers

These folks are out on the dance floor. There are two main subgroups, Line Dancers and Two-Steppers, which can be classified as Advanced, Intermediate, and Beginner. They are unaware that the Pickers and Grinners don't care much for their kind. Some don't even like country music, they just like to dance. Others feel that dancing is their way of showing appreciation for the music.

A lot of people may be unfamiliar with some of the jargon dear to every country dancer's heart: line of dance and dance-floor etiquette. It is important that line of dance not be confused with line dancing; they are separate but related. To clarify:

- "Line of dance" (L.O.D. in real dancer lingo) refers to the counterclockwise flow of dancers around the floor or the direction line dancers face when starting out.
- "Line dancing" occurs when people line up in rows and execute a prelearned choreographed routine.

★ "Dance-floor etiquette" refers to manners as much as it does to turf rights.

A few clubs confuse dance etiquette with some disc jockey dictating what to dance and when to dance it, going so far as to start the count so everyone will be dancing to the correct musical phrase. I have been in at least one club, and have heard of others, where dissenters are asked to leave if they don't dance what the despotic DJ calls. In my book this is not dance etiquette, it is a totalitarian state and people need to know the difference. After all, this is America and we're supposed to have freedom of choice. Some people have actually told me they prefer a controlled atmosphere like this because they are incapable of figuring out what to dance to a given beat. Unfortunately, this creates dependency when education is what's needed. Once, at the aforementioned club, the DJ forgot to call 5–6–7–8 before a line dance and the sheep of the world just stood there not knowing what the heck to do. If they had learned timing in the first place they wouldn't have had any trouble figuring it out. So for those of you who don't know, listen up! Country dancing starts on the downbeat and the bass or the drum establishes the beat for a song. A two-step is done in two-quarter or half time (down/up) and starts out after the eighth beat, or 5–6–7–8, while the waltz is done in three-quarter time (down/up/up) and starts out after the sixth beat, or 4–5–6. This is because the first beat is a heavier sound than the fifth beat in the two-step and the fourth in a waltz. If you still have trouble figuring out when to start, do what Dick and Geneva Matteis, who teach at the Rhinestone Cowboy in Newport News, Virginia, recommend: Wait until the singer starts to sing, or wait for the next lyrical sentence to begin. That way, your footwork will match the music. This is called "phrasing." Most certified instructors teach this, so neophytes should take advantage of any free lessons before trying to do their impression of the Texas two-step. There's just no way around it: You have to know how to dance in a Country Club, especially on the choreographed line dances. Most all clubs offer beginning to advanced lessons–free or for a minimal fee–several nights a week for both partner and line dances. Remember, you can never take too many classes, even if you're a better dancer than the instructor, and even if you only learn what *not* to do. Lessons also can help out-of-towners who know how to dance catch on to any regional variations.

With the burgeoning interest in line dancing, the etiquette issue has become increasingly important for a peaceful coexistence among all dancers. Things can get downright territorial between couples and line dancers, with people going so far as to knock each other down should they encroach on the other's space. There are some solutions to this problem, however. For example, the Saddle Rack in San Jose, California, simply separates the two. Couples only are allowed on the large floor in front of the stage, while the smaller floors in the back are devoted to those who like to go it alone. In addition to posting its rules, the club prints them on the monthly dance lesson schedules.

Here is what to expect at the Saddle Rack:

* Please, no drinking or smoking on the dance floor.
* Head's up! Watch where you're going! Swingers, watch out for others.
* Collisions happen! If you bump into someone, say, "Excuse me" or "Sorry," even if it really wasn't your fault!
* Faster dancers pass on the right. Slower dancers move to the slow lane. Watch for traffic stacking up behind you. Please don't cut across the center of the floor.
* Keep line of dance moving forward. Don't back up in the fast or slow lanes unless everyone is doing the same dance.
* If the band calls a line dance, do the line dance they call or use the time to socialize with your friends or get a drink.

Country dancing is like driving on a freeway during rush hour in unmarked lanes. You need to know the rules of the road to avoid collisions. The "on-ramps" in this analogy are the corners, so wait until there is a break in traffic and proceed. "Bpm" (beats per minute) rather than "mph" (miles per hour) establishes the speed on this freeway. Dance instructor Geneva Matteis says that there are four basic speed, or tempo, groups:

* Ballad–50 to 90 bpm. Buckle-shiners and some line dances.
* Slow–90 to 125 bpm. Pattern partner or sequence dances, waltz, two-step, West Coast swing, and some line dances.
* Medium–125 to 160 bpm. East Coast, two-step, waltz, and some line dances.
* Fast–160 and up. Clogging, polka, and some line dances.

To calculate bpm, count the number of beats in five seconds and multiply by twelve. For example, if there are ten beats in five seconds, it would be 120 bpm and a slow-tempo song.

It's important to keep your eyes on the road and not on your feet so you will be able to steer your way through the masses. In Texas–especially in the Dallas area–many of the young bucks like to double-time their steps, so the pace is even faster. The main thing is to keep moving, that's why these dances are called "progressive." Should gridlock occur, take smaller steps and dance in place until traffic gets moving again, and don't try to execute any fancy moves.

The standard progressive dances, such as the two-step, waltz, and polka, always travel in a counterclockwise forward-moving direction. It should be made clear to newcomers that fast and slow "lanes" are imaginary. This is just one of those things you are supposed to figure out, although a handful of clubs, such as the Stampede in Quincy, Michigan, have delineated them for dancers. Fast dancers generally travel along the outer perimeter of the dance floor, while the slower and "stop-and-go" dancers are on the inside, but not in the very center, which is reserved for swing dancing, line dancing, clogging, or plain old-fashioned freestyling or buckle-shining. Line dancers usually are inclined to take over the entire floor, but they should allow a good four to six feet of space along the outer edge for partner dancers. Ron Threlfall, who with his wife, Sally, teaches dance at Kelly's Grand 'Ol Opry in State Line, Idaho, hands out flyers to students with a floor diagram on it. The Threlfalls also explain the rules at the start of every class. Ron says Kelly's has no real problems between line dancers and couples dancers because each respects the other's right to be on the floor.

If you are new to a honky-tonk and want to fit in, it's always advisable to sit back and soak up the scene while taking advantage of a longneck special before getting up to dance. Watch how people are dancing and follow suit. The most popular dance is the two-step, whose origins date to the 1800s when it was done polka style to march-style music. The two-step became popular in the United States shortly before World War I and was gradually incorporated into the foxtrot. There are many variations, but according to the United Country-Western Dance Council, the preferred two-step consists of six- or eight-count combinations of either **quick, quick, slow-slow** or **quick, quick, slow-quick, quick, slow** patterns, executed in a sliding manner. But whatever the dance, just remember to do as they do in the bar you're in because each club has its own idiosyncrasies. For example, if folks are clogging, buckle-shining, line dancing, or freestyling and haven't allowed space for "train" dancers, i.e. progressive dancers, it is best to sit out the dance. Likewise don't attempt any stop-and-go dances such as the El Paso, Wooden Nickel, or Colorado ten-step if there is no room or if everyone else is traveling forward. It also is not a good idea to do a lot of turns, ducks, or tunnels on a crowded floor, nor is it the best time to try to teach someone to dance. In many honky-tonks throughout Texas and Oklahoma, folks will two-step to every song, save for an occasional waltz. Never mind that it may be a cha-cha beat, these people can–and do–two-step to anything. Remember you're here to have fun, not start a fight. It basically comes down to this: Go with the flow of traffic. If everyone is freestyling, then maybe that is what you should do as well, or stake out a small area on the floor and move only within that space.

Now all this doesn't mean that you are not allowed to step foot on the dance floor if you don't know how to country dance. You have every right; everybody was a beginner at one time. So if you just want to let loose and boogie, find a spot somewhere in the middle and do your thing. And if you want to line dance but haven't a clue as to what to do, don't stand on an outside row, go to one on the inside. That way if everyone is standing where they should be, only those who know the dance will be on the outer edges and hopefully you will have people who know what they're doing on all sides where you can watch them.

Someone just getting into the country dance scene should always look for a partner who dances at the same level or higher. The latter has the advantage of helping you pick up new skills, but there is also the danger of picking up bad habits, which is why everyone needs to take lessons now and then. Conversely, an experienced dancer should not feel put out by dancing with someone who is at a lesser skill level–as I said, everyone was a beginner once. Of course, this is where the hierarchy of dancers enters in. There are three broad categories:

- Advanced. All levels of competitive dancers fall into this category, from Novice and Division IV on up to the Masters, most of whom go dancing to see and be seen–or at least that is the image they seem to project. They can be either couples dancers or line dancers. Some appear to resent the presence of others in their space and can be either impressive or obnoxious, depending on if they're having an on or off night.
- Intermediate. Good to exceptional dancers who enjoy dancing, but who are not inclined to compete–"street dancers," as Sally Threlfall calls them. By choice they are not in the same league as their competitive counterparts. These people don't usually dress like their partners, unless they've been married for fifty years, and they don't go ballistic over a botched move. They may get out only on the weekend or a few times a month, but when they do, they have a good time.
- Beginner. The ones whose steps and manner of dress are uncertain fall into this category. They should be encouraged rather than discouraged.

The primary objective of honky-tonking is to have fun. That means everybody who wants to dance should get to without others behaving in a rude or condescending manner toward them. Folks who get out only one night a week don't want or need anyone pressuring them or spoiling their fun–especially if they paid a cover charge. So relax. There is no need to get stressed out if a partner doesn't execute a move perfectly. As choreographer and dance champion

Barry Durand of Rockville, Maryland, says: "There are no wrong moves in country dance."

Among dancers, the battle lines are clearly drawn between two subgroups: Two-Steppers and Line Dancers. Line dancing, like two-stepping, has been around for years, but has grown in popularity in the 1990s. Two-steppers feel that they were here first and resent line dancers for various reasons, some of which will be addressed momentarily. But first, the benefits of line dancing:

- It is highly aerobic.
- It draws new converts into the fold.
- You don't need a partner to dance.

Unfortunately, most line dances change as quickly as the songs do, and a lot of clubs try to teach as many different ones as possible to keep drawing new customers. So the dance you learn today you may never do tomorrow. It is far more important to master some of the standards, such as the Tush Push, Sleazy Slide, and Slappin' Leather, than those choreographed for a specific song. It is also good to have these standards, as well as the two-step and waltz, in your dancing repertoire so you can fit in wherever you go. There are literally hundreds of line dances, so the chance of learning and doing them all in a honky-tonk is minimal, which is why many people form their own dance groups and sponsor dances in a rented hall. If line dances are not practiced on a regular basis they are easily forgotten. For those who get out every night this can be nirvana. And it is quite amazing to watch those who improvise and deviate from the "vanilla version" (more dancer lingo). If you are one of those brave souls trying to pick up the dance, however, and happen to be stuck behind someone doing the chocolate-marshmallow-with-cherries-on-top version (throwing in splits and jumping jacks), by the end of the dance you will be able to supply the nuts.

For those who only get out on the weekend, myself included, we just can't keep up with all these dances and we want to be able to two-step and enjoy ourselves without having line dancers monopolize the entire floor. A lot of honky-tonkers strongly oppose line dancing and don't feel the least bit sorry about voicing their opinions. For example, Redneck, an Albuquerque-based touring band, sells T-shirts that say: "Real cowboys don't line dance." And Wayne Vieler, owner of Kodiak Jack's in Petaluma, California, who has choreographed his share of line dances, tells how he and some friends were going to have T-shirts screen-printed, each with one letter on the back, that would spell out "NOT ANOTHER FUCKIN' LINE DANCE" when they lined up. "And that was in 1980!" he says.

So what do people have against line dancers? In a word, attitude. Serious two-steppers say that even though line dancing has attracted people who normally wouldn't listen or dance to country music, they are people they would rather not associate with. This is because some line dancers are unmannerly and act "holier-than-thou"; they think their dancing is what's hot and two-stepping is what's not. Erstwhile honky-tonkers vehemently contend that line dancing belongs in a disco or a gym and has no redeeming social value because you can't interact with anyone except in a sort of pack mentality. Rhonda Gore-Scott, a co-owner of the Cowboy Palace Saloon in Chatsworth, California, says that even though her club draws a good number of line dancers, some patrons feel line dancing exists solely for self-gratification and, therefore, should be practiced in the privacy of one's home. It all boils down to personal preference and that is why you can choose to go to a Traditional or New Breed club, depending on if you want to dance with someone or go it alone.

Other matters that require attention include something I call "David's Dilemma." David Prieto of Valencia, California, is relatively new to the country dance scene. He and his wife, a former competitive salsa dancer, took up line dancing and got hooked. When they went to their local Country Club, they grew bored waiting through the many partner dances just to get in the few line dances they knew. "It seemed like you would dance for ten minutes and then wait for an hour," David says. Meanwhile his wife figured that she would learn some partner dances and the two-step so she could dance more. She rounded up some neighborhood friends to go out a couple of times a month for a ladies night out. Because she was already an experienced dancer, she picked up country dancing in no time and was in demand as a partner. When David and his wife went out together, men she had met on her nights out without her husband had no qualms about coming over and spiriting her away. David found himself left in the sawdust, so to speak, which prompted him to take up two-stepping. To his dismay, he wasn't up to speed with his wife and more often than not found himself dancing with her friends. What's a husband to do? Isn't the reason you get married so you will always have a partner? Husbands, however, are not the only ones who have experienced David's Dilemma; so have wives, girlfriends, boyfriends, and casual dates. And it is not just this situation that needs to be addressed–so on to the questions and the answers.

Q. Do you always "dance with the one who brung you"?

A. At Adair's Saloon in Dallas, the answer is simple: "You daince with who brung you or no damn daincing." Adair's, however, is a beer joint of the first order that sticks to tradition (check out its jukebox and you'll see). The club has been in business long enough to know that if this rule isn't followed, trouble may ensue. This, too, is what you must do if you are with your spouse or have asked someone to be your date for the evening. It is simply common courtesy to pay attention to your own date or spouse and not someone else's.

Most honky-tonks are not in business to dictate with whom their customers should dance, however. People (even couples) switch partners all the time because, like David and his wife, they dance at different skill levels. Going back to the freeway analogy, someone used to speeding at 180 bmp may find it tedious to shift gears and dance at 50 bpm with a not-so-skilled significant other. Face it, country dancing is addictive and a fun way to exercise; it sure beats working out in a gym with a bunch of sweat-suited fatties to C+C Music Factory. If dancing is your sport and you're good at it, why not do it around slim cowboys and cowgirls in tight jeans to music you like? The accomplished dancer may welcome the chance to dance with someone equally skilled, but this may be at a loved one's expense. This can make or break a relationship. Of course, now we're entering the whole realm of interpersonal relations between male and female and the matter of trust enters in. It may be that you trust your date or mate implicitly, it's the other person you don't. I'm no counselor, but I have lived enough and seen enough to tell you that you must decide what is more important: the dancing or the relationship. You need to voice any concerns and accommodate each person's emotional and physical needs. The key, however, is to work things out before you enter a club; there's no reason to do it in a public place. Usually the more experienced dancer is the one who says: "Everybody changes partners; it's just a dance." And they mean it. Chances are these folks don't drink much anyway so alcohol won't cloud their sensibilities and everything will be perfectly innocent. But anything can happen when you take good music and great dancing and mix in alcohol. That's reality.

So if you both agree that it is okay to dance with others, fine–just don't expect everybody to have the same arrangement you do. Some people just don't switch partners when they are with someone out of respect for that person. So do not go up to another person's spouse or date expecting a dance. The proper, and polite, thing to do is to check with their partner. This may sound archaic, but honky-tonks are a throwback to the past. Just remember, if you truly care about the person you are with, you will put yourself in his or her place.

Q. What are some ways to compromise when it comes to David's Dilemma?

A. The answer to this question is as varied as individuals are and everyone is capable of figuring out their own solutions. For example, David and his wife wrote a pact with sections covering “Ladies’ Night Out,” “Our Night Out Alone,” “Couples Night Out,” and “General Understanding” to eliminate arguments stemming from “Differences of Opinion” related to country dancing. They also agreed not to correct, criticize, or change one another’s opinions, dance style, skills, or dance steps. Last I heard, things were working out much better for them.

But for those of you who are unsure of making your own decisions, don’t want to write up an agreement, or need a neutral party to step in, here goes. First, you can take a break from dancing for a while and then start back at a different club where no one knows either of you and you are forced to dance with each other. Or the die-hard dancer could go to a gay cowboy bar where there are plenty of good dancers and not have to worry about someone of the opposite sex being interested. Of course, then you might be concerned about members of the same sex. I have danced in several gay honky-tonks and have never had a problem with anyone hitting on me because everyone is there for the same reason–to dance. And I have found a lot of women lead better than some men. Women have danced together for years in all sorts of situations, usually because there aren’t enough men to go around, so there is no reason to feel strange about it. Likewise, in days of old, cowboys used to dance with other cowboys because women were scarce on the range. (See the “Turf Club” section in Chapter Six.) What I am saying is that dancing with someone of the same sex does not make a statement other than maybe there just aren’t enough qualified dance partners of the opposite sex to go around.

If you simply can’t agree on a solution and your spouse insists on dancing with other people, then pull yourself up by the bootstraps and find yourself several very attractive partners at your skill level. Chances are it won’t take long for your loved one to realize that what’s good for him or her is good for you, too.

There is also the type of person who thinks it’s okay to dance with others but that their significant other cannot. For example, I dated a man a few years back who felt it was his every right to dance with other ladies during the week when I was at home with my kids. When we went out together on weekends, he felt it was his duty to keep his little stable of hoofers happy, while I stood by and watched. One night a man asked me to dance and my date absolutely lost it, cursed and shoved the unwitting man across the room. Never mind that my date was dancing, hugging, and kissing every woman in the joint. It is the age-old double standard. Listen guys, if you dance with others, we can, too. Simple as that. If you don’t like it, then pay attention to your mate or date.

Q. How can you tell if the person you're eyeing is with someone?

A. Wedding bands are your first tip-off. And if a couple is dressed in matching outfits this is usually a "hands-off" signal. They are either a) competitive dancers who don't want to waste time dancing with those of lesser abilities, b) married, c) so madly in love they cannot bear the thought of being apart for a three-minute song, or d) all of the above. If you are looking for a real cowboy to dance with, don't worry: They wouldn't be caught dead dressed like dude ranch Kens and Barbies. Serious dancers can get fairly rabid and are more likely to break into an argument over a pivot missing its stopping point by a few degrees than over someone stealing their date for a two-step. This is one reason why some married couples don't dance with each other–it keeps the peace at home. If said date is in fact guilty of said pivot infraction, believe me, neither partner will mind if the other is whisked away by someone else.

Q. Should a less experienced dancer give up or try to match the speed of a more experienced partner?

A. Do not give up. This will change with practice. The mark of a good dancer is someone who can accommodate people of all skill levels. So men, if a lady tells you she doesn't know ducks and tunnels, then don't force her into these moves. The same holds true for women. If a man is just starting out, don't try to lead unless he wants you to. As was pointed out earlier, dancing with someone more experienced helps you learn new things, so don't balk. In dancing guys have the harder job, they have to lead. It is not fair for women to get upset with them when all they have to do is follow. Leading is complicated, and women shouldn't get mad until they have put the boot on the other foot and tried it themselves

And while we're on this subject, there is nothing more obnoxious than a bossy dance partner (or one who sings off-key in your ear), man or woman. In all aspects of life, nothing turns a person off more than "do this, do that" behavior. Dancing is supposed to relieve stress, not exacerbate it. There is always a time and place to practice and correct, but never in a public place with someone you are dancing with for the first time or with someone you would like to keep as a friend.

Q. What about women who like to lead?

A. Lloyd Thompson calls this a "positive follow," which some men may welcome. It takes the pressure off the man. But remember this is a honky-tonk; men are allowed to dominate, if only while leading a dance. Ron Threlfall says, "Guys, it's your job to put her feet where you want them."

Q. Does country dancing change people?

A. Yes, both physically and mentally. Dancing tones your body and improves your cardiovascular system and self-image. But any addiction–even an innocent one like dancing–can alter a personality. You need to keep it in perspective and not become obsessive compulsive about it. For example, I once knew a nice shy guy with two left feet who transformed himself (with practice) into a competitive dancer who refused to dance with anyone he deemed unworthy of his newly acquired abilities.

Q. Is it okay to turn someone down for a dance?

A. Of course. You needn't dance with everyone who asks, but sometimes you could be the difference in making a poor dancer a better dancer. If you choose not to dance with someone, just be polite about it and then sit out the dance. No explanation is necessary. A simple "No thanks, I'm sitting this one out" should suffice. Everyone has his reasons for not dancing certain dances or to certain songs or with certain people, and no one should take it personally. But it is extremely rude to turn down one person and then dance with another on the same song. Likewise, it is rude if the person you have turned down badgers you as to why you did. If he or she simply refuses to take no for an answer, alert a bouncer.

Q. Is it permissible to cut a dance short before a song is over?

A. In some cases, which I'll cover in the next question, but as a rule, no. Tough it out. I had a man walk away from me once just because he didn't like the place where I worked. He asked, I told him, and he stalked off the floor in a huff. I figure he did me the favor. But I have seen other people get exasperated with a partner's inabilities and leave and come back with someone else, all in the course of one song. This is just plain rude. One dance is not going to kill your reputation as a dancer. In fact, you may be surprised when people tell you what a talented dancer you are because you can make anyone look good.

Q. "Is that a pistol in your pocket or are you just glad to see me?"

A. Actress Mae West may have been the first to utter these immortal words on the silver screen, but countless women since have uttered it mentally on many a honky-tonk dance floor.

One reason many people feel comfortable country dancing is because it is done either at arm's length or by oneself. There is absolutely no need to get close to someone unless you want to, but doing so should be a mutual decision. Most women are more likely to slow dance with someone they know or with somebody who just swept their boots off on a few fast numbers. The honky-tonk regulars know who the irregulars are anyway, so it is likely they will not dance with someone new until he or she has proved they can dance (see the following question). The majority of country dancers and cowboys are gentlemen, however, who know the meaning of self-control. They are more likely to do a slow two-step than a buckle-shiner with a woman they don't know as a show of respect. If they do slow dance, they will offset their right hip against the lady's left to avoid full frontal contact.

So of whom need you beware?

a. Those who have never stepped foot in a honky-tonk until this very night. They just plain don't know how to country dance yet, so they will do what they know by instinct.

b. The very drunk. You either have to have a brutal sinus infection or be minus your sense of smell altogether not to recognize these guys. Take a whiff, and you be the judge of whether it's worth the risk. It may be all they can do to stand up, which means they will definitely depend on their dance partner for support.

c. The recently separated. These guys have been pent up so long that at the first hint of freedom they're ready to try anything with anybody, even fully clothed. Watch out!

d. All of the above. These are the most dangerous and desperate of all!

So you have been forewarned. Now don't misunderstand, this doesn't mean you shouldn't dance with beginners. Everyone does his or her share of mercy dances by default. If you have been dancing all night, however, and prefer not to be up close and personal with someone you have never seen before, just tell him or her ever-so-sweetly and politely, "No thank you, I'm taking a break, but you can catch me on the next two-step." If they can dance, they will come back. If they cannot, they'll simply move on to their next mark and you will have saved yourself a mortifying three minutes or so when you see them grinding away against a less-savvy soul.

In the quite-likely event that you have downed a few too many tequila shooters or strawberry daiquiris (cowgirls love these) and have experienced a momentary lapse of reason, simply tell your partner that it is much too hot to dance that close. If he gives you a knowing wink and says, "You got that right, baby," walk off the dance floor. It's okay in this case. The guy is being a jerk. If he won't take no for an answer and drags you onto the dance floor against your will, just tell one of the bouncers, who will have a word with him or ask him to leave. It's security's job to watch out for the ladies and take care of obnoxious patrons.

A good rule to follow is this: Never slow dance with a stranger–unless he or she is someone you really want to know up close and personal.

Q. How do you get a dance partner if you are new to a honky-tonk?

A. Country dancers can be pretty selective. I've seen it over and over, because I've been there. You walk into a honky-tonk, the band is smoking, and your boots won't keep still. But you don't know anybody and they don't know you. Human nature is to go with a sure thing, so if no one notices you keeping time with the music, then it's time to speak up. The best way to prove that you are an able dance partner is to watch and see who matches your ability and then ask that person. Once other dancers see that you are no novice, dance requests will follow. I've found that it always helps to say you're from out of town and would like to dance with someone who can show you the regional variations. They are usually more than willing.

Q. Can a woman ask a cowboy to dance?

A. You bet. These are the 1990s and women have been doing it for years now, so don't be shy. There are a couple of ways to ask. You can go the usual route and say, "Would you care to two-step?" or you can lure him onto the dance floor by looking him straight in the eye and beckon him with your index finger without having to say a word. The latter method is quite effective and chances are he'll be flattered. The worst he can say is no, then you just move on to someone else–just like a man does.

Q. How many times can you dance with someone before they think they own you?

A. Twice. Any more than that, watch out. Yes, you may go back for thirds or fourths or fifths, but if you have no intention of going to breakfast with this person, you'd best spread out dances among partners. Once a man lamented to me about how he had danced with a woman the night before and by the end of the evening she wouldn't let him sit down or dance with any of his regular partners. He was an exceptional dancer and in demand. It distressed him somewhat because his other lady friends weren't getting to dance much and he feared they were getting the wrong idea about him and this other woman. His first mistake was continuing to dance with her. Usually you know if you want to spend more than five minutes with someone after a couple of dances. By the end of the second dance, it's up to either one of you to cut it off. Simply ask your partner to save you another two-step later on and walk off the floor. Then it is solely up to you whether you dance with that person again.

Q. After a dance is over is it necessary for the man to walk the woman back to her seat or where she was standing?

A. A real cowboy, and by that I mean a real gentleman, does. It shows a certain amount of class as well as a good upbringing. If you weren't brought up this way, just remember it is never too late to acquire manners. If a man goes his own way after a song is over and makes a beeline for someone else, then it is okay to turn him down for other dances. It's up to you if you want to explain why.

Q. Should people socialize or drink on the dance floor?

A. No. The dance floor is for dancing. If you aren't dancing, get off the floor and do your talking. Be polite. It's that simple. And never walk across the floor carrying a drink. It's too easy for someone to run into you and spill it, which is dangerous to everyone–especially if the floor is cement. There's nothing worse than having to dodge a wet spot and even after it has been cleaned up, that spot is ruined for the rest of the night because it becomes tacky and you can't slide properly.

Q. When do you take off your hat?

A. Off the dance floor a hat is doffed as a show of respect or when showering, sleeping, undergoing brain surgery, or scooping water for your horse. About the only time you need to take it off in a honky-tonk is when you're slow dancing and want nothing to come between you and your partner; then hold onto it behind your partner's back. Cowboy hats look good, so why take them off? Where do you hang a three hundred dollar hat in a public place anyway? Coatroom attendants may not know the proper way to handle them, and it just isn't worth the risk. Besides, then the whole hat-hair issue enters into the picture. The more you take a hat on and off, the more you'll suffer from hat hair. Dancers especially should remember this when they try to execute a fancy move and put their hat on a partner's head, which is only permissible if the person in question is a regular partner and you are used to fighting anyway. Most people, however, do not appreciate a sweat-soaked piece of straw or beaver plunked atop their heads without fair warning. Bear in mind, too, that hat hair is not a pretty sight and the smell isn't much better. Just keep them to yourselves, and if you do take them off for whatever reason, make sure you don't put them on backward!

Q. What can one do about sweat-drenched hair?

A. Either keep your hat on or tie a bandanna around your head and wear it under your hat to catch runaway perspiration. Ladies who don't wear hats can keep long hair in a braid, bun, or ponytail or go to the "Cowgirls" room and blow it dry with the hand dryer. Simply angle the nozzle upward and let her blow. It works like a charm and keeps you looking great.

Q. What about sweat-soaked shirts?

A. There is an old saying: "Horses sweat, men perspire, and ladies glisten." However, this was not said in reference to country dancing, during which everybody sweats–regardless of sex. Dancing is exercise, and men and women with healthy lymph systems will sweat, some profusely. Some folks repair to the "Guns" and "Holsters" rooms to take a quick sponge bath with paper towels. Still others bring along extra shirts and change during band breaks in their cars or behind the open doors of their pickups in the parking lot. Of course, you both run the risk of not making it back inside if you like what you see or if police are patrolling the area. But at least these folks know they are a lot more appealing to dance with if they are dry. That is, of course, unless you don't mind getting down and dirty with your dance partner.

Q. How do cowgirls carry their money?

A. One of the most ridiculous sights I see are women trying to two-step with purses dangling from their shoulders or fanny packs bouncing on their butts. This is not cool–and cowgirls are cool. So leave those bags at home unless you have an overriding desire to let people know you're new to honky-tonking. As a rule, cowgirls do not carry purses; they carry enough money for a phone call, the cover charge, their first drink, and maybe a taxi ride home in the front pocket of their Rockies or Wranglers. Then they let the cowboys take it from there. Yes this is sexist, but, again, we're talking cowboy bars here. These places are bastions of sexism and some of us like it that way. Honky-tonks are one of the few places in America where a lady can still find a man who will call her "darlin'," open a door for her, buy her a drink, lead a dance, and walk her to her seat. If you don't like it, go to the rap club down the street.

For those wearing dresses or skirts, secure your cash inside your bra or in the pocket of a snap-button shirt or blouse. You may also opt to use a small purse such as the one Coach makes that attaches to a belt. Or you can do as your mama always said and keep it in a boot. Some western wear outlets such as Sheplers sell boot wallets that attach to a boot strap with a Velcro strip, but these can irritate dancing fools. There is also an ankle cuff with a zippered pouch on the market. Of course, you could always stash your cash inside a boot sock, but do this only if you are wearing jeans–don't try it with a skirt. I once lost twenty bucks this way because as I danced, Andrew Jackson worked his way up and someone else took him home.

Q. How does a cowboy carry his money?

A. Jethro, a western wear salesman in Atoka, Oklahoma, who goes only by his first name, says cowboy impostors are the ones with a long wallet or a checkbook stuffed in a back pocket. A real cowboy doesn't let it all hang out. They have wallets that fit inside a pocket, usually a front one. This is done mostly, Jethro says, because a cowboy is less likely to lose it when he rides or falls. Besides it's a whole lot easier noticing if some outsider is trying to lift your bankroll when it is in a front pocket.

Q. What do you do with a chew once you've finished with it?

A. Disposal methods vary, but discretion is the key. For example, Butch Markle of Hanna, Wyoming, swallows his. Jethro, the western wear salesman, stuffs it in his cheek like a chipmunk, while his friend Jimmy Lee recycles his by spitting back into the pouch it came in. "Keeps it moist," Jimmy says. "It also keeps other people from bumming a chew off you!" Still others expectorate into glasses or empty beer bottles. But Michael Naughton, a card-carrying Professional Rodeo Cowboy Association committee member from Flagstaff, Arizona, says "nothing's worse than a bunch of 'floaties'–a real cowboy wipes on his jeans." Michael adds, "I once dated a girl who chewed and she wiped, too."

In the old days, spittoons positioned at various spots around a bar solved this problem. Although chewing is as popular today as it was way back when, spittoons are visibly absent. It may be because more people use snuff, which can be swallowed. It is usually fairly simple to identify those who chew; they have cylinders of Skoal in the back pockets of their Wranglers. Just be aware, however, that cowboy wanna-bes will stick cylinders of Bubble Tape back there instead.

Q. Why don't honky-tonkers applaud for the band?

A. Because they are rude. I'm sorry. There's just no other way to put this. There are some who do, but the majority don't. It sounds pretty sad when only one or two individuals clap. Having dated my share of musicians, this happens to be one of my pet peeves. These are the makers of the music. They get up there and sing out their souls and nobody seems to notice. Some dancers clap, but they are more likely applauding themselves. Watch them during a band break or in a country disco when all that is playing is recorded music. They still clap.

Q. Is dancing permitted when a national act is performing?

A. Vince Gill, the CMA "Entertainer of the Year" for 1994, reportedly has said: "I ain't no jukebox." I don't know in what context this comment was made, but it could be that he prefers not to be treated like a machine that plays music on demand in some corner of the room while everyone ignores him. So the answer is no–not unless the artist, Marty Stuart is one, tells you it's okay to get up and dance. Otherwise stay put and enjoy the music. And don't forget to applaud!

Q. Why do some bands take requests and others don't?

A. Again, these people are not jukeboxes and they usually have a play list that they must follow to fill their forty minutes of playing time. Some singers will announce if the band takes requests, but wait for a break–do not approach them in the middle of a song.

Q. What about tipping the bartenders and waitresses?

A. If you get good service, tip. These people work their fannies off and have to put up with more than their share of harassment. It's only fair. The 15 percent rule applies, however, it seems that honky-tonkers tend to be overly generous or overly stingy depending on how much they've had to drink. You may even want to tip the band.

Q. What can be done about beer breath?

A. It's not just beer breath–it's gin, vodka, and whiskey breath. People seem to forget this stuff stinks, especially if intake has been heavy or they have been smoking as well. There have been many times I have had to shut down my nasal passages while dancing with someone who has overindulged. I do not think one has to be rude, but if it is unbearable you can always offer a stick of gum or a breath mint to the offending party. I always carry gum just for this purpose and Ron Threlfall at Kelly's always carries Tic-Tacs for anyone who needs them. If the offending person can't take a gentle hint like this and turns down the offer, lead them to the Breathalyzer in the corner or make a mental note not to dance with said person again that evening.

Q. Is there such a thing as "fighting etiquette"?

A. Yes. In honky-tonks today, fights are still quite common, even though many go unnoticed because security steps in before things have a chance to go from bad to worse. Still, there are some unspoken ground rules for barroom brawls. It seems that fights almost always start for no good reason. I've seen them happen simply because an envious woman wanted another's fancy clothes and because someone brushed against someone who didn't want to be touched. Most fights occur because somebody is unable to hold his or her liquor and act in a civil manner. And more often than not it's an outsider or a woman stirring up the trouble.

Nowadays situations are simply not allowed to get out of hand because club owners want to create a safe environment for their customers. Many times it is the owners themselves who immediately put an end to rowdy bar behavior. For example, a sign behind the bar at the Cowboy Palace Saloon in Chatsworth, California, says: "Forget the dog, beware of Rhonda." Rhonda Gore-Scott, one of the club's co-owners, is a lissome blond who doesn't look the type to wallop an unruly patron–but she can and she will. She has been known to jump over the bar and escort a troublemaker outside, holding his ear like a bad schoolboy. Then there is Jason Palumbo, the slim young buck who owns the Cowboy Saloon and Dance Hall in Laramie, Wyoming. Jason, a former wrestler and jock of all trades, takes on the rabble-rousers and prides himself in never having lost a fight. Once, he says, he took on the town bad boy and the police personally thanked him. Ken Lance takes a softer approach, talking to the perpetrators in a fatherly way, saying such things as, "Now boys, you wouldn't want to get old Cowboy Ken in trouble, would you?"

So what are some of the unspoken rules for barroom brawls?

- ⋆ Don't get in a fight if you don't know anything about a bar.
- ⋆ Take it outside so innocent parties won't get hurt.
- ⋆ Don't fight unless you have to.
- ⋆ Don't use knives or weapons.
- ⋆ Know your limitations. That is, know how much you can drink and still keep your wits about you.

If you are not adult enough to go out and enjoy yourself without getting into a fight, know that you may suffer some serious consequences. Besides being hauled off to jail, you could very well be banned forever from a honky-tonk.

Q. How late should youngsters stay in a club?

A. Clubs differ on this policy. Most liquor laws prohibit honky-tonks from allowing anyone under twenty-one inside. Others permit their presence in areas away from the bar. Some require that the child be accompanied by a parent or guardian. More and more clubs are instituting nights or days when the whole family can dance together (check the directory in the back of the book for clubs that offer Family or Teen Nights). In any event, most clubs that allow children have a set time when they must vacate the premises. Still, there are those that leave it to the judgment of a parent or guardian. Parents should keep in mind, however, that a lot of people go to honky-tonks to escape kids. When I take mine to a honky-tonk, we usually leave by 9:30 P.M.– and that's on a Family Night when they are allowed to stay until closing.

Q. Is a woman obligated in any way if a man buys her a rose?

A. No. Some guys think that buying a woman a rose buys into her good graces. It is a sweet gesture, and I always appreciate receiving a rose, but a woman is in no way obligated to do anything more for the man who bought it than to say, "Thank you." These flower ladies have a nice little business going, and anyone who has bought a rose in a honky-tonk knows they are priced well above fair market value. Some men, like Scott Beaty, simply refuse to buy a rose under such circumstances. "That's what all-night florists are for," he says.

Q. Does going to breakfast with someone mean that you will be going home with that person?

A. No. The "Rose Rule" applies here, too. Going to breakfast is one of those nice little rituals among the honky-tonk set where the events of the evening are recapped while you replenish your body with calories lost during dancing. Breakfast also has the added benefit of soaking up some of those suds imbibed during the course of the evening and getting some caffeine in your system for the drive home. It can be done by yourself, with someone, or in a group. And you are in no way obligated for anything more than breakfast– especially if it was Dutch treat.

A WORD ABOUT Barroom Bovines

4

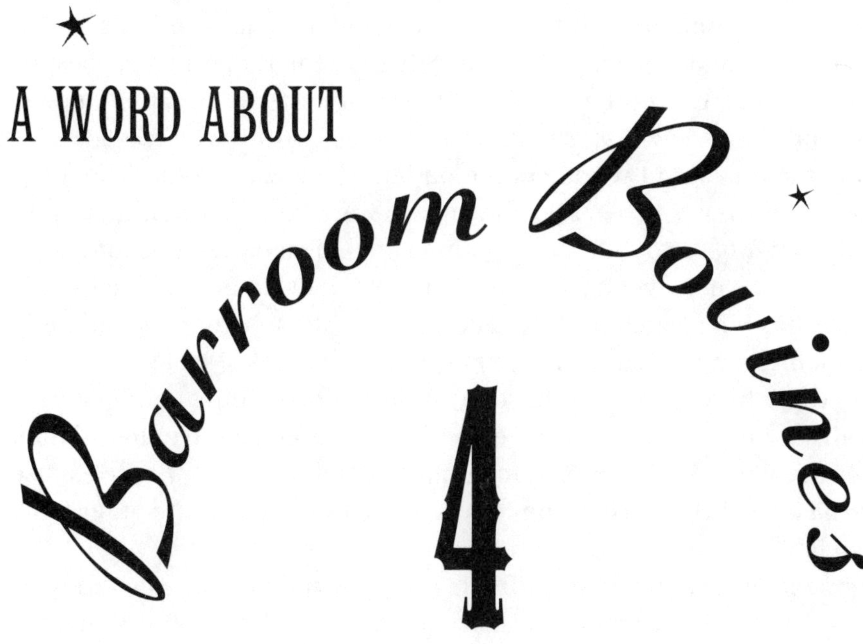

A lot of people see guys dressed in Wranglers and Resistols mount barroom bovines and assume they're cowboys. Don't. They may walk the walk and talk the talk, but that doesn't necessarily mean anything. This is not to say cowboys never ride mechanical bulls. Plenty do. After all, they created these critters to hone their bull-riding skills. Still, it is more likely that they will want to practice on the real thing.

There are several reasons real cowboys rarely ride these mechanized creatures, especially in a barroom setting. First, they have an image to protect. They don't want to be lumped in the same category as some drugstore cowboy. Second, mechanical bulls are highly unpredictable and are a lot harder to ride than the real thing. At least this is why Tony and Dean, two bull riders from Australia I met at the Ken Lance Sports Arena and Dance Pavilion, say they don't ride. Anyone who has seen *Eight Seconds,* the film about world champion bull rider Lane Frost, who died at the tender age of twenty-three after the bull he was riding gored him, or has been to a rodeo might beg to differ. Bull riding is the most dangerous and most often entered rough-stock event in rodeo, so it's a bit hard to believe a cowboy would shy away from a pretend bull. A mechanical bull isn't going to get mad and try to hook or trample, but it can spin around real quick–just lay low after your fall so it won't hit you. Tony and Dean swear the mechanical bulls are worse, though, and no amount of female persuasion could cajole either of them into demonstrating proper bull-riding technique. Dean had a legitimate excuse; he was nursing a few broken ribs from a recent throw. Tony, on the other hand, had none. No how, no hell, no way . . . end of discussion!

The critters make for good entertainment, though, and club owners know this. Cowboys like it when women ride, sort of a throwback to Debra Winger in her *Urban Cowboy* phase. I, myself, enjoy the heck out of these things, but then I have always had a fondness for the mechanical ponies out in front of K mart. And, yes, it does feel good when the bull is going nice and slow. Cowboys find a certain excitement in watching a female undulate on a mechanical bull, which would never happen on the back of a Brahma. Cowboys also like it when the wanna-bes down a few beers and are ready to show off. To paraphrase the Bible: "Ride goeth before a fall." Nothing, and I mean nothing, is funnier to a cowboy than watching some cocky guy in Dockers and a polo shirt wearing a pair of python boots (if you haven't read Chapter Two, do so now!) sign an injury release and plunk down a few dollars only to get bucked off in a matter of seconds. Said person usually ends up dangling helplessly from the handle by a boot, laughing his fool head off. He'd better laugh now because one thing is certain, he won't be laughing come morning, when he feels the results of his wild ride in muscles he didn't know existed. Bear in mind that if I had not witnessed this very incident, I would not be relating it here.

"Usually I try to make 'em look like a hero in front of their friends," says Ken Lance, a rodeo cowboy and owner of the aforementioned arena. "If I don't, they won't come back and I won't make any money. There *are* times though . . ."

You see, cowboys have a lot of common sense and always have a pretty good reason for everything they do.

So maybe real cowboys don't care much for these critters, but if you don't have access to a Brahma and have a hankering to ride, a barroom bovine is the next best thing. On a real bull you're a champ if you can hang on for eight seconds and look good. A ride on a mechanical bull, however, typically lasts about thirty seconds, give or take a few, depending on the demeanor of the operator. There is no real way to practice for riding one of these either. Face it, those K mart ponies just don't cut it. I once saw some Easterners at a party "mount" an Oriental rug hung over a couple of clotheslines while guys on either end jerked the lines in an attempt to "buck" the riders. It was pretty pitiful, but at least they were trying. Your best bet is to tell the bull operator it is your first time and ask him to have mercy on you. This is a ploy you can use quite a bit if you're not a regular. After a few slow rides, you may find yourself wanting more of a challenge and then you can ask the operator to kick up the juice.

Barroom bovines come in all shapes and sizes, just like the genuine article. You've got your *Urban Cowboy* type, leather-sided contraptions that look nothing like an animal, or ones with Fiberglas bodies made to resemble the real thing. In Oklahoma, they take on a personality all their own. For example, the one at Tumbleweed in Stillwater has a saddle, Ken Lance's is customized with cowhide, floppy ears, and a braided-rope tail with a bow on the end, while "Maxie" at Cowtown, U.S.A., in nearby Tecumseh, is your basic homemade model covered with red indoor-outdoor carpeting. Ladies, do not, and I repeat do not, ride either of these types in skirts or shorts (again, if you haven't read Chapter Two, read it now!) unless you want to experience serious rug burn on your inner thighs.

Mechanical bulls are less prevalent in the 1990s than they were in 1980, at the height of *Urban Cowboy's* popularity, but they are still around. Oftentimes they are just brought in for "Buck Off!" nights or special events such as the "Cheyenne Chute Out," sponsored by the Cheyenne Cattle Co. in Wichita Falls, Texas. There contestants pay a five dollar entry fee, which goes to the Lane Frost Scholarship Fund, to ride "High Voltage." This event draws a lot of real cowboys and those who go the distance receive a T-shirt and qualify to compete for $2,500 in prizes. First-place winners receive "Chute Out" belt buckles, just like at a real rodeo.

Club owners are well aware of the potential legal problems these creatures pose. That's why you must sign a form absolving them of any liability should injury occur. Of course, some of you may wonder why the heck anybody would want to do something where it's almost guaranteed you'll fall. I know one guy who says, "I have a rule: I don't ride wild animals and they don't ride me!" It's not an activity for the faint of heart, that's for sure. But people ride bulls for the same reason others zoom down a snow-covered slope on two thin slices of Fiberglas at God-knows-how-many miles per hour–for the thrill of it. Still, if you have a history of back or neck problems, it is advisable to forgo either activity altogether.

If you are hell-bent on riding a mechanical bull, Ken Lance says to "keep a leg on either side and your mind in the middle." Here are several other points to remember:

- ★ Know that you will be watched. In some clubs, such as the Saddle Rack, each ride is broadcast on big screens in every corner of the club.
- ★ Put your wallet in your front pocket. This way you are less likely to lose it when you fall and your hindquarters will be evenly distributed.
- ★ Wear a leather glove (clubs provide these). It helps you grip the hand-hold better and protects virgin palms from blistering. Some honky-tonks even have cotton gloves for you to wear underneath the leather one to provide extra padding and to absorb sweat brought on by severe adrenaline surges. Be advised, however, that someone else has probably used it first and it may be a tad damp.
- ★ Grip with your nondominant hand. That is, if you are right-handed hold on like hell with the left, and vice versa. Keep the top of your hand against the bull with fingers curled up and over the hand-hold. If you use your dominant hand, you may be sorry the next morning because it will feel as if arthritis has set in about thirty years too soon–even more so if you didn't wear a glove.
- ★ Hold your free arm up. In rodeo, bull riders are permitted to hold on with only one hand and they can be disqualified if they touch either themselves or the bull. The same rules apply at a "Buck Off!" or "Chute Out," but that free arm also helps you balance and stay on.
- ★ Scoot up. Keep your crotch close to the grip.
- ★ Squeeze your thighs. This helps you hold on, too.
- ★ Take it slow. Build up your skill before going full tilt.
- ★ Go with the bull. When the bull's head goes down, lean back some, but not too much; and when the bull spins, go with the spin.

PART TWO

Clubs with Staying Power

Arizona

5

The main thing you need to know here is that the Arizona two-step, or the half-time, is done more than the Texas two-step. And the state offers some mighty fine clubs in which to practice. Down in Tucson, there's the Maverick (Traditional) and the Cactus Moon (New Breed). The Phoenix area is home to many New Breed clubs, including Denim & Diamonds, Graham Central Station, and Rockin' Rodeo; Traditional offerings include Mr. Lucky's and Toolies Country Saloon and Dance Hall, which will be profiled in this chapter. Up in Flagstaff, they're all pretty much Traditional in nature, but none can compare with the Museum Club.

The Museum Club
3404 East Route 66, Flagstaff
602/526-9434

DIRECTIONS: From I-40 take exit 201/Country Club to Historic Route 66. The Museum Club is on the right.
DRESS CODE: Ropers, Rockies, and Wranglers.
DANCE DYNAMICS: Arizona two-step, buckle-shiners. Line dancers beware!
HOURS: Open seven days a week from noon to 1 A.M. Happy hour daily from 2 to 7 P.M.
MUSIC: Live music nightly, except Monday.

The Museum Club's former general manager Gary Nelson likes to tell about the time a band struck up the first few chords of "Achy Breaky Heart." A few people, clearly out-of-towners, jumped up to line dance and the lead singer yelled, "Not!" into the microphone before launching into a more traditional country song.

In case you hadn't guessed, this is a real redneck stomping ground. There's a mixed drink you can order at the bar called the Redneck and one of the more popular bands is Redneck from Albuquerque. Yes, the same band that sells the "Real Cowboys Don't Line Dance" T-shirts. So you're correct in assuming that folks here don't take too kindly to disco cowboys. If you choose to line dance you may do so at your own risk, but the dance of choice on the four-hundred-square-foot hardwood floor is the Arizona two-step, or the half-time (so called because it takes half the time and half the space). I call it the "two time" because one man can dance with two women at once. As a rule, you won't see the Texas two-step here unless someone from out of town is doing it. On a smaller dance floor such as the Museum Club's, the Arizona two-step enables everyone to dance without impeding one another. The dance itself slowly moves counterclockwise with a step-together, step-together with a pause-step back and a few in-place turns for the ladies while the man dances in place. For those accustomed to a more progressive two-step, it can be a bit awkward at first. Take my advice though, and ask someone like doorman Larry Paolella to teach you. (Having once been a newcomer himself, Larry, a tall, beefy Italian from Philadelphia, is more than happy to play dance instructor.) That's what I did. Once you catch on, the dance is a lot of fun. It isn't all that hard to pick up and you won't annoy the locals by going against the dance-floor grain. Luckily it's a simple enough dance. And remember, the club offers free lessons for the uninitiated on Thursday nights.

This is the club that *Country America* magazine chose as its "King of Clubs" in 1994. The Museum Club also was named as one of the nation's ten best roadhouses by *Car and Driver* magazine in 1992. In 1994 it received the Governor's Award for Historic Preservation, and was listed in the Arizona Register of Historic Places as well as the National Register of Historic Places. Current owner Martin Zanzucchi, an old-car buff who bought the club in 1984, plays up the fact that the club is Flagstaff's original Route 66 landmark and led the petition drive to have Santa Fe Avenue restored to its original name.

"Old cars and old bars, that's part of the love affair with the highway," he says. He should know, because he was born and raised in Flagstaff. You can learn all about the Arizona stretch of the "Mother Road" in a video that plays continuously on a small television at the front of the club, where other memorabilia, such as a Bob Wills poster and Willie Nelson's contract for six hundred dollars a night, are on display. Call it Martin's Mini-Museum.

You might say this club is rooted in history. Back in 1915, Dean Eldredge, who owned a local taxi business, bought land east of town so he could build a place to house his taxidermy hobby. He used ponderosa pine from nearby forests to build what is still the largest log cabin in the state. Eldredge turned part of a forked pine upside down to create the wishbonelike entrance, and five live trees were incorporated inside the building. He dug deep enough so as to encase the trees in concrete so they would stay stable long after they died.

The Dean Eldredge Taxidermy Museum and Trading Post officially opened for business in 1918 and offered stuff-while-you-wait service. Eldredge apparently stuffed everything from buffalo ($50) to canaries ($2.50 for closed wings and $3 for open wings) and even horned toads! He was fascinated with freaks of nature like six-legged lambs and two-headed steers. Then a man called "Doc" Williams bought the dead-animal museum in 1936 and turned it into a first-class roadhouse called the Museum Club. It traded hands over the years, and for a time in the 1950s was known as the "Muscle Club" because of the bikers, the booze, and the brawls. That changed when former professional musician Don Scott bought the club in 1963 and put the focus on the music. Willie Nelson was a frequent visitor during those years when he had an ongoing friendship with Scott's daughter, Donna.

The Museum Club is basically the same today as it was back then. It still looks like the great outdoors indoors, what with the trees that mark the four corners and center of the dance floor and the eighty mounts on the walls left over from its taxidermy days. No wonder people call it "The Zoo." Martin takes great pride in owning such a landmark and has a vested interest in preserving the Museum Club. It was here that his parents met and also where he met his wife, Stacie. Martin is nothing less than meticulous in the upkeep of the club and the trees and floors are polished daily with lemon oil. He has added new plumbing since he bought the place in 1978, as well as the mahogany bar in the back of the club that dates back to the 1880s. The bar was built in Wisconsin and used to be a prop at the old Legend City amusement park in Phoenix.

There's something else you should know about this club. It's haunted. Tales are told of empty chairs starting to rock and fires lighting on their own volition in the fireplace at the front of the club. Gary Nelson tells of having bottles hurled at him at 3 A.M. when he was the only person in the club. Probably one of the more fascinating stories involved Richard Bentley, a handyman Martin hired in 1984. Richard used to live in the apartment above the club where the former owners, Don and Thorna Scott, lived in the 1960s and 1970s. Richard awoke one winter night to find a blond woman sitting on his chest, pinning his arms down. She allegedly told him not to be afraid because "only the living could hurt him." He struggled out of her hold and dove out of one of the club's front windows. He went to a motel and called Martin at 3:30 A.M. Martin says the next day Richard quit and left Flagstaff for good.

Those aren't the only spirits that have made this club famous. The recipes for two of the Zoo's better-known mixed drinks, the aforementioned Redneck and the Neon Moon, are featured in *The Route 66 Cookbook* by Marian Clark. Bartender Jen Ringle says the cowboys prefer Bud and Coors, however. So if you know you're going to drink a few too many of either, call ahead for one of the free round-trip taxi rides the Zoo provides for its patrons within the city limits.

Steve Talaga, the club's current manager, says the Zoo also had another nickname–"The Park and Fight." But that all changed when Martin bought the place. Steve says the club's policy is simple: "If you're caught in a fight, you're out of the bar for sixty days." Nope. Not many problems here anymore. And Steve says they do watch out for the ladies.

The Zoo attracts a fair amount of football players, too. The main attraction the Sunday night I was there was Phoenix Cardinal Jim McMahan. Usually though, the focus is on the live entertainment, a tradition that Martin has continued from the days when "Pappy" Scott used to own the place and would bring in all his musician friends. Martin books an assortment of local and regional bands (the night I was there the band was Las Vegas's Western Rain). With a club capacity of 250, Martin says he can't justify the expense of booking the really big names.

On your way out, be sure to look at a pamphlet hanging by the door promoting Dean Eldredge's taxidermy business: "Wanted, Freaks, Antique Guns, Prehistoric Indian Curios . . . an hour spent here will never be forgotten."

And Martin promises that "the same holds true today."

Toolies Country Saloon & Dance Hall
4231 West Thomas Road, Phoenix
602/272-3100

DIRECTIONS: From I-10 exit at 43rd Avenue. Go north on 43rd and turn right on West Thomas Road. Toolies is on the right.
DRESS CODE: All manner of western wear. Most Arizonans wear Ropers, Wranglers, and Rockies, but many women wear skirts here. No tank tops or motorcycle apparel.
DANCE DYNAMICS: Texas two-step, Arizona two-step, West Coast swing, waltz.
HOURS: Open Monday through Saturday 8 A.M. to 1 A.M.; Sunday from 10 A.M. to 1 A.M. Family Night is 5 to 8 P.M. on Friday.
MUSIC: Live music nightly.

Toolies is the kind of place where a stranger can kick up his heels and make himself right at home. Like many suburban honky-tonks, its shopping-center location disguises what lies behind its doors. Inside, the old meets the new. One might think it was a saloon circa 1890 were it not for the electronic sounds coming from the game room (and the fact that it's virtually smoke-free). But this is an all-purpose modern-day honky-tonk that has won its share of local and national awards and offers everything from a boot shine to a general store.

Toolies, the hottest Traditional country dance spot in Phoenix, has walked away with the "Best of Phoenix" awards for several years running. Over the years it has been nominated for both the Academy of Country Music (ACM) and the Country Music Association "Nightclub of the Year" honors. Nationally, 1993 was the club's best year to date when it won the ACM "Nightclub of the Year" title and its owner, Bill Bachand, was named ACM "Talent Buyer/Promoter of the Year." Toolies also was nominated in 1993 for the CMA "Nightclub of the Year." Locally, in 1994, *New Times* magazine rated it best in its "Country Bar" and "Off-Track Betting Parlor" categories, the *Arizona Republic* touted it as "Best Arizona Nightclub," and *Seniors* magazine as "Best Place to Country Dance."

You won't hear any canned music here–it's live every night of the week. Bill does his homework and keeps tabs on who's hot in country music and books acts from all over the United States. In fact, it's the musicians themselves who highly recommend Toolies, which has been featured on the Nashville Network's *On Stage* program. Ask them which clubs they enjoy playing the most and Toolies is always mentioned. Pickers say it's because

Bill gives them first-class treatment and wrangles cut-rate deals with nearby hotels to help keep road costs low.

The funny thing is, Bill never fancied himself a nightclub owner, let alone a country one. He grew up with Motown in Dearborn, Michigan, and had a thriving career in commercial real estate. Bill bought the struggling west-side institution in 1984 when it was nothing more than a smoky, decade-old honky-tonk that booked good bands and attracted a decent clientele. Bill gave the operation to his wife, Joan, to run, until he could make a quick turnaround on his investment. But it kept doubling until it got to where they were turning away three hundred people a night on weekends, and they decided it would be foolish to sell. In 1986 the club moved three doors down to its present location. Toolies now encompasses twelve thousand square feet of space and can accommodate up to nine hundred people on a given night, and its two-thousand-square-foot dance floor of smooth oak is a big attraction. Children are allowed in for the family barbecue dinner from 5 to 8 P.M. on Fridays and at all concerts featuring national acts.

California 6

Honky-tonks in California run the gamut from very Traditional to very New Breed. It seems that folks here are into line dancing more so than in other parts of the country, and you can pretty much get away with wearing any western combination you can pull together. Californians tend to test the fashion limits . . . I know this from having lived in the state for seven years.

There are so many new clubs in southern California, it's hard to keep up with them all. But if you get the chance be sure to check out the Crazy Horse Steakhouse and Saloon, a five-time ACM "Nightclub of the Year," in Santa Ana. Other Traditional types to see are Beaver Creek Saloon in Escondido, Cactus

Corral in Palm Springs, Cocky Bull in Victorville, Longhorn Saloon in Canoga Park, and the Western Connection in San Dimas. Popular New Breed nightspots include Cowboy Boogie Co. in Anaheim; InCahoots Dance Hall & Saloon in Fullerton, Glendale, San Bernardino, and San Diego; Country Rock Cafe in Lake Forest; and Graham Gilliam's Denim & Diamonds in Huntington Beach, Santa Monica, and Woodland Hills.

In the central part of the state, check out Jim's Place in Clovis and Scotty's in Chico, both Traditional honky-tonks. New Breed offerings include Graham Gilliam's Denim & Diamonds in Citrus Heights and InCahoots in Sacramento.

Up north, I am not aware of many Traditional clubs, but Josey Wales in Vallejo was the closest I found. There are plenty of New Breed clubs, though, so check out Kodiak Jack's in Petaluma and the Cadillac Ranch in Concord, Fairfield, Pleasanton, and San Leandro.

For the clubs I chose to profile, I picked two to the south and two to the north. All are different, all have demonstrated longevity, and all should be an experience you'll not soon forget. They are the Cowboy Palace Saloon in Chatsworth, the Palomino in North Hollywood, the Saddle Rack in San Jose, and the Turf Club in Hayward.

The Cowboy Palace Saloon

21635 Devonshire Street, Chatsworth
818/341–0166

THE COWBOY PALACE SALOON
The last real "Honky Tonk"

DIRECTIONS: From I-405/San Diego Freeway, I-5/Golden State Freeway, or Route 27/Topanga Boulevard, exit on Devonshire Boulevard. The Cowboy Palace is between Canoga and Owensmouth avenues.

DRESS CODE: Anything, as long as you're dressed.

DANCE DYNAMICS: Two-step, ten-step, Cowboy Cha-Cha, Tush Push, waltz, western swing, West Coast swing. Some line dancing.

HOURS: Open seven days a week from 2 P.M. to 2 A.M. Free dance lessons Monday through Thursday and Saturday at 7 P.M., Sunday at 3 P.M.

MUSIC: Live music nightly.

"The last real honky-tonk" is how the Cowboy Palace bills itself, and it comes pretty darn close to fulfilling that claim. In fact it more than meets all the qualifications of a tried-and-true honky-tonk, which is a rarity these days and even more of a rarity in southern California. The Palace sits on the edge of civilization on a stretch of road that's urban on one side and rural on the other. Regulars "park" their mounts at the fifteen-horse hitching post out back after riding in from nearby ranches to sit for a spell, dance, shoot the breeze or some pool, and generally unwind without having to pay a cover charge.

The first thing you'll see as you enter the honky-tonk is a wall of photographs of bands that have played here. Booths are situated around the perimeter of the club and the unregulated dance floor (that means no called dances) is to your left, the bar to your right. The decor is down-home, all unfinished pine and corrugated metal with hat and boot collections donated by customers, who range in age from twenty-five to fifty. Trawling is minimal because everybody here is like friends and family. And the best part is that you're never more than ten feet away from the four-hundred-square-foot hardwood dance floor. In fact, the entire square footage of the club–3,500–equals that of many a Texas dance floor. As co-owner Bob Rustigian says, "Everyone is involved and not isolated."

"It's the country background versus the city background," explains co-owner Rhonda Gore-Scott. "We were taught to be leaders, not followers."

Rhonda, who was raised on country music in Woodbridge, Virginia, "couldn't think of owning" a country disco. "Those clubs are very anonymous . . . you are not going to know the owners," she says. "Here, if a toilet gets clogged, I go in with a plunger and unclog it.

"We have our finger on the heartbeat of our customers," she continues. "We know if they've lost a horse; we care about them, that's the way we are and the customers are the same."

There is no identity crisis here. The T-shirts say, "I'm not a F.U.C. (Fake Urban Cowboy) I'm for real" and they mean it. Even though the Palace is close to Los Angeles, the yuppie quotient is never more than about 10 percent, Bob says. This club knows what it is and from whence it came; it was and always has been a country bar ever since it opened in 1970. And as long as Bob and Rhonda own it, country it will stay. The two business partners met when they worked together as real estate agents. They had in common a love of country music and dancing and both longed to own their own honky-tonk. So they looked near and far, even in Rhonda's hometown, and came close to buying the old Hillbilly Heaven (see the chapter on Virginia), but the deal never materialized. When the Cowboy Palace came on the market in 1991, Rhonda and Bob bought it in a heartbeat.

Since then the two have made few changes, but the ones they have made are for the better, such as the hardwood dance floor and the "Watering Hole," a designated area where thirsty dancers can get their own drinks of water after working up a sweat. They also serve buckets of beer, which hang from the rafters when not in use, during the entertainment. You can get four bottles in a bucket of ice for eleven dollars. Not everybody opts for beer, though.

As Rhonda points out, "A large part of our clientele doesn't drink." For those customers she has developed nonalcoholic drinks like "Bunkhouse Coffee" and "Safe Sex on the Range."

Being a southern girl and a frustrated cook, if there is one thing about the Palace that Rhonda would change it would be to serve food on a nightly basis. But local liquor laws prohibit the selling of food at hard-liquor establishments, so the club gives it away at free western barbecues every Sunday and Monday night. The only catch is you must eat what you take. The club has a special permit from the fire department so Rhonda is able to barbecue the burgers and chicken and simmer her own special sauces on the grill out back. "The only thing I can't do on it is bake," she says. So she whips up the bread pudding and brownies at home. And you must know that the potato salad here doesn't come out of a carton; Rhonda makes it herself with her own special dressing.

"As stupid as it sounds, it's a place where anything can happen, movie stars and TV actors love to hang there," says Chad Watson, whose band is one of about a half-dozen that play the club. He's been a featured performer here since 1988. "Buffalo Springfield band members have come in and sat in with me."

Chad lived in Nashville for ten years, toured with Charlie Rich for fifteen years, played bass for Ronnie Milsap, and wrote songs for Acuff-Rose Music. He has been backing Janis Ian since 1985. So it's no wonder that in the course of a night he and his band perform a lot of original material as well as "everything from Jones to Stones." Wednesday night is talent night, and Chad says they get some pretty polished acts in from L.A.

Originally from Independence, Missouri, Chad, a hulking Hank Jr. look-alike, is one of those musicians who can actually two-step and waltz and likes it. He has never line danced though, probably never will. Most people don't here–it's the ones who filter in from L.A. proper who do.

Being on the fringe of Los Angeles as it is, the Cowboy Palace also gets its share of tourists. Bob likes to tell about the time a group of Japanese came in and requested a cowboy cocktail, so "we gave them all Budweiser beer."

This little watering hole has several claims to fame. Its forty-eight-foot bar is the longest in the area, which is one reason many movies, *Twins* and *Pontiac Moon* among them, and commercials (Leggs pantyhose and Bud Light beer) have been filmed here. This isn't too hard to fathom, seeing's how movie producer Clive Barker is a regular at the Palace. So is ACM "Pioneer Award" winner and CMA "Hall of Famer" Cliffie Stone.

Rhonda says that she and Bob actually spend more time at the club than they do at home, "so we insist everyone behave. It's very seldom that someone comes in that doesn't. If they don't, I take care of them. If there's any upset women, I send Bob to take care of them." (You may want to refer back to the Manners chapter in Part One. Remember the "Forget the dog, beware of Rhonda" sign?) "I'm not afraid of anything or anybody," the pretty blond says. So if you're looking to stir up trouble, don't mess with Rhonda or she'll kick your butt and banish you forever from the best honky-tonk you're likely to find in the Golden State.

The Palomino
6907 Lankershim Boulevard, North Hollywood
818/764-4018

DIRECTIONS: From the Ventura, Hollywood, and Golden State freeways exit on Lankershim Boulevard. The Palomino is between Hart and VanOwen streets.
DRESS CODE: Anything goes. Dress in vintage clothes on rockabilly nights.
DANCE DYNAMICS: Freestyle, jitterbug.
HOURS: Open seven days a week from 11 P.M. to 2 A.M.
MUSIC: Live bands nightly.

Let's get one thing straight: Expect to find more Rodeo Drive cowboys at the Palomino than rodeo cowboys. This is North Hollywood after all. And don't expect to do much two-stepping either. The dance floor is just a small triangle of tile located in front of the stage where people mostly swing or bop around if they dance at all. Here the focus is on the music, not the dance.

"Come here if you want to hear the cutting edge of country," says owner Sherry Thomas. Country, in this case, meaning the roots of country–heavy on the blues, rockabilly, and hillbilly. Singer Dwight Yoakam cut his teeth at the Pal.

Still, if you have a partner and want to try to two-step, show up on Tuesday night for Ronnie Mack's free-admission "Barn Dance," when three to four local bands are showcased during the evening.

The Pal is located just a few miles up the road from Universal City's Country Star, which Sherry disdainfully refers to as the "Hard Rock Cafe of country." It's the flagship of a chain of country eateries and is all slick and new, backed with big bucks from Vince Gill, Wynonna, Reba, Charlie Crook, and Loriann Chase. Call it Planet Nashville, but whatever you do, don't call it a honky-tonk!

The Palomino, on the other hand, is the Bluebird Cafe of California, and a Pickers club of the first order. Such country icons as Hank Williams Sr.,

Johnny Cash, Buck Owens, Kitty Wells, and Waylon Jennings played on the Pal stage at one time or another because in the early days of country music an act had to take its show on the road to make any money.

"Virtually every country singer in the past has played here," Sherry says. "The younger crowd coming up wants to get back in touch with that."

Seeing herself as having a responsibility to provide a venue for up-and-coming singer-songwriters, she reinstituted the weekly talent nights in 1994.

The club was so renowned at one time that it walked away with ACM "Nightclub of the Year" honors fifteen times. It won fourteen years straight, from 1965 to 1978, losing out to Gilley's in 1979. The Pal's last win was in 1980.

The Palomino almost didn't make it in the running for this guide because in recent years the musical focus had been on rock. Enter Sherry, widow of Tommy Thomas, who founded the club and ran it with his brother, Bill, during its heyday. After Tommy passed on to that big honky-tonk in the sky, Sherry packed up and left SoCal to raise her two young sons in Oregon. She remained a co-owner with a nephew, who managed the club. Sherry stepped in in 1994 to revive the dying Country Club and hopes to return it to its glory days, back when scenes from movies like Clint Eastwood's *Every Which Way But Loose* and *Any Which Way You Can* were filmed here.

Not only had the club deteriorated in the years since she'd left, but the neighborhood had as well. She knew it was going to be a big job restoring the three-hundred-seat club, and expects to spend at least twenty-five thousand dollars in materials doing much of the work herself with help from friends. Sherry even enlists the help of the homeless, paying them to do odd jobs for a day. The Pal has remained immune from vandals and gangs haven't "tagged" her building because word is out on the street that she's a good person. Still, if you're a little wary of walking back to your car in the side lot, one of the bouncers will be more than happy to escort you. By the way, the parking lot is dirt here, too.

The Saddle Rack
1310 Auzerais Avenue, San Jose
408/286-3393

DIRECTIONS: If traveling north on I-280/Sinclair Freeway, exit on Race Street and turn left on Auzerais. If traveling south on I-280/Sinclair Freeway, take the Meridian Avenue North exit and turn right on Auzerais. The Saddle Rack takes up the entire block between Meridian and Auzerais.

DRESS CODE: Almost anything goes. No gang colors or tank tops.
DANCE DYNAMICS: Everything from two-stepping to line dancing.
HOURS: Open Wednesday through Saturday, 7 P.M. to 1:45 A.M.
MUSIC: Live music; two bands on Friday and Saturday.

There's only one word to describe this place–kicking! Once you've parked over in the dirt lot off to the side because the main lot is full, and once you get past all the ciggie butts stamped out by the curb, be prepared to jump boots first into a madding crowd like you've never seen before. The Saddle Rack is about half a block long and with fourteen hundred people inside, absolutely electric on a Saturday night. Expect an energy buzz from hereon in. The place is absolutely humming. Listen. Hear it? Now look cool and walk deliberately through the masses toward the center of the room, back near the mechanical bull that's going full tilt. Okay, you're almost there. See the bar with the awning around it? Stop. You have arrived. This is where all the regulars hang out. And they can dance, too. Grab yourself a cowboy and get two-stepping on the main floor in front of the stage that's reserved for couples. If you want to go it alone, better head over to any of the other four dance floors, where line dancing is permitted. They're tucked away in the back so the cowboys won't have to watch. That way they can keep with their kind and you with yours. Trust me. It's better this way.

Suzy Bramhall, one of several bartenders, is kept plenty busy, dispensing as many hugs and kisses for her customers as she does drinks.

The Saddle Rack, which opened for business in 1976, is about the oldest running country dance hall in these parts. People come from all over northern California–Stockton, Livermore, San Francisco–to let loose here. There are dance lessons on Wednesday and Thursday nights and two bands on weekends. It gets its share of national country acts, too, on occasional Sunday and Monday nights. Garth Brooks is one of the bigger names who has performed here.

Beth, a regular, looks more the marketing person she is during the week than the cowgirl she is on weekends. She's been coming here so long she doesn't need to dress country. All the cowboys, like Jess and Don, both ranchers, and Jim, a team roper, know she can dance.

Jim dances like a Texan because his family is from Longview. They moved to California just before he was born twenty-nine years ago. He rodeos, two-steps, and calls women "darlin'" so Texas is as Texas does–even if it's in northern California.

Turf Club
22517 Mission Boulevard, Hayward
510/881–9877

DIRECTIONS: From the San Mateo Bridge/Route 92 go east until it becomes Jackson Street. Turn left on Mission Boulevard. The Turf Club is on the left at the corner of A Street and Mission. From the Oakland Bay Bridge/I-80 go east and exit south on Route 17/Nimitz Freeway. Turn left on A Street and right on Mission Boulevard.

DRESS CODE: Anything goes, western wear is not mandatory.

DANCE DYNAMICS: Two-step, waltz, various line dances.

HOURS: Open seven days a week from 10 A.M. to 2 A.M. Dance lesson Saturday, 7 to 10 P.M.

MUSIC: Jukebox, disc jockey, and occasional live music.

While some of the older honky-tonks are listed on the National Register of Historic Places, co-owner Dan Burris says the Turf Club should be on the National Register of Hysterical Places.

Decorwise, this bar is pretty much like any other country bar: wagon wheels, rustic wormwood paneling, a smooth hardwood dance floor, a jukebox full of country songs. And a sign above the bar reads, "Best little outhouse in the West."

"My dad came here once," Dan says. "He was seventy-two at the time, and said, 'I'm really impressed! I've been to the bathroom four or five times tonight and nobody's said a word to me.' I said, 'Dad, they're gay, they're not blind–you're seventy-two years old for God's sake!'"

I can see straight rednecks rolling their eyes and saying, "Only in California!" Think again. There are gay cowboy bars in every corner of this country. And guess what? Gays go to hetero honky-tonks, too, you just aren't aware of it. Bear in mind, however, that sexual preference is all that separates straight rednecks from gay rednecks, who relate to country music and dance just as much as the next cowboy.

"The whole thing of it is having fun," says Dave of Berkeley.

Usually the only way you can tell if you're in a gay honky-tonk is by who is dancing with whom. And at the Turf Club you may not even know at all because, as Dan says, "Quite a few straight women come here to dance so their husbands don't have to worry about them. There's a good mix of both men and women.

"One thing about a gay country-western bar," he adds, "is that if somebody asks you to dance, it's just to dance."

Same as in a hetero honky-tonk.

Plusses here are that there is never a cover charge and dance lessons last three hours. Instructor Ron Points says this is because he spends a lot of time walking through the steps. This night, he is teaching the finer points of the LDC Express line dance on the three-hundred-square-foot floor.

"Toes, toes, balls, balls," he explains. "Now doesn't that sound good?"

Of course he is referring to the balls of the feet, but the students appreciate his sense of humor.

In days of old, cowboys used to dance with other cowboys because women were scarce on the range, so, in a sense, gay honky-tonks bring the origin of country dance full circle. Back then cowboys "filly branded" the one designated to dance the lady's part by tying an apron around his waist. Today, however, dance partners are referred to in a more nonsexist way: Leaders and Followers, which, as dance instructor Bill Dunigan of Virginia says, is not to be confused with "Tops and Bottoms."

Over the years there has been some debate on whether cowboys were bisexual. As William Dale Jennings wrote in his book *The Cowboys,* "Men do not cease to be men simply because there are no women around."

Country music knows no boundaries, and with the recent influx of younger more enlightened singers some old attitudes are changing. Garth Brooks, whose lesbian sister, Betsy Smittle, plays bass in his band, has been at the forefront of this movement with his song "We Shall Be Free," which supports homosexuality. Another recent example is the Red Hot + Country recording project, in which country singers the likes of Willie Nelson, Johnny Cash, Kathy Mattea, and Mark Chesnutt teamed up with the AIDS charity Red Hot to raise money for AIDS research. And, of course, the ongoing "Country Music AIDS Awareness Campaign Nashville" features thirty-five country singers in public service spots.

Dan, who barrel races in the International Gay Rodeo Association, says running a honky-tonk is "a hard business on a relationship." He should know, since his business partner, Larry Gray, was his life partner for eighteen years. They have owned the bar since 1985 and switched to a country format the following year. The Turf Club, which originally opened in 1932, has been a gay bar since 1960. It's not exactly a Traditional or a New Breed club; it's somewhere in between in that there is a disc jockey some of the time and live music the rest of the time. Dan says that both straight and gay acts perform here; just call ahead to find out what the format or act is for a given night.

Colorado usually is associated more with skiers than with boot-scooters–but both are in abundance. There are a good deal of neon cowboy bars and family-oriented Country Clubs, especially in the Denver area, but I was hard-pressed to find a real, honest-to-goodness honky-tonk. I looked in Pueblo and Colorado Springs, but came up empty-handed, so I decided to check out a couple of clubs whose names had come up time and again: the Grizzly Rose Saloon and Dance Emporium in Denver and the Sundance Steak House and Country Club in Fort Collins.

People I knew raved about the Grizzly Rose, the 1993 CMA "Club of the Year," but after experiencing it for myself I realized they liked it because it was very big, very new, and very hot. It was 1992, and the club had been in business only two years. As it was, the night I went it was overrun with line dancers who wouldn't make room for couples. By 1994, Denver dancers had defected to the even newer, even hotter Stampede Mesquite Grill and Dance Emporium in nearby Aurora. I tried to enlist the help of some local dance instructors in my search, but messages I left went unanswered. Brenda Eads West, who grew up in Denver, told me to try Ollie's Roundup–"where the real cowboys went." But, alas, Ollie's has gone the disc-jockey route and caters to competitive dancers, which is good for them but what about the rest of us? Scratch Ollie's. Many smaller clubs, such as Club Corner in Wheat Ridge, have a track record, but I was searching for one with that special something. So I kept looking.

Glenn Miller, who lives in Fort Collins, told me to check out some clubs in his area: the Sundance, the Cow Palace, and Bruce's Bar in Severance. The Sundance celebrated its tenth anniversary in 1994, and by honky-tonk standards is still young. The Cow Palace seemed a likely possibility, but it was only a few years older than the Sundance. Glenn assured me that Bruce's was what I was looking for because it had real personality. So Bruce's it was, even though it was a bit out of the way.

Bruce's Bar
345 First Street, Severance
303/686–2320

DIRECTIONS: Severance is about fifty minutes from Denver and fifteen minutes from Fort Collins and Greeley. From I-25 take Road 74 to Severance. Turn left on First Street. Bruce's is on the right, across from the post office.

DRESS CODE: Anything goes, but don't get too fancy. Jeans, baseball caps, and plaid shirts will suffice. Some women wear long dance skirts.

DANCE DYNAMICS: Mostly two-steps, buckle-shiners, and some western swing.

HOURS: Open seven days a week from 5 A.M. to 10 P.M. during goose season, which runs from late October to late January, and closes at 2 A.M. on weekends. All other times, open from 10 A.M. to 10 P.M. during the week and closes at 2 A.M. on weekends.

MUSIC: House band Friday, Saturday, Sunday; jukebox Monday through Thursday.

Let's put it this way, there isn't much to Severance except Bruce's Bar. In fact, Severance (population 106) *is* Bruce's. Owner Bruce Ruth not only runs the town bar but also rents out a hundred or so duck blinds on a nearby reservoir. Sure, there's a filling station, a liquor store, and a post office, but the Eaton Chamber of Commerce (Severance isn't big enough to have its own) says that Bruce's is the only real enterprise. So it's no wonder that the sign welcoming visitors into town bears Bruce's motto: "Where the Geese Fly and the Bulls Cry." Of course, Bruce did contribute a thousand dollars to pay for the sign.

The first thing you see as you pull into the dirt lot next to Bruce's Bar is a mural on the side of the cinderblock building that says: "Nuts to You Says Bruce." Some people might take offense at the mural's statement, but, like the town sign, it refers to Bruce's specialty of the house, Rocky Mountain oysters, which are not served on the half-shell. These culinary treats–also known as prairie oysters, bull fries, or calf fries–are made from the part of the bull that is cut off to make him a steer, which explains the painting inside the bar of a castration in progress. Picketing bulls carrying "Unfair," "Very Unfair," and "You Don't Know How Unfair" signs are painted on the building's exterior.

Bruce's Bar, which sells close to thirty thousand tons of these deep-fried delights each year, has been in business since 1957. Over the years the bar has been featured on the *Today* show, in local newspapers, in *Penthouse* and *People*–and now this guide.

People come from all over the world not only to sample the "swinging steaks," as manager Betty Schott (who has worked here since 1958) calls them, but also to dance. But don't expect to log much time on the sunken, L-shaped tile dance floor, which translates to fifteen hundred square feet, during the week unless you bring your own partner and dance to the country jukebox. In other words, don't show up on a Tuesday like I did if you want to dance. It's not until the weekend rolls around that the place gets hopping. That's when Ruthless, the house band, plays to a packed house of 250 every Friday, Saturday, and Sunday. Be forewarned, however, that if it's raining outside, it may be inside as well; and you'll have to dodge buckets as you two-step around the dance floor. Just don't kick the buckets over! By the way, did I mention the all-you-can-eat special on Rocky Mountain oysters every Friday and Sunday night?

Sandy Trowbridge, a sturdy waitress in sensible shoes, has worked here since 1984. She's as friendly and helpful as the day is long, and offered my friend Glenn and me a tour of the kitchen, where we saw a sink filled with raw prairie oysters. In case you haven't guessed, Bruce's is the kind of place where some customers exit and enter through the kitchen, right past Dennis Guffy, who slices, breads, and deep fries the gigantic gonads.

There are mounts of stuffed geese in flight and a bulletin board in a corner with lots of Bruce's memorabilia, including a photo of Bruce and Denver

Bronco John Elway. If you're lucky, you might even run into a few Broncos. It's a favorite spot of the team's and Sandy says she counted "ten of them in here Monday night."

Bruce himself is often seen in his establishment greeting his customers by name; he has calmed down somewhat from his wilder days, when he was known to shoot out the lights with his Colt. Yes, you guessed it, no problems with rowdy bar patrons here!

There is never a cover charge at Bruce's, and children are always welcome with a parent or guardian until 9 P.M. So go ahead and bring the whole family, and, as Betty says: "Have a ball."

Country dancing is pretty popular in this state. It was, after all, a woman from Boise who choreographed the original Boot Scootin' Boogie line dance, of which there are several variations depending on what part of the country you live in. That was eight or nine years ago, when Asleep at the Wheel released the song (long before Brooks & Dunn ever did). I had no problem figuring out which honky-tonk to write about in this state because dancers everywhere recommended Kelly's Grand 'Ol Opry in State Line. And even though the honky-tonk is still young (it opened in 1983), it was the oldest in the state that I knew of.

Shorty's Country Western Saloon in Boise had been in the running, but it was two years younger than Kelly's. The only other Country Club there was Rock 'N' Rodeo, which opened in 1992. The Green Triangle Bar in Chubbock near Pocatello is popular, as is the Corral in Lewiston, but I wasn't headed their way. So Kelly's it was. Now for the hard part: Where the heck was State Line? It wasn't in my Rand-McNally atlas, and the state had more than one state line. Was it nearer to Boise or Pocatello? Or was it upstate near Coeur d'Alene? I found it quite by accident, just off that small stretch of I-90 between Spokane, Washington, and Coeur d'Alene, where you see all the "Don't Californicate Idaho" bumper stickers.

Kelly's Grand 'Ol Opry
6152 West Seltice Way, State Line
208/773-5002

DIRECTIONS: From I-90 take Exit 299W to Seltice Way. Kelly's is two-tenths of a mile north of the interstate.
DRESS CODE: Anything goes.

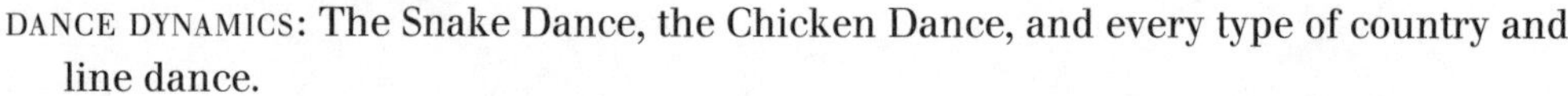

DANCE DYNAMICS: The Snake Dance, the Chicken Dance, and every type of country and line dance.
HOURS: Open Friday and Saturday from 6 P.M. to 2 A.M. Dance lessons from 7 to 9 P.M.
MUSIC: Live music.

"This honky-tonk is home for me," says the carved wooden sign hanging above the entrance to the dance hall inside Kelly's. These words, actually lyrics of a song that owner Kelly Hughes wrote in 1993, echo the heartfelt sentiment of many a honky-tonker. Yet Kelly feels very strongly that a honky-tonk should be home only on the weekends, which is why his club is just open Friday and Saturday nights.

"We're geared to drawing working-class people," he says. "When Friday comes they can go out, hoot, holler, shout, dance on the tables, and basically let loose."

Come Friday his patrons are ready to do just that. A line of close to eight hundred people stretches out into the dirt parking lot, which looks to be as long as the ninety-six-foot-long dance hall itself. Notice, I haven't yet called it a bar.

"My goal is never to be a bar owner," Kelly says. "It's not so much drinking anymore; it's like back in the '40s in the big dance halls. It's actually ballroom dancing to country tunes, except we do it in a circle."

Well, let's just say they do it in a circle sometimes. They also do it in a lot of lines and on a lot of tables. That's why the tables aren't fancy. Kelly encourages his customers to get up on them and dance as the evening wears on. Later, Kelly himself leaps off the stage to lead the crowd in the Snake Dance, a crack-the-whip style of dance that always ends up in the "Cowboys" room, and the Chicken Dance. From the dance names, it may seem like Kelly's houses a cult that practices some pretty strange rituals, but the Chicken Dance is actually German in origin.

Kelly's is also home to many area dancers, including the Coeur d'Alene Country Unlimited dance team and two-time international line-dance champ Lisa Kruse of Spokane, Washington. But look for the best dancers early in the evening; they usually leave by ten when the younger crowd is out in full force. Instructors Ron and Sally Threlfall are largely responsible for creating this dance community. As Ron says, "We have people who drive sixty miles through mountain roads to dance at Kelly's." And ladies, here's the good news: There's usually more men than women dancers. Elsewhere in the country the opposite is true.

Ron and Sally are what you could call "solemates," and approach teaching simply and with a sense of humor. They break things down step by step and their goal is to have people "street dancing," which is dancing not to compete but to have fun, before the night is over. They also teach dance etiquette at the start of each lesson and the rules are posted.

A lot of kids here are rodeo cowboys, according to Sally, who like to do the "no-step swing," also known as western swing. "That's when you're just trying to keep up so your arms don't get jerked out of the sockets!"

The dance floor is 3,264 square feet of black and white tile that gives a touch of class to the otherwise down-home atmosphere, complete with worn-out boots nailed to the rafters.

One thing you should know about Ron is that he is a walking, talking, dancing miracle. He suffered a major aneurysm in 1992 and was left paralyzed on his left side. A few weeks after he was released from the hospital, he was back on the dance floor at Kelly's teaching from a wheelchair. After more determination than rehabilitation, he was walking and then dancing again. In late 1994, he underwent a triple bypass and is back in his boots again.

You see, it's not just the dancing that makes Kelly's stand out. It's people like Ron and Sally–and Kelly.

Kelly began singing when he was eight, trying to belt out songs louder than Charley Pride and Ferlin Husky did on the records his parents played. His first singing job came when he was in the ninth grade, and he earned fifteen dollars a night. By the time he was seventeen, Kelly got a part in a movie called *The Last American Cowboy*, starring Ben Johnson and Mariette

Hartley. The film never made it out of production, so Kelly kept singing. He played the Northwest nightclub circuit and by the time he reached twenty-one, he had a dream of owning a place where he could bring in national acts.

From the outside, Kelly's looks to be nothing more than a rambling red barn that has been added onto right and left. As Ron says, it was "nothing more than a goddamn pole barn." But Kelly wanted the place even though it was one step away from being condemned. He had no start-up income, but persuaded the owner to let him fix it up and try to make it into something. Just weeks later, Kelly and some of his high-school friends had the place up and running. "It was the busiest place around," Kelly says, until three months later when "somebody burnt me down." His friends pitched in once again and in only forty-seven days, Kelly's was back in business.

Kelly, who is a talented singer and songwriter, has no aspirations of going to Nashville. So the Kelly Hughes Band opens for the many Nashville acts that come this way, including Bobby Bare, Vince Gill, Hank Thompson, and Patty Loveless. The singers' names and play dates are stenciled on strips of paper posted on the rafters and behind the stage. Whenever possible, Kelly works with Blake Dowen over at Seattle's Riverside Inn to coordinate talent for the clubs and work out package deals.

In short, this honky-tonk is, as Kelly puts it, "an Idaho boy's dream come true." On second thought, "it's any boy's dream come true."

Kentucky

The hot New Breed club in the Louisville area is Coyote's Music and Dance Hall. But, of course, there are no real stories for it to tell yet. I would have liked to have gotten over to Wilder to Bobby Mackey's place, a slaughterhouse-turned-dance hall that is allegedly haunted, but I already had a spook-filled honky-tonk. What I didn't have was anything like the Do-Drop Inn in Louisville.

Do-Drop Inn
1032 Story Avenue, Louisville
502/582–9327

DIRECTIONS: From I-64 take Exit 7/Story Avenue. Go down four blocks. The Do-Drop is on the left.
DRESS CODE: Anything goes.

DANCE DYNAMICS: Buckle-shiners, freestyle, and the occasional two-step.
HOURS: Friday and Saturday from 8 P.M to 4 A.M.
MUSIC: Live music.

Most dancers here don't know their left foot from their right, but come Saturday night when there's a chance to win dinner for two at a local eatery, six courageous couples hit the 1,250-square-foot hardwood floor with spuds precariously positioned between their foreheads. The music starts out slow and ends fast. The last couple to remain dancing with their tuber tucked tightly between their frontal lobes wins the prize. Co-owner Trudy Walters says they started doing the Potato Dance in 1962 but did away with it in 1994. At this writing, ownership is thinking of starting it up again. Hopefully they will. It is one of those rituals that makes a honky-tonk individual and something you must see to believe.

Two-step is a language that largely goes unspoken here, and don't even think of line dancing unless you want to attract plenty of stares. I did find a couple doing the Montgomery County Shuffle, a dance similar to the El Paso with cha-cha steps. Aside from the shuffle and the Potato Dance, the variety ranges from freestyle to buckle-shiners; regular folks don't have the time or money to spend on uppity dance lessons.

This is your typical cement-floor honky-tonk where Grinners have been content to enjoy music, beer, and friends for more than thirty years. And this is what makes the Do-Drop Inn special: No famous faces or claims to fame, just a down-home good time in a church-social atmosphere–except for the beer and the smoke.

Clubs in Kentucky have some of the latest closing times in the country, which means folks can party at the Do-Drop until 4 A.M. on Friday and Saturday. And unlike other clubs in Louisville, the Do-Drop is licensed to serve liquor on Sundays. Better yet, Trudy feels comfortable saying that the cover charge is and always will be a buck-fifty.

Montana

10

A common misconception about Montana is that where there are cowboys, there must be cowboy bars. Surely the state that is home to Hank Williams Jr., Wylie & The Wild West Show, and Tim Ryan must have a proliferation of honky-tonks. Wrong. There are plenty of bars and lots of casinos in the more populated parts of Montana, but you'll be hard-pressed to hear live country music and do some serious two-stepping on a weeknight. In fact, the few country music clubs that do exist often have rock-and-roll or karaoke nights. And, yes, they even line dance here. As it happened, I spent more time looking for a honky-tonk than I did honky-tonking. I found more cowboys–two–in a Helena laundromat than I did in any cowboy bar. Perhaps I was looking in all the wrong places. I decided to ask.

Gary was sitting in his car listening to country music and waiting for his clothes to dry when I approached him. He wore a black T-shirt bearing bull rider Tuff Hedeman's likeness. Gary, who was still too young (twenty) to go in any cowboy bar, offered his impressions anyway. A lifelong Helena resident and country music fan, Gary says he is an anachronism in this town. Folks here have been associated with "cowboy this" and "cowboy that" for so long that they want to escape the cowboy way altogether, he says. Heck, he continues, that's why they don't dress cowboy here. Cowboys are more likely to wear T-shirts, jeans, and ball caps so as to disguise their origins. Gary should know, his two roommates are rodeo cowboys.

"Bozeman has more cowboy kids than this town," he said. "Basically, if you're into country music here, you don't really fit in. I fit in in Dillon–it's a little hick town, a little farm town–better than I do here. That's the place to be on Labor Day. It's Montana's biggest weekend."

I told Gary I had checked Bozeman the day before and couldn't find any honky-tonks there at all. He shrugged.

"I don't know. I've always loved this state," he continues. "I've never really wanted to leave this state. If you leave, you've got to deal with traffic and stuff. But the more I talk about it, the way nobody's into country stuff, I wonder why I'm still here."

My next target, Mike, wore a black cowboy hat.

"The best places are in the smaller towns," Mike says. He himself is from Kalispell up to the north. "There's a place in Nevada City where *Lonesome Dove* was filmed. You ought to head down to Virginia City. There's an old place there."

So I checked out the Pioneer Bar in Virginia City, and, as it turned out, Mike's idea of a real cowboy bar is the same as most Montanan's: No dancing, just drinking. There are better prospects elsewhere. The Tobacco Root Tavern and Supper Club in Harrison and the Norris Bar in Norris each have a dance floor and live country music on weekends. Up in Columbia Falls there is the Blue Moon, which could well be the oldest operating honky-tonk in the state, but I wasn't able to get up that far to find out. Across the state in Billings is Drifters, which has been in business since 1979 and has live music on Friday and Saturday.

Linda Pabst, a country music booking agent in Billings, says several factors have contributed to the demise of Montana's honky-tonks. First of all, Montana is the fourth-largest state in land mass, with one of the smallest populations. Urban areas, which translate directly to honky-tonks, are few and far between. A lot of ranchers just don't go out at night because they rise with the sun, work hard all day, and hit the sack early. Linda cites a big oil and lumber boom in the 1970s, followed by the change in the state's drinking age from nineteen to twenty-one in the mid-1980s. Things were so bad, she says, that Billings lost 21 percent of its population in a year. Then, as if things weren't bad enough, a five-year drought ruined the state's agriculture. People just didn't have the time or money to go out honky-tonking. By 1987, 25 percent of honky-tonks had filed for bankruptcy and "the old-line clubs went belly-up.

"That's why there are no really old clubs," she says, "and people's social habits have changed."

Club owners found they could make more money from legalized gambling so many of them focused on casinos. If people want "name" entertainment, it is relatively available. County fairs now bring in the big acts and the state's major concert venue is Yellowstone's Metra, with twelve thousand seats. Newer country music clubs close as quickly as they open; for example, Duelin' Daltons, one of the older clubs I had heard about, had recently undergone both a name and format change. It is now Mustang Sally's and caters to rock-and-rollers.

"A honky-tonk should be where you can take your girlfriend or wife and have a true country band–not all this rockabilly–and where you can get some service," says Bob Bice, lead singer for the Vigilantes.

Bice has played in honky-tonks for forty-five years, and ran down the list of honky-tonk possibilities for me. I finally settled on a club in Helena where his group had once played.

Silver Spur
2000 North Montana Avenue, Helena
406/449–2512

DIRECTIONS: From I-15 take exit 192/Prospect Avenue. Take Prospect to Montana Avenue and turn right. Go over the railroad tracks and the Silver Spur is just past Poplar Street on the left.

DRESS CODE: Anything goes, from ball caps and blue jeans to matching western outfits.

DANCE DYNAMICS: Two-step, waltz, freestyle, and buckle-shiners.

HOURS: Open Monday through Saturday noon to 2 A.M.; Sunday 4 P.M. to 2 A.M.

MUSIC: Live music on weekends only.

From the moment you first see the Silver Spur, you can tell it's a honky-tonk. The kitschy 3-D neon spur sign on the Quonset hut made of corrugated metal is your first clue. Your second is inside on the shelf behind the bar: a gigantic jar of pickled turkey gizzards. Yep. You're home. See, the clock behind the bar is set on bar time, fifteen minutes fast.

The Silver Spur, open seven days a week, is a great stopping-off place in the afternoon on the way home from work. It was voted "Best Country Bar" in Helena by a local paper and is also one of the oldest honky-tonks in the state, having been established in 1952. The current owner, Tammy Laib, and her husband, Myron, have been running the Spur since 1993. Tammy's whole family loves country music; in fact, her sister won the local "True Value Showdown" held at the club in 1994, and you can tell from the Showdown video playing on the TV behind the bar and her voice that nepotism had nothing to do with her placing first.

As Linda Pabst says, it's very hard to sustain a country music club in this state. The Laibs agree. Myron says the video poker and keno machines bring in the bulk of the money. And they have had to experiment with different formats some nights during the week just to stay afloat. At this writing, the Spur features reggae nights four times a year, Wednesdays are devoted to recorded rock and roll, and Thursday is karaoke. Excuse me, you say, but this can't be a honky-tonk if there is karaoke. Remember? I said it could if there were mitigating circumstances. And in the Spur's case, there are. If karaoke means the difference between surviving and going out of business, then so be it. There is, after all, live country music on weekends and a jukebox full of country songs . . . and don't forget those turkey gizzards! You won't want to cuss here, though. If you use a four-letter word, you'll be asked to leave.

Myron says most dancers here are married couples, who dress in matching western outfits to two-step, waltz, jitterbug, and line dance on the 810-square-foot rectangular parquet floor. Tuesday dance workshops cost two dollars a person (beginners at 6 P.M., intermediates at 7 P.M., and partner dances at 8 P.M) in all of the above dances as well as East and West Coast swings, polka, and cha-cha. Be aware that dance lessons are canceled in July and August, when business is slower than usual.

Don't expect to hear Bice and his band play here other than on a fill-in basis. Myron says the old-style music just doesn't draw like it used to and he has to hire younger bands, like the Red I Express, a group of Native American cowboys from Great Falls, to satisfy his patrons. The format is basically 90 percent country and 10 percent rock and roll.

As Myron says, "In different areas, different things go."

When most people think of Nevada, it's images of neon nights, floor shows, bad lounge acts, and legalized gambling–all flash and cash–that come to mind. As in Montana, the cards are stacked against honky-tonks here; distance, population, and gaming work to their disadvantage. Nevada, as a whole, is fairly fickle where honky-tonks are concerned. Businesses cater to folks who want to see floor shows and gamble more than they do to two-steppers. Names can be deceiving, too; what sounds like a honky-tonk may be nothing more than a bar or a strip joint. But don't be too discouraged, for this glitz-saturated state somehow garnered its fair share of wide-open spaces, country music and dancing, and cowboys and rodeos.

It's a good drive between the major cities of Reno and Las Vegas, with precious little in between. Even though many cowboys live and work in northern Nevada, Country Clubs up there seem to close their doors with a flourish. At this writing, Reno and Lake Tahoe have only one neon cowboy bar each, the Rodeo Rock Cafe and Wild West, respectively. Mr. B's Casino, part of a truck-stop complex about 140 miles east of Reno in Mill City, is the closest thing you'll find to a Traditional honky-tonk, and its name doesn't even sound country. On the other hand, Bruno's Country Club in Gerlach (population 200), noted for its five bars, doesn't even have country music or dancing. The same holds true for the Delta Saloon, which Mark Twain used to write about, and the Bucket of Blood over in Virginia City.

Fortunately the situation has always been better downstate where more people live. In the early days of Las Vegas, the casino industry was founded on a western theme and most hotels had names like El Rancho, Last Frontier, and Horseshoe instead of Mirage and Luxor. Vegas Vic, a gigantic neon cowboy on Fremont Street, greeted passersby with "Howdy, pardner." Helldorado Days, when the city celebrated its western ways with a parade and rodeo, was another constant reminder of the cowboy element.

During the year, most of the country dance action in Las Vegas is east of town, on or near the Boulder Highway, where Traditional clubs like the Silver Dollar and Sam's Town Dance Hall go head to head with New Breeders like Rockabilly's and Dylan's Dance Hall & Saloon. But come the first week of December, when the National Finals Rodeo (NFR) is in town, Las Vegas is transformed into honky-tonk heaven. Virtually every major hotel and casino books country megastars and features country dancing. Two major country dance competitions coincided with Country Music Week and the NFR in 1994: the Desert Sands Fest, sponsored by Country-Western Dance International, and the Las Vegas Finale, sponsored by the United Country-Western Dance Council.

Sadly, this honky-tonk attitude doesn't exist year-round because of the theme-park mentality that has overtaken the city of late, but some vestiges of Vegas's distant western past remain. There is still Helldorado, minus the parade, and Vegas Vic, even though Fremont Street is now encased in glass, and there is still the Silver Dollar.

Silver Dollar
2501 East Charleston Boulevard, Las Vegas
702/382-6921

DIRECTIONS: Located on the corner of 25th Street and East Charleston Boulevard near where the Boulder Highway becomes Fremont Street.
DRESS CODE: Anything goes.
DANCE DYNAMICS: Two-step, waltz, East Coast swing, buckle-shiners.
HOURS: Open twenty-four hours a day.
MUSIC: Live music nightly.

In a town that has seen cowboy bars pop up like sagebrush in the last few years, the Silver Dollar is one of a dying breed. It's old-guard country, a real honky-tonk. You won't find what owner Bill Ladd, a man with a say-howdy voice, calls "new wave" country here. There are no line dancers and no disc jockeys, and the only videos you'll see are about rodeos. You will find a separate area with pool tables, a jukebox full of country songs, and live country music seven days a week, 365 days a year.

The Silver Dollar has always been somewhat off the beaten path for most tourists, and its clientele is a mix of the young, the old, and the restless. It's where locals like "Stormy," a thirtysomething police officer, and my shirttail aunt, "Bo Peep," who is pushing ninety, go to two-step on the eight-hundred-square-foot hardwood dance floor.

When you pull into the parking lot you may notice a dusty maroon Cadillac sitting out front with license plates that say: "THE DUKE." Yep. John Wayne is alive and well at the Dollar. The car belongs to bartender Johnny Moats, who says Bill hired him back in 1966, not long after he had bought the club. Johnny is nattily dressed in black. It accentuates his belt buckle, which, upon closer examination, pays tribute to "John Wayne, the Duke American." No, Johnny's middle name is not Wayne; it happens to be Richard.

The dress code, which warns against the wearing of T-shirts, is posted on the back of the front door, but Johnny says it isn't enforced anymore. "Everyone comes in dressed in anything," he says.

This club has seen its share of big names, including Merle Haggard, Willie Nelson, and the Duke himself, pass through its doors. Once a construction worker from Henderson named Beau Tucker brought his nine-year-old daughter, Tanya, here to sing, and the rest is country music history.

Built in 1931, the honky-tonk was originally called the Saddle Club. Bill bought it in 1965 and changed its name. It has been revamped twice over the years and now accommodates four hundred people. The Dollar has basically beat all odds for a honky-tonk in this plastic town; but what else could we expect from Bill, who once wrote a book about gambling called *To Quit a Winner*?

The large bar with inlaid video poker games seats forty-seven and is the center of action on weeknights. More dancers are out on the weekends, but you probably would do best to bring your own partner.

New Mexico

12

It wasn't easy finding a honky-tonk in New Mexico. For one thing the state is mostly desert and heavily populated with Hispanics and Native Americans. It is tough to get a liquor license near a reservation these days. In fact, there are little more than a thousand liquor licenses in the entire state. So I searched from the high country to the low country and all points in between. After disqualifying all the neon cowboy bars in Albuquerque, I checked out Taos–Michael Martin Murphey country–and Ruidoso–playground of the Southwest. Nothing. So I set my sights closer to the border and landed in Las Cruces, near Billy the Kid's old stomping grounds of Mesilla. At the very least, I knew someone here who would give me the straight skinny on any club worthy of the title "honky-tonk."

So it was here, at the base of the Organs, a mountain range so named for its resemblance to a pipe organ, that I connected with an old friend and found the closest thing to honky-tonk heaven I was to find in the Land of Enchantment.

The Desert Sun
1390 West Main Street, Las Cruces
505/523-5705

DIRECTIONS: From I-25 exit at North Main Street (Highway 70 becomes North Main). The Desert Sun is on the left, just before North Main intersects with West Picacho Avenue and Spruce Street.
DRESS CODE: Cowboy hats and ball caps for men; boots and jeans for everyone.
DANCE DYNAMICS: Two-steps and buckle-shiners. Line dancers, beware!
HOURS: Open Monday through Saturday, noon to 2 A.M.; Sunday, noon to midnight.
MUSIC: Two jukeboxes and a live house band.

The Desert Sun is pretty much what one would expect of a New Mexico cowboy bar: flat roof, pink stucco exterior, wooden beams, carved wooden double doors. A stylized orange and yellow sunburst on the front of the building simply says, "Desert Sun." Inside, it is dark. Really dark. All red and black, the Early Bordello period of decor. There are no false pretenses here. Locally the Desert Sun is known for drawing an older, blue-collar crowd, the "mellow set" as my friend Scott calls them, while the younger set heads down the street to Cowboys–minus Scott. What you see is what you get, an unassuming place filled with unassuming folks–real people. It's the kind of place bikers have been known to frequent, and one of the regulars, Chip (his girlfriend's name is Cookie), has "Harley-Davidson" tattooed on his forehead. In an age where it is getting hard to find a honky-tonk, let alone one with a jukebox chock-full of country songs, the Desert Sun goes one better with two.

The nine-hundred-square-foot hardwood floor is smooth as can be and has a fair number of straightforward two-steppers on a Thursday night dancing to music provided by the Brenda Bruer Band, which is the house band. Brenda's dad is one of the owners and her husband plays in the band, too.

Dance dynamics at the Desert Sun are simple. "We don't . . . like line dancing here," one of the owners warns. "Line dancing is like *Urban Cowboy*, here today and gone tomorrow." He adds that "line dancers drink only water or Coke, which means no business for us"–a common refrain voiced among club owners everywhere.

Yes, Scott had found me a real honky-tonk.

North Carolina

13

This state used to be known for its cloggers and mountain music, but that hasn't hindered it from inspiring a good number of country dancers and some darn good country music. In Raleigh, the Longbranch Saloon is the place to go for serious country dancing, and in Charlotte, Coyote Joe's is a popular New Breed club. But my friend and colleague Kent Jenkins, a North Carolinian by birth, told me about one of the last real honky-tonks there: Country City U.S.A.

Country City U.S.A.
4809 Wilkinson Boulevard, Charlotte
704/393-1149

Country City U.S.A.

DIRECTIONS: From I-85 take the Billy Graham Parkway/Airport Drive exit, which takes you to Boyer Street and turns onto Wilkinson Boulevard/Routes 29 and 74. Country City is on the right.

DRESS CODE: Casual.

DANCE DYNAMICS: All types of country dancing. Line dances on band breaks.

HOURS: Open Wednesday through Saturday 8 P.M. to 2 A.M. Closed Monday and Tuesday.

MUSIC: House band nightly.

Not too far off the Billy Graham Parkway, perched atop an asphalt hill with an upstart neon cowboy bar to its left and a rent-by-the-hour-day-or-week motel to its right, sits Country City U.S.A. The red and white stucco structure isn't much to look at, but it's the kind of place folks like Tim of Gastonia visit at least once a week. Tim calls himself "an old redneck truck driver" and Country City "the boulevard of broken dreams."

But to former Marshville resident Randy Traywick it is anything but. Traywick is singer Randy Travis's given surname, and it was here that he got his start in 1977 when he won a talent contest at the club. Randy's tale is the stuff of local legends. Lib Hatcher, who managed the honky-tonk at the time and was sixteen years his senior, was so taken by his voice that she hired the seventeen-year-old. Randy had had a brush with the law, but Lib told a judge Randy worked for her full-time and was not drinking or using drugs. Her testimony kept Randy out of prison and she promised to make sure he stayed on the straight and narrow.

At that time Country City was across the street from its current location and was owned by the late Bill Jordan, who sold the club to Lib in 1979. Lib moved the club to its new facility in 1981. Susan Lewis, who was then Bill's wife, bought it back in 1983 shortly after Lib and Randy left for Nashville to achieve national recognition and later marry.

Now it is Susan who greets the regulars by name as they enter the club, and she also joins them on the 750-square-foot horseshoe-shaped hardwood dance floor to take in a dance or two herself. Come summer, there is also dancing under the stars on the adjacent outdoor patio. Couple dancing is the name of the game here, especially when the Chrome Elvis band plays. Chrome Elvis–which takes its name from the slide used on the steel guitar–

has been the house band here since 1989. The dances vary from two-steppers and waltzers to flat-footers and line-dancers to freestylers and buckle-shiners. It's just a pretty all-purpose honky-tonk.

One thing to be aware of is that Country City is a private club that charges a five dollar yearly membership fee. It takes about three days for the state to issue the membership card, but folks just passing through can simply pay five dollars to enter as a sponsored guest of a member on Friday and Saturday or two dollars on the other weeknights. As in Utah, just ask someone at the door to be your sponsor.

The nice thing about Oklahoma is that when you talk about Country Clubs, people don't automatically think of golf courses. There are some pretty darn good places to honky-tonk in this state and folks here will drive a country mile several times over to get someplace where they can let loose for a night. Sadly, the legendary Cain's Ballroom in Tulsa, once owned by Bob Wills, has done much to advance country music, but now operates only as a concert hall during certain months of the year. The offerings of Traditional clubs worth mentioning these days are the Arbuckle Ballroom in Davis, Brander's in Lawton, Chastain's Club in Oklahoma City,

Ernie's Country Palace outside of Yukon, and the Hall of Fame in Tulsa. Among the New Breed clubs, check out Chisholm's Club, InCahoots, and Graham Country Dancing in Oklahoma City.

The music in this state is as good as it gets because Oklahoma breeds country singers like it breeds cattle, and many singers, including Hoyt Axton, Spade Cooley, Joe Diffie, Vince Gill, Wanda Jackson, Toby Keith, and the Tractors, have hit the big time. So I decided to write about the musical birthplaces of two Oklahoma artists who are responsible in part for reshaping the face of country music as we know it today: Reba McEntire and Garth Brooks. Reba got her start at the Ken Lance Sports Arena and Dance Pavilion singing with her brother and sisters, while Garth used to hang his hat at Tumbleweed Dance Hall and Concert Arena.

Ken Lance Sports Arena and Dance Pavilion

Ken Lance Road, Ada
405/265-4423

Ken Lance
SPORTS ARENA AND DANCE PAVILION

DIRECTIONS: From Ada take Route 3 West toward Stonewall. Turn left onto Ken Lance Road, which is just beyond the Union Fork exit. The honky-tonk is roughly halfway between Ada and Stonewall.

DRESS CODE: Ropers, Wranglers, and Rockies.

DANCE DYNAMICS: Two-step, waltz, western swing, and buckle-shiners. Line dances on band breaks.

HOURS: Saturday from 9:30 to 1:30 P.M.

MUSIC: Live bands.

As you drive dead straight into the black of night from Ada toward Stonewall, you may start to wonder if you'll ever find this place. I did. Not to worry. Folks here–sometimes a thousand or more, but fewer in the summer–don't show up until 10:30 P.M. So keep going. Just when you think you might have missed it, a life-size likeness of a steer high upon a platform comes into view. Like a beacon, illuminated brightest white by floodlights, it beckons. A marquee lets you know this is the Ken Lance Sports Arena, so turn here. A ways down, you'll see it on the left, with a parking lot attendant directing the flow of traffic with a flashlight through the gate and over the cattle guard.

You are now in "Ken Lance, Oklahoma," as the owner of the same name refers to it: a honky-tonk and rodeo arena surrounded by red oaks and rolling hills. Ken calls himself "the original urban cowboy." A member of the

Professional Rodeo Cowboys Association, Ken sticks mostly to trick and team roping now that the years are gaining on him. And he's real proud of the fact that his daddy rodeoed and two-stepped up until he was eighty-nine. He died at age ninety-one.

Ken says country stars "from everybody to nobody" have played here, including Red Steagall, Ray Price, George Jones, and George Strait. He's especially proud of Reba McEntire, who sang for the first time in public here and went on to gain national fame after he introduced her to Red Steagall, who set the wheels in motion for her becoming a four-time CMA "Female Vocalist of the Year." Their pictures grace the walls inside the dance hall. There's even a section at the entrance devoted to those who have passed on to "Honky-Tonk Heaven." Ken says he can't afford Reba now, but that her brother and his kids still sing here. Big-name acts are expensive these days and "I can't hardly go over ten dollars a ticket here or people think you're robbing them," he says. Instead, Ken books young stars on the rise like Tracy Byrd.

Ken lives the good life with his wife, Linda, and his two dogs, Stoney and Rusty Lance, on the same acreage as his enterprise, which once was nothing more than an overgrown watermelon patch. As luck would have it, his symbol is the horseshoe, which is evident in the ring he wears, on a kitchen tablecloth, and in a lighted sign above the "Cowboy Cafe" in his dance hall.

As you step out of your car and sink into the soft red Oklahoma dirt, country music floats through the air like a cloud and you know coming here was well worth the trip. In this part of America, being a real cowboy is as much a part of the lifestyle as is the rural ritual of a honky-tonk Saturday night. Just ask Mitch Henley of Enid, a heeler in team roping, who started coming to the arena with his folks when he was three. The honky-tonk adjacent to the rodeo ring is about as rough-and-tumble country as they get these days. "There's always a good brawl here during the rodeo," Mitch says, referring to the Ada Pro Rodeo that has drawn up to five thousand folks here the first week of August almost every year since the place opened in the early 1960s. Mitch says, "Everybody kind of has a good time until somebody bumps into somebody else." Blame the young bucks who like to blow off steam and haven't yet learned that solving a problem with fists isn't the answer. The bouncers get a hold of the rowdy ones, and then Ken tells them in his gentle Oklahoma drawl: "If y'all want to get it on, we'll go out to the rodeo ring and draw a circle and y'all can get it on." It's rare that anyone ever takes him up on the offer.

Ken employs plenty of security to control any "situation" that may arise. It's people like "Tiny," the dean of bouncers, who keep things under control. As one of Tiny's minions says, "It's Tiny's world; we all just live in it." Still, in spite of security's best efforts, rest assured there will be a scuffle almost every Saturday night–the only night the dance hall and bar are open.

You wouldn't think that there would be much of a problem with fights here because the club is in the dry county of Pontotoc and it's what's known to Oklahomans as a "not" club–not old enough to drink. It is only licensed to sell beer and wine coolers, so eighteen-year-olds and up are allowed to enter but can purchase only water or soft drinks at the front bar; the one at the far left is for "Overs" only. Identification is checked at the door when guests pay the five dollar cover charge and hands are stamped with either "Over" or "Under."

Some of the smoothest two-steppers in the country come here to dance and if you watch real close, you may learn the secret of their success. Of course, the answer might lie in the 5,600-square-foot hardwood floor, which is raised above the concrete foundation to make it more user-friendly; Ken keeps it primed with just the right amount of dance wax. The dance hall has been added onto two or three times over the years and now accommodates fifteen hundred people, sometimes more.

During the course of an evening, Ken can be seen bustling about, greeting customers, introducing cowboys to cowgirls, and checking things out behind the bars and such. "I'm kind of like horseshit," he says, "everywhere!" It's amazing that he has so much energy. Doesn't he ever tire? Sure, but the sixty-seven-year-old, who says he still feels like thirty-five, says that as he's aged he's had to adapt to the younger set's hours so he takes a nap during the day. What is the average age of his customers? "Well, I don't really tooth 'em, but I'd guess about twenty-seven," he says. And Ken sees no need to open more than one night a week (you'd be wise to call ahead and make sure the place is open, as Ken has been known not to open now and then) because he gets by on the money he makes on "butter 'n' egg day." "Money don't mean nothin' to me," he says. "It's only a dollar and you only spend one at a time, but it sure beats diggin' post holes." The Saturday-night-only policy also frees up his week for more important things, like roping, building motorized roping calves, roping, playing with his dogs, and roping.

Be forewarned that it's hotter than heck inside the dance hall. But, dancers, don't dare wear a skirt or midriff top here–this is the country and you've got to look cool in those jeans and long-sleeved shirts even if you aren't. Women, of course, can wear sleeveless shirts. Find a spot near the fans, which are situated in strategic areas throughout the club. The good thing is that the smoke factor is virtually nonexistent; maybe it's because so many people chew here. Ken sees no reason to add air-conditioning because he "wouldn't sell near enough beer" if he did. "Where else can you dance, sweat, reduce, and have a good time doing it? Five bucks for five pounds." Not a bad deal, when you think about it. Dancers, be aware that your first cup of ice water will cost you a quarter, but if you bring back your cup, refills are free.

Sonny, who operates the mechanical bull, says he gets anywhere from thirty to sixty riders a night. You get more buck for your bucks here, too. A two dollar ride lasts about thirty seconds, compared with other clubs that give you eight seconds for three to five dollars.

When Ken Lance dies, he says he wants his funeral held in the rodeo arena and his white Cadillac raffled off.

"I want everybody to have a good time," he says.

And what will his tombstone say?

"Just a damn good ol' boy."

Tumbleweed Dance Halls & Concert Arena
Lakeview and Country Club Roads, Stillwater
405/377-0076

DIRECTIONS: Go north on Route 177/Perkins Road and turn left on Sixth Avenue and right on Country Club Road. Tumbleweed is on the left at Lakeview Road.
DRESS CODE: Ropers, Rockies, and Wranglers.
DANCE DYNAMICS: Two-step, shuffle, buckle-shiners, line dances.

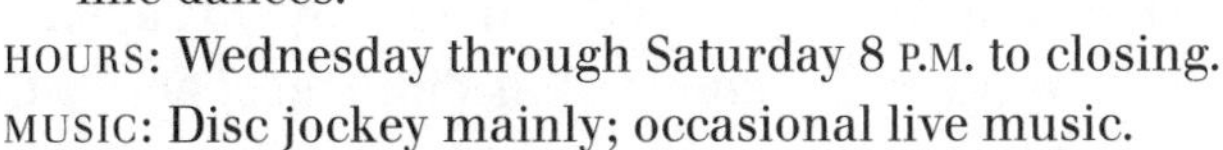
HOURS: Wednesday through Saturday 8 P.M. to closing.
MUSIC: Disc jockey mainly; occasional live music.

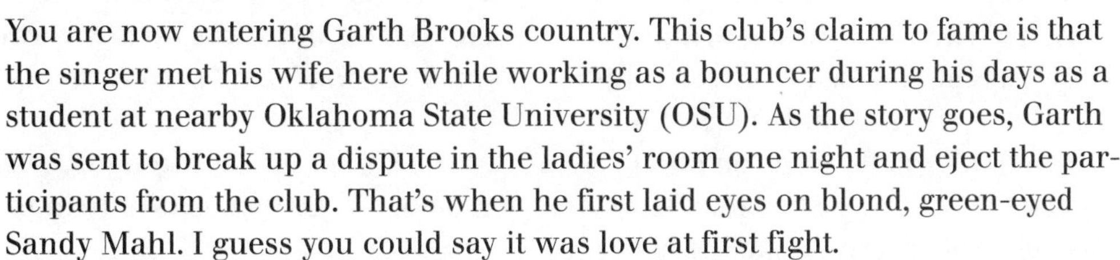
You are now entering Garth Brooks country. This club's claim to fame is that the singer met his wife here while working as a bouncer during his days as a student at nearby Oklahoma State University (OSU). As the story goes, Garth was sent to break up a dispute in the ladies' room one night and eject the participants from the club. That's when he first laid eyes on blond, green-eyed Sandy Mahl. I guess you could say it was love at first fight.

Garth also had a band back then called Santa Fe that played here, and he opened at what was then an adjacent rodeo ring after he got his recording contract. Now the sports arena is an eight-thousand-seat amphitheater for outdoor concerts, featuring such artists as Brooks, Chris LeDoux, and Tracy Lawrence.

This is young country here partly because of the club's proximity to OSU and partly because the club is classified as an entertainment facility, allowing it to admit eighteen-, nineteen-, and twenty-year-olds. Yes, it's a "not" club, too. As a result, young folks drive in from all over Oklahoma to take advantage of the lower admission age, even though they cannot purchase alcoholic beverages because the legal drinking age is twenty-one. IDs are checked at the door and, just like at Ken Lance's, hands are stamped "Over" or "Under" for the bartenders to check.

After 10 P.M. there's an elbow-to-elbow crowd at the 'Weed and an energy that manifests itself in an audible hum throughout the club. Count yourself lucky if you can find space to two-step or shuffle on the club's 3,200-square-foot floating maple floor. The owners, Hank and Sherry Moore, bought the club so they could have a place to dance and didn't realize it would bring an end to their dancing days. They now get their exercise shuffling around, taking care of business.

Tumbleweed is one of those somewhere-in-between clubs. It has a disc jockey most of the time, but also offers a fair share of live music to keep things interesting. During the year the 'Weed sponsors several major events, such as the annual picnic and concert in July, its anniversary party in September (which George Jones actually showed up for in 1995), and the annual Testicle Festival.

Excuse me? Actually, the Testicle Festival is just the affectionate nickname for the club's Annual Calf Fry. Remember Bruce's Bar in Colorado? That's right. Prairie oysters. About forty-eight hundred people turn out to chow down on the local delicacy. It is traditionally held each spring the Sunday before "dead week," or final exam week at OSU. The gates open at 2 P.M. and the ten dollar admission fee covers drinks, food, and concerts by three bands. Prices are kept low, Sherry says, to cater to a college kid's budget. There's free soft drinks and beer from 2 to 5 P.M. and dinner is served from 4:30 to 6 P.M. That's when Bart Towne whips out his secret recipe and slices up anywhere from eight hundred to fifteen hundred pounds of gonads and breads them and deep fries them to perfection.

Actually, calf fries aren't half bad. They taste sort of like chicken nuggets, only they are more the consistency of overcooked liver. Just drown them in ketchup if you don't like the taste.

After you get your fill of calf fries, go out to the concert arena for a helping of country music. At the 1993 festival the Great Divide Band, Brent Self and the Tumbleweed Band, and Chris LeDoux, whose worn-out tape Garth used to sing about, performed. A dance follows the concert from 9:30 P.M. to midnight with live music. And remember, children are only allowed at special events the 'Weed sponsors–including the calf fry.

Oregon

15

This may be lumberjack country, but there must have been cowboys here in droves at one time or another. Why else would the Cattlemen's Heritage Foundation operate a Cowboys Then and Now Museum in Portland? There is also a yearly rodeo at the exhibition center in the Portland Union Stockyards near the Columbia River. The state's most famous rodeo, however, is the Pendleton Round-Up, which usually ranks in the Top Ten rodeos for earnings. It is here where you'll find Oregon's most authentic cowboy honky-tonk, but, sadly, the Let 'er Buck Room is only open at roundup time (mid-September), as is the case with Pendleton's Happy Canyon Dance Hall.

The Spinning Wheel in Salem allegedly had the same guy singing there for twenty-some years. When I called to check it out, the voice on the other end of the phone answered, "Neon Cactus." Yikes! The club had gone neon on me. I'd have to keep looking. The Flying "M" in Yamhill sounded like a definite possibility, being a log cabin tucked away in the woods and all, but the cabins and motel were booked through the weekend. There was the country lounge at Mr. B's truck stop, but it was too new, as was Rock 'N' Rodeo and the Roadhouse over in Gresham. The Red Steer next to the Portland stockyards offers country dancing, but it is actually a classy supper club. I began to think Oregon had nothing to offer in the way of an older honky-tonk until local country dance instructor Wally Quinn told me about the Drum. The name didn't sound too country, but Wally assured me it was the oldest club in town–besides, that's where he teaches!

The Drum
14601 SE Division Street, Portland
503/760-1400

DIRECTIONS: From I-205 North exit right on Division Street. The Drum is on the left between 145th and 148th avenues in the southeast quadrant of the city.
DRESS CODE: Street clothes, skirts, coordinating western outfits.
DANCE DYNAMICS: West Coast swing, Cowboy Cha-Cha, two-step, line dances.
HOURS: Open seven days a week from 11 A.M. to 2 A.M.; closes at 4 A.M. on Friday and Saturday.
MUSIC: Live music nightly.

The Drum looks too new–all brick and tile and nicely trimmed trees–to be an old honky-tonk. But don't let its manicured appearance fool you. The place has been in business continuously since 1963. It moved from across the street in 1985 to its current location. And like the club, its manager, Dee Pierce, is a local institution.

So how long has she been at the Drum?

"I'm Mom here," Dee says. "I've matched a lot of people up. In fact, I've seen one guy meet and marry different women three times. That's how long I've been here."

Actually, Dee began working at the club just two years after it opened and was responsible for instituting dance classes here in 1980. Dance classes are now offered Sunday through Thursday by various instructors for a buck a body. Dee is an instructor and has choreographed two of the club's specialty dances, "Dee's Around" and "Sweet Pea."

On the Thursday night I was there, Wally Quinn was teaching a West Coast swing lesson. "There is no such thing as a dumb question unless you don't ask it," he tells the group. Believe me, West Coast is one dance where everyone always has a lot of questions. It is fairly difficult to learn and takes practice. (I myself have yet to master it.) It is what's known in dancer lingo as a "slotted" dance; that is, it's done in a straight line that extends an arm's length in front and in back of the man, who pretty much stays in one spot. The woman basically does all the work and the man just stands there and looks cool, pulling her this way and that.

The Drum is actually a lounge adjacent to Ricardo's La Fiesta restaurant, known for its "B-52," a humongous fifty-two-ounce burrito that serves sixteen hearty appetites.

The club is not so slick inside as out. It looks more Mediterranean than cowboy, except for the profiles of Indian chiefs on the wall (ah, that's why it's called the Drum!) and the saddle stools at a table near the bar. This is Oregon after all, not Texas. At least they're trying to make it look western. Short skirts and boots are not out of place because that is what most the women wear here. Others show up still in their work clothes and heels!

Dee says the club "is consistent and that people know what to expect from us. It's also the kind of place where you can bring your parents and not be embarrassed." And women don't have to be embarrassed about asking a man to dance here, either.

Music is probably one of the best things about the Drum, which offers live music seven nights a week from 9:15 P.M. until 2 A.M., except on Friday and Saturday when the band plays until 4 A.M. The music is first rate and so are the dancers, who span virtually every generation. Two-steps, East and West Coast swings, the Cowboy Cha-Cha (which is different from the East Coast dance of the same name in that it is a traveling partner dance and not a line dance), and a few line dances are all done on the smooth-as-can-be 990-square-foot oak floor. No parquet for this crowd! With the band singing and the lights down low, the Drum not only sounds like a honky-tonk, it looks like one, too.

Texas

16

I have but one regret in life: I was not born a Texan. Texas is unarguably the honky-tonk capital of the world, and, as they say, everything is bigger here. The state is big. The roads are big. The clouds are big. The honky-tonks are big. And the dance floors are *really* big–every dancer's dream.

You'll find hundreds of country music clubs scattered throughout the Lone Star State, but the concentration of the oldest and best basically follows a "J" pattern in central Texas, with the exception of Cypress off to the right. The top of the J runs from Abilene, Mingus, Fort Worth, and Dallas to Longview, while the hook consists of Austin, New Braunfels, San Antonio, Helotes, Bandera, and Luckenbach.

The three oldest dance halls are the Luckenbach Dance Hall, which opened in 1849 and hosted dances until the 1960s; Gruene Hall in New Braunfels, which opened in 1878 and is profiled in this section; and Tin Hall in Cypress, which opened in 1890. Luckenbach only has entertainment on some Saturdays, while Gruene Hall is open daily. Still, there is a lot of history at Luckenbach and you should check it out; just call ahead to see when it's open. Few non-Texans have heard of the Tin Hall in Cypress over Houston way, but it also deserves a look. It's known for bringing in many major acts.

Most people outside Texas probably associate the state more with Gilley's. But ever since the Pasadena institution closed, nothing of its kind has replaced the legendary club in the Houston area. And be wary of "gentlemen's" clubs with names that sound like honky-tonks, lest you find yourself sipping longnecks served by scantily clad waitresses.

The most difficult task is narrowing the field of honky-tonks to a mere handful, because in this state they're all pretty darn good, especially Adair's Saloon and Cowboys in Dallas, Blue Bonnet Palace in Selma, Cibolo Creek Country Club in San Antonio, the Caravan in Amarillo, Eddie's Country Ballroom in Manvel, John T. Floore's Country Store in Helotes, and Reo Palm Isle in Longview.

Another thing you need to know about Texas is that liquor licenses vary from club to club and county to county. Country Clubs here range from hard-liquor dispensers to beer joints and from BYOB establishments that just sell beer, wine, and mixers to "private clubs" where members only may purchase alcoholic beverages. Children are generally welcome in most all the honky-tonks except for the New Breed clubs. Be sure to call first to find out a club's policy on minors.

The dance of choice is the Texas two-step, with regional differences within the state. Dallas dancers like to double-time the steps, with cowboys doing a tight arm-hold around the women's necks and the women hooking their left thumbs through a belt loop on their partners' Wranglers. In Houston, things are smoother and more laid-back, and you're more likely to encounter a classical ballroom hold, also known as the "closed cowboy" or "bra-strap" hold. And ladies, men are the ones who usually dance backward here.

The waltz is the second most popular dance in Texas, followed by buckle-shining and freestyle rock and roll. The Cotton-Eyed Joe, which is danced only to a song of the same name, is also done across the state. It can be danced solo, in a couple, or in a line of people that branch out like spokes on a wagon wheel. Usually the Cotton-Eyed Joe is followed by the schottische, a

German dance that also is danced only to one song. The schottische, which is made up of grapevines and hops, is very easy to pick up, and, like the Cotton-Eyed Joe, can be executed in lines of people. Remember, it was the Germans who brought dances like the polka and the schottische to America and they heavily populated Gruene, Luckenbach, and New Braunfels.

So now that you have a general idea of what to expect in the great state of Texas, pull on those Ropers and Wranglers (that's what they wear here) and let's get to those "kicker bars," as the Texans say.

Arkey Blue's Silver Dollar Night Club
308 Main Street, Bandera
210/796-8826

DIRECTIONS: From Highway 16/Cypress Street turn right on Main Street. Arkey Blue's is on the right in the first block.
DRESS CODE: Ropers and Wranglers, plaid shirts; some women wear skirts, baseball caps okay.
DANCE DYNAMICS: Two-step, waltz, and buckle-shiners.
HOURS: Open seven days a week from 10:30 A.M. to 2 A.M.
MUSIC: Jukebox/live music nightly and house band on Saturday.

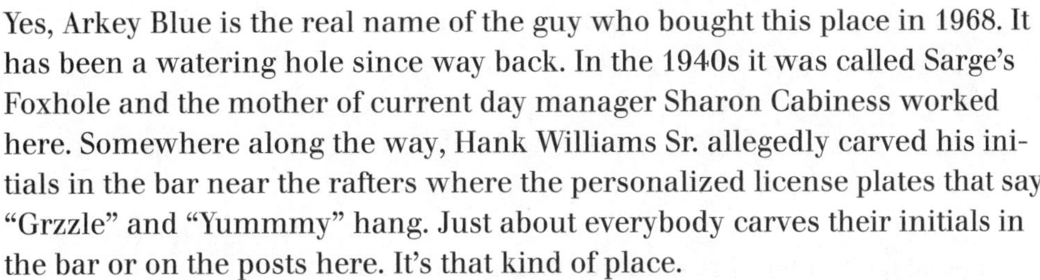

Yes, Arkey Blue is the real name of the guy who bought this place in 1968. It has been a watering hole since way back. In the 1940s it was called Sarge's Foxhole and the mother of current day manager Sharon Cabiness worked here. Somewhere along the way, Hank Williams Sr. allegedly carved his initials in the bar near the rafters where the personalized license plates that say "Grzzle" and "Yummmy" hang. Just about everybody carves their initials in the bar or on the posts here. It's that kind of place.

A certain randiness permeates the air in Bandera during deer-hunting season, which runs from the first week of November to year's end. For two solid months the town's testosterone level is well above normal, which is plenty high in the "Cowboy Capital of the World." Men can be found anywhere and everywhere at this time, and they are unabashedly on the prowl. Women are sought out and appreciated here, if only for a night. Arkey Blue's self-penned songs attest to this. He sings of love found and lost and found again all in the course of a night.

From the moment you walk down the narrow staircase into "Arkey's place," as everybody calls it (they may as well drop the Silver Dollar altogether), you will recognize this as a honky-tonk for the books. It's not just the sawdust sprinkled about on the twenty-four-hundred-square-foot cement floor. It's not just the velvet paintings of Elvis and naked ladies. And it's not just the bumper sticker slapped on the side of a speaker on the stage that says, "Steel Players Do It Sittin' Down." Nope. It's the clientele itself. "Doc" Frank Nuanes for one. Doc is not the type to let an unfamiliar face go unnoticed, and is as much Arkey Blue's as Arkey Blue himself.

Put a buck in the jukebox and you can get ten tunes, many of which are Arkey's. About the only new songs are by neotraditionalists Mark Chesnutt, Alan Jackson, Doug Supernaw, Hank Williams Jr., and the like. Drinks, like the club and the jukebox, are pretty retro: Coca-Cola in a glass bottle–just like in the old days. Kitschy cowboy collectibles are everywhere. The red restroom walls are covered with graffiti; burlap curtains serve as "doors" to the two stalls.

Just outside is a nice patio with trees where people hang out during the summer. Engraved brass plates hanging by the fireplace name several couples who have met and married at Arkey's. Believe it or not, only one couple married here has ever untied the knot.

The club, which normally holds 150, fills up quickly. So get there early and be sure to respect the "Reserved" signs on the tables. Arkey Blue and his Blue Cowboys (Doug, Sonny, Gary, and Harvey) usually play on Saturday night.

Arkey's is BYOB and only sells beer, wine, setups, and local microbrews, some very low in alcoholic content. Children are welcome anytime as long as they are accompanied by a parent or guardian.

Arkey himself is somewhat of a local legend at age forty-six. His song "Daddy's Sick Again" was played as part of the background music in *Texas Chainsaw Massacre,* and another, "Misty Hours of Daylight," was featured in the soundtrack of *Race With the Devil.* Some of the scenes from that movie were filmed in the Silver Dollar. And at closing time, Arkey will still be there–not on stage but holding court at his table in the center of the room.

Billy Bob's Texas
2520 Rodeo Plaza, Fort Worth
817/624–7117

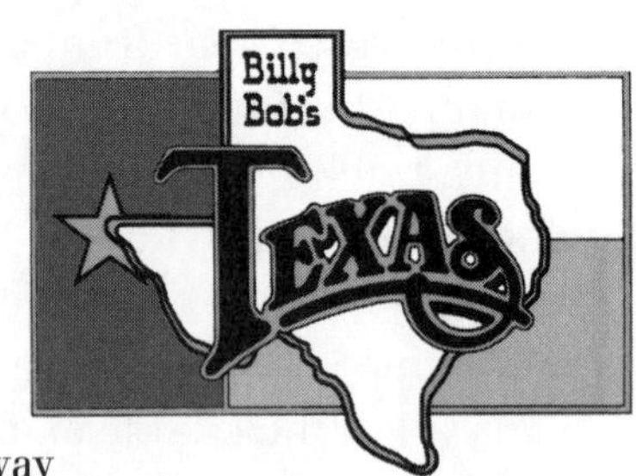

DIRECTIONS: From I-35 West to Fort Worth, cross Loop 820 and go right on Exit 54A or B (NE 28th Street/Highway 183) for two miles to the Fort Worth Stockyards. Turn left on Main Street (Highway 287-81). Billy Bob's is on the left at the corner of NE 26th Street and Rodeo Plaza. Parking is north of NE 26th Street.

DRESS CODE: Almost anything goes.

DANCE DYNAMICS: Texas two-step, waltz, buckle-shiners, some line dancing.

HOURS: Open daily from 11 A.M. to 2 A.M.; Sunday noon to 2 A.M.

MUSIC: Live entertainment nightly.

Billy Bob's Texas bills itself as "The World's Largest Honky-Tonk" (actually, it's more of an entertainment complex with a honky-tonk attitude for the whole family). Even when Gilley's was open, this place was bigger, with a hundred thousand square feet under one roof. Just pull into the twenty-acre parking lot and come on in.

After you pay the admission fee, walk down the hall and ooh and aah over the handprints hanging on the wall of artists who have performed here. It looks as though Alan Jackson has the most lipstick kisses, but to reach Garth Brooks someone would have to be boosted up; from the looks of it, a fair number of fans went to the extra trouble.

Billy Bob's has so many tales they could fill the state of Texas. Did you know only five hundred tickets were sold for Garth Brooks's first gig here in August 1989, most of which went to his fan club in Stillwater, Oklahoma? Did you know George Strait opened here for Rusty Weir in 1982? Did you know Alan Jackson played for free the first time he performed at Billy Bob's? Did you know Merle Haggard made the *Guinness Book of World Records* here by buying the largest round of drinks ever? And it was here that the record for the most bottles of beer sold in one night–sixteen thousand–was set during a Hank Williams Jr. concert.

In the early 1900s the club was nothing more than an open-air cattle yard in the Fort Worth Stockyards. It was enclosed in 1936 and the missionlike towers were built. Then the annual stock show moved to the Will Rogers complex and the building was vacant. In its next incarnation in the 1950s it was a department store that was so large the stock boys had to wear roller skates to get from one end to the other. Then Billy Bob Barnett bought it and turned it into an amusement park in 1971. What we now know as Billy Bob's Texas opened for business in 1981 under a partnership formed between four Fort Worth businessmen: Holt Hickman; Dan Jury; Steve Murrin; and Billy Minick, a former champion bull rider.

There aren't any mechanical bulls here, just the genuine rip-snorting article that both semipros and pros sign up the Monday before to ride every Friday and Saturday at 9 and 10 P.M. The indoor arena has a natural slope from the entry to the showroom stage, which makes for perfect concert viewing. The original function, however, was to facilitate runoff from the cattle pens and allow for easy cleaning. According to Pam Minick, head of advertising and promotion (and Billy's wife), cowboys who compete at Billy Bob's can earn more than a thousand dollars in a weekend. At fourteen bulls a night, more than twenty thousand bovines have bucked here since the club opened. Before and after the contests, the rodeo cowboys hang out in the Let 'er Buck Saloon across from the arena.

Virtually every big-name country act in recent years has played at Billy Bob's. There's live entertainment nightly, with major stars performing on Fridays and Saturdays at 10:30 P.M. You can take in the show for the price of general admission, which is never more than $7.50, or you can reserve a seat in the main showroom that will cost somewhat more. The Friday I was there Tracy Lawrence sang to a sold-out showroom in which hundreds of young bucks milled about dressed like, you guessed it, Tracy Lawrence. And it's okay to two-step, waltz, swing, or buckle-shine during the concerts, though you may not want to if you're sitting front and center in the main showroom. If you don't have prime seating, you can still get a close-up view of the singer on any of two big screens or thirty-one monitors situated throughout the club. After dancing the night away, take advantage of the breakfast buffet that starts at midnight.

It's Billy Bob's commitment to country music that earned it national recognition as the ACM's "Nightclub of the Year" in 1981, 1985, 1992, and 1994, and the CMA's "Club of the Year" in 1992 and 1994. Pam says the main problem the club faces in winning the CMA honor is that it "is on the cusp" between qualifying for "Club of the Year" and "Venue of the Year." To qualify as "Club of the Year," capacity must be two thousand or less, and two thousand or more for "Venue of the Year." Billy Bob's total capacity is six thousand, so it ends up getting compared with small clubs like the Crazy Horse Saloon in Santa Ana or huge venues like Dollywood in Pigeon Forge, Tennessee. Billy Bob's likely squeaked by with the CMA honors because the showroom only seats eighteen hundred.

Many movies and television shows have been filmed at the club over the years. Some on the big screen include *Necessary Roughness, Pure Country, Over the Top*, and *Baja, Oklahoma.* Small-screen shows include *Dallas* and *Walker, Texas Ranger.* Billy Bob's also has its own syndicated television show: *Billy Bob's Country Countdown,* cohosted by Pam and singer Michael Twitty. The Nashville Network uses the club as a venue for its *On Stage* concerts.

There are never-ending possibilities of things to do here. Parents and children alike can play video games, have their pictures taken on the stuffed bull, shop in the gift store, or take dance lessons from instructor Wendell Nelson on one of the club's two dance floors. Lessons run in eight-week cycles. Classes are free on Thursday at 7 P.M. The 2 P.M. Saturday line-dance class, at which children seventeen and under are welcome with a parent, and the three classes that run from 4 to 7 P.M. on Sunday cost three dollars per person. If you find yourself running low on cash after all this, just head over to the money machine up front and replenish your wallet.

Broken Spoke

3201 South Lamar Boulevard, Austin
512/442-6189

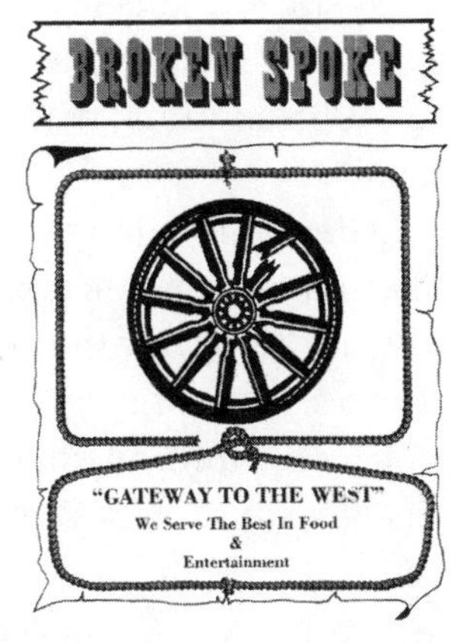

DIRECTIONS: From I-35 South/Route 81, exit west (right) on Ben White Boulevard. Turn right on Lamar Boulevard. The Broken Spoke is on the right.

DRESS CODE: Anything goes.

DANCE DYNAMICS: Texas two-step, waltz, swing. Line dancing highly discouraged.

HOURS: Open Tuesday through Saturday 10:30 A.M. to 2 A.M.

MUSIC: Jukebox and live music.

Deep in the land of Lone Stars and Shiner Bocks, in a section of Austin once known as "Bubba Land," sits the Broken Spoke, the stuff of which honky-tonk legends are made. All parts add up to make the whole. The massive oak. The dirt parking lot. The classic-country jukebox. The best chicken-fried steak in the state of Texas. The stories. The hundreds of country music stars that have passed through its doors. The sign that says, "Parking for Misplaced husbands out back." And the other one that says, "Through this door pass the best country music dancers in all the world."

That means you. Just don't blow it like those line-dancing German tourists did the night I was there. But we'll get to that later. Once inside, you'll think you're in another time, another place. Heck, you are! As they say, Texas is another country. The dining area is right up front with the jukebox and the pool tables and that's where you need to order up a platter of the best chicken-fried steak (breaded beefsteak smothered in cream gravy) in these parts. After you finish, head past the bar where the "Aggie Chainsaw" (a rusty hacksaw) hangs overhead and into the Tourist Trap, the club's mini-museum. (Wait, listen to what one bartender is telling the other: "That lady wanted a line-dance song. I told her when she came in there was no line dancing here." This is a real honky-tonk!) Okay, back to the Trap. In the first glass case, the same one LBJ's hat is in, is the thick white platter Randy Travis dined on. You see, the singer was in Austin promoting a movie and got a hankering for some home-cooking and naturally headed over to the Spoke. He didn't have time to finish his meal before other commitments called, so he took it with him. A few hours later a messenger returned with clean utensils and the platter with this message scrawled on it: "The chicken fried steak was great. Thanks. Randy Travis." The Tourist Trap is full of such memorabilia and the Spoke is full of such stories. This is where Willie Nelson hangs out when he's in town; he even filmed scenes from *Honeysuckle Rose* here. Look in the Trap for his 1968 contract, when he first played the club for eight hundred dollars a night.

After you're done reading all the citations from the Oklahoma and Texas lawmakers, the magazine stories, and the autographed pictures, you're probably ready to pay the cover (usually three dollars during the week and six dollars on weekends) to enter the dance hall and scoot your boots on that fourteen-hundred-square-foot cement floor to the music of Alvin Crow and his Pleasant Valley Boys, one of the more popular draws at the Spoke. Kind of reminds you of Hank Thompson and the Brazos Valley Boys, don't they? Bet you didn't know George Strait and Ace in the Hole used to open for Alvin. And look where it got him! Alvin, on the other hand, is quite content singing in Texas dance halls. He and his band do songs like "Okie From Muskogee," but then again, Alvin is an Oklahoman by birth.

Posted on a wall in the seating area off to the left of the dance floor is the "Ten Commandments" for Spoke waitresses, which includes such admonishments as, "Wear makeup" and "Be happy–no one likes a grump."

Owner James White loves to tell about the heart and soul of the Spoke. Did you know Roy Acuff, Ernest Tubb, and Bob Wills all played here? You do now. Pretty soon it'll be time for James to do his nightly ritual: singing the "Broken Spoke Legend," which he wrote. That's when Becky Jenkins, the dance-wax lady whom James affectionately refers to as "Little Miss Bashful Hunk of Heaven" and who's dressed in overalls James bought her for her birthday, will roll the big wagon wheel with the broken spoke back and forth in front of the stage while James sings: "You can take all your rock joints and discos and you know where they can go. . . ."

Another ritual is the "Breaking of the Spoke," which is carried out at the club's birthday bashes (pun intended). That's when James let's some lucky woman try her hand at breaking out a spoke on a wagon wheel. The first wheel cost James seven dollars in 1964; now they cost a hundred dollars. Speaking of birthdays, the Spoke just celebrated its thirtieth on November 10, 1994. Scheduled entertainers included Alvin and the boys, the Geezinslaws, Don Walser, Chris Wall, and Gary P. Nunn. Surprise guests of the evening included Jerry Jeff Walker and Mark Chesnutt, who lamented the fact that he had yet to play the Spoke. That's something he can't say anymore.

James started building the Spoke in 1964, the day after he got out of the army, on a vacant lot about a mile from where he grew up outside the city limits. He dreamed of building a dance hall, a place where the whole family could come, and set out to make it happen with help from a lot of friends and good old boys. Building permits weren't required back then, so he had the place up and running in forty-six days. He and wife Annetta (it's *her* chicken-fried steak recipe) have kept it pretty much the same since then, with only a few add-ons over the years.

A fitting motto for the Broken Spoke could be: "If it ain't broke, don't fix it; and if it is broke, don't fix it either." After all, the club's symbol is a broken wagon wheel. But other things bear this out; the roof, for starters. A few years back it started leaking like a sieve, so James just jerry-rigged a second roof of corrugated metal on the inside to catch the runoff, which falls into a gutter along the ceiling and then is carried to an exterior wall and, thus, outside. It's also the kind of place where prices are "whited out" on the menu and changes are written in by hand. Duct tape rejoins linoleum that has separated over the years. All of these things just add to the club's charm, along with the red-, white-, and blue-checkered tablecloths; the folding tables and chairs; and the plywood stage. The acoustic ceiling panels above the stage are peppered with indentations from the bows of many a furious fiddle player. They have managed to replace a missing ceiling panel that had been removed so the "Big Un," six-foot-seven-inch Ray Benson, lead singer of Asleep at the Wheel, wouldn't have to stoop when he performed on the stage.

Now back to those line dancers. Cindy Lay, the cover charge lady, gives them a good-natured scolding and tells them there'd better not be a next time.

The Cabaret Dance Hall
801 Main Street, Bandera
210/460-3095

DIRECTIONS: From Highway 16/Cypress Street turn right on Main Street. The Cabaret is down another block on the left.

DRESS CODE: Ropers and Wranglers, plaid shirts; some women wear skirts, baseball caps okay.

DANCE DYNAMICS: Two-step, waltz, and buckle-shiners.

HOURS: Open Thursday 11 A.M. to 10 P.M., Friday and Saturday 11 A.M. to 1 A.M., and Sunday 11 A.M. to 10 P.M.

MUSIC: Live band.

Bandera is the Hill Country's dude ranch center, a place where people from all over the world come to escape. Part of the escape mentality is to let all hell break loose; why worry about tomorrow? Established in 1936, the Cabaret is the town's oldest dance hall. This is where local hero Arkey Blue first sang in these parts years ago.

The cover is five bucks a head, but the band more than compensates for the price. This is young country. The place is full of twentysomethings scooting around the 1,950-square-foot hardwood floor. The songs are the ones you hear on the radio and the tone is upbeat, not so much about leaving as loving.

Cheers
815 North Grandview, Odessa
915/334–9941

DIRECTIONS: From I-20 go north on Grandview Avenue, past Second Street/Route 80, to Eighth Street. Cheers is on the left at the corner of East Eighth Street and North Grandview.

DRESS CODE: Ropers, Wranglers, Rockies, and cowboy hats for everyone. A few women wear straight skirts or shorts. No tank tops.

DANCE DYNAMICS: Texas two-step, waltz, freestyle.

HOURS: Open daily from 5 P.M. to 2 A.M.

MUSIC: Pre-recorded music and disc jockey. Live music at concerts only.

This is not so much a story about Cheers as it is the story of the men behind Cheers, and I don't mean Norm and Cliff. I'm talking Herb, Phil, Ray, Charlie, and Terry. As a Country Club, Cheers is pretty predictable: Recorded music, disc jockey, a packed house, silver saddle suspended above a smooth hardwood dance floor. But it is special in that this Country Club started it all in 1973 for the Graham Brothers, who now own the largest group of country nightclubs, twenty-one and counting, in the nation. At one time they owned as many as forty-three clubs, but they sold off most of the smaller ones. If you've ever heard of Dallas Alley, Denim & Diamonds, Graham Country Dancing, Graham Central Station, Mudbugs, Cactus Moon, or Rockin' Rodeo, then you've probably heard of Cheers, too. The outfit also owns some rock-and-roll clubs called West L.A.

Herb Graham says he "started dabbling" in the club business in 1968. Cheers actually was established in 1972 as a rock club called the Other Place, but switched to country a year after opening. That same year, Herb opened clubs in Waco, San Angelo, and Longview.

Although Cheers, being the flagship Country Club of the operation, can't compare to its newer sister clubs, like the Shreveport Denim & Diamonds that's billed as "an acre of dancin', romancin' and great country music" or Phoenix's Graham Central Station, there are similarities:

- The trademark mirrored saddle that was designed for the Graham Brothers and is much copied by other country discos.

- The music format. All the clubs in the Graham operation (except Dallas Alley) feature recorded music played by DJs who follow a Top 40 list compiled by the head office; the lists features forty-eight minutes an hour of country music and twelve minutes of other types of music, primarily rock. Like the saddles, this formula is also copied by other country discos.
- A packed house.

Cheers covers only eight thousand square feet of ground and has a three-hundred-square-foot dance floor where primarily the Texas two-step and the waltz are done. On the rock-and-roll sets, it's just good old-fashioned freestyle. Don't expect to line dance here. West Texans are pretty set in their ways when it comes to dancing. It's that familiarity thing. (A word of warning: Thursday is rock-and-roll night.)

The club also does a good bar business, in part because of the way the liquor laws are structured. You can't buy liquor at package stores after 9 P.M. or beer after midnight, but clubs can sell both until 2 A.M.

Herb Graham has definitely hit upon a recipe for success. While some may complain that this is honky-tonk homogenization, others welcome the consistency. That translates to a safe environment, large dance floors, spacious clubs (the average is thirty thousand to thirty-five thousand square feet), quality sound systems, virtually smoke-free buildings, huge parking lots, and food and drink specials that are hard to beat.

Herb's story is one of hard work and survival. He didn't have any formal schooling before age thirteen because he was working the cotton fields in Heavener, Oklahoma, to help support his eight brothers and sisters. By age thirty, he worked eight hours a day for a local trucking outfit and then he was off to his rock club from 7 P.M. until 2 A.M. So if you're tempted to denigrate any of the Graham clubs as just another country disco, save the criticism for the competition and remember his story. Even at fifty-seven, Herb Graham is still watching out for his family. His brother Phil is a co-owner, and diversified with Herb into the banking business in 1982. The Graham-owned Texas Bank now ranks around sixth on the top one hundred of large community banks. Phil also oversees the design of the clubs. Another brother, Terry, a former musician, promotes them; a third, Ray, takes care of the lights and sound systems; and a fourth, Charlie, is another co-owner. A fifth brother, Gary, has his own clubs and recently sold a few to his older brother, including Tucson's Cactus Moon. There is also a sense of family that Herb Graham instills among his employees, eleven of whom have been with the organization for twenty years.

Even though Herb could live anywhere in the world, this humble man still chooses to base himself in Odessa because "I like it here." So does his wife, a former hairdresser. She never goes to the clubs though, preferring to spend her time with the thoroughbreds she and Herb raise. In fact, they named the first Denim & Diamonds after one of their racehorses.

All the Graham clubs bring in national acts periodically for special concerts. Cheers has featured local-girl-made-good Ronna Reeves, Pirates of the Mississippi, and Michelle Wright, among others.

Herb actually prefers the blues over rock or country music, but he knows that in this business you have to go with the trends, which sometimes means switching formats, if only for a night or two during the week.

"The club business is really a three-night business," he says, "and you have to do an alternate format to fill the club up."

Herb's secret to success is his hands-on style. As he admits, "It's pretty hard to do 'hands-off.'"

Gruene Hall

1281 Gruene Road, New Braunfels
210/606–1281

GRUENE Hall
Texas' Oldest Dance Hall

DIRECTIONS: From I-35 South, take the Canyon Lake exit and go west one and a half miles on FM 306. Turn left on Hunter Road, which is only a half-mile long. Hunter dead-ends at Gruene Road. Gruene Hall is straight ahead.

DRESS CODE: Anything goes. Shirts must be worn at all times.

DANCE DYNAMICS: Texas two-step, buckle-shiners. Line dance at your own risk.

HOURS: Open daily from 11 A.M. to midnight; closes at 1 A.M. Saturday.

MUSIC: Live music every night except Monday in summer; Thursday through Sunday the rest of the year.

Entertainment Weekly said it best when it classified Gruene Hall as the kind of place "where a guy would as soon wear ladies' underwear as line dance." Co-owner Mary Jane Nalley says the only people she's ever seen line dancing here are children. And John, the bartender, tells of the time when John Fitzpatrick, a former lineman for the Dallas Cowboys, mowed a couple of line dancers down in their tracks. Consider yourself forewarned. It's mostly two-steppers you'll find gliding smooth as ice skaters over the well-worn sixteen-hundred-square-foot hardwood dance floor at the oldest operating dance hall in Texas.

The hall, named for its founder, Heinrich D. Gruene (pronounced Green), has been in business continuously since it was established in 1878. It was then the town's social center, hosting every event from weddings to badger fights. It is listed today in the National Register of Historic Places.

To understand Gruene Hall, you must know something about the town it's in, says Mary Jane, which is an old German cotton-farming community situated halfway between Austin and San Antonio on the banks of the Guadalupe River, the largest recreational river in the state.

She and her business partner, Pat Molak, bought the hall in 1975. Pat always dreamed of owning "an old joint." "When we came it was like a ghost town," Mary Jane says. Together they have worked to make the hall a profitable venture. The pair also owns an old mercantile store and cotton gin where they run the Grist Mill Restaurant.

The hall still looks the same as it did in the old days. The six-thousand-square-foot-structure resembles an old barn with flaps on the sides that fold up to let air circulate in the summertime through screens backed with chicken wire. And here is some Gruene Hall trivia for you: singer Hal Ketchum built those doors that open into the dance hall when he was employed as a master carpenter at Bushwackers up the street. There are long wooden tables inside and a front bar section. Outside there is a beer garden and horseshoe area. Gruene Hall is licensed only to sell beer and wine and the clock is set on bar time, fifteen minutes fast.

Autographed pictures of some of those makers of the music grace the walls in corners of the club. Among those that have sung on the stage, backed with a bucolic mural of a river and trees, are Garth Brooks, Lyle Lovett, Rodney Crowell, George Strait, and local hero Hal, whose songs you know.

But local bands, whose songs you don't know, also play here, including a bluegrass group called the Volunteer Fire Ants from Wimberley. You can sit back with the rest of the Grinners and tap your toes, listening to such original compositions as "Another Reason to Barbecue" and "When the Dealer Calls Your Hand," whose chorus goes something like: "I'll be there when the shit hits the fan." If this ain't a honky-tonk, I don't know what is.

Mary Jane credits a video Travis Tritt filmed here with giving Gruene Hall national exposure. It also has been featured in a Miller Beer commercial, and Dennis Quaid and Meg Ryan shot footage here for their film *Flesh and Bone.*

Film crews and celebrities aside, Gruene Hall draws a varied clientele. About 350,000 tourists step through its doors each year in addition to the regulars, who range from children to Southwest Texas State students to senior citizens.

The Ponderosa Ballroom
3881 Vine Street, Abilene
915/698-2102

THE PONDEROSA

DIRECTIONS: From I-20, exit at North Clack Street/Highway 84 South. The road will become Danville Drive and Winters Freeway. Exit north on Sayles Boulevard and turn right on Industrial Boulevard, then left on Vine Street. The Ponderosa is on the right.

DRESS CODE: Boots, jeans, and hats. Some women wear regular dresses–not cowgirl dresses. No tank tops or muscle shirts.

DANCE DYNAMICS: Texas two-step, swing, freestyle.

HOURS: Open seven nights a week. Bar special from 7 to 9 P.M. nightly.

MUSIC: Live bands Friday and Saturday; disc jockey Monday through Thursday.

A sign inside the Ponderosa Ballroom states: "Minors washing stamps off will be barred until age 21. No Exceptions." To a young Texan, this could be a punishment worse than death. No more pool. No more dancing. No more country music. Ouch!

Up until 1994 the house band was that of longtime owner L. C. Agnew and his Dixie Playboys. L. C., who took up the fiddle at age eleven and can play just about every instrument except mandolin and saxophone, has played backup on the Louisiana Hayride and in bands for Gov. Jimmie Davis, Red Sovine, and Billy Walker. Now local and regional bands take the stage every Friday and Saturday night because L. C. sold out to a group of partners, J. R. Holland, David Thedford, and Donny Pratt. When asked if he planned to keep it country, Donny retorted, "This is Texas, isn't it?"

Ask a stupid question . . .

The friendly, kicked-back ballroom draws a mostly older clientele, except for the eighteen-, nineteen-, and twenty-year-olds in the pool room. It's definitely a no-frills warehouse of a club with a 2,500-square-foot cracked cement dance floor that's as slippery as all get out. Chicken wire holds in exposed insulation in spots and the aqua and chrome Formica tables and matching chairs are a throwback to the fifties.

The bands, too, can be reminiscent of the fifties–such as Johnny Dee and the Rockets. Yep, you guessed it, rockabilly. Shades of the Palomino. They're very good, though, which is probably why the cover charge the night I was there was eight dollars–it varies depending on the band.

You can get a rodeo beer (beer on the rocks) at the front bar in view of a large photo of John Wayne.

Even though L. C., a soft-spoken man in his early sixties who operated three other clubs over the years, just sold the place, he still hangs out here. A musician friend, Tommy Dodson, first put him onto the place. Tommy saw the vacant building on Vine Street and told L. C. it would make a great club. L. C. took a look at it and liked what he saw, leased it, and readied it for business. His five-man band moved over from Carpenter's Hall, which L. C. ran from 1965 to 1975, and provided entertainment while L. C.'s wife ran the bar.

Come closing time, keep in mind the little ritual called "Pick-Me Time," practiced mainly in Texas and Oklahoma. It works like this: The cowboys come in late and don't buy anything to drink, whereas the ladies have been drinking since 9 P.M. It's a sure thing that by eleven, several couples will be paired off.

White Elephant Saloon

106 East Exchange Avenue, Fort Worth
817/624-9712 or 817/624-1887

DIRECTIONS: From I-35 West to Fort Worth, cross Loop 820 and go right on Exit 54A or B (NE 28th Street/Highway 183) for two miles to the Fort Worth Stockyards. Turn left on Main Street (Highway 287-81) to East Exchange Avenue and turn left again. The club is on the right across from the Stockyards Hotel. Street parking is available or you can just park at Billy Bob's and walk over.
DRESS CODE: No nudity.
DANCE DYNAMICS: Texas two-step, waltz, buckle-shiners, some line dancing.
HOURS: Sunday through Thursday noon to midnight; Friday and Saturday noon to 2 A.M.
MUSIC: Live entertainment nightly.

Esquire magazine named the White Elephant Saloon one of the hundred best bars in America. This intimate watering hole, which reopened for business in 1976, evokes the Old West. It's patterned after a saloon of the same name from the 1880s that offered women, strong drink, and gambling in the section of Fort Worth once known as "Hell's Half Acre." Lonesome cowboys facing a long hard drive on the Chisholm Trail would stop in for one last night of rabble-rousing before heading out with the cattle.

Its recent claim to fame is that the White Elephant plays the part of CD's Place, the hangout in *Walker, Texas Ranger*, starring Chuck Norris. But it is better known in these parts for the great shoot-out between White Elephant owner Luke Short and former city marshal Jim Courtright the night of February 8, 1887. Apparently there was a dispute between Short, a partner of Wyatt Earp and one of the West's better gamblers, and Courtright over the saloon's gambling practices. They took the argument outside, and when the smoke and dust settled, Courtright lay dying. Accounts of what really happened that night vary, but the shooting was ruled a fair fight. Short then sold his interest in the saloon and moved to Kansas. Six years later, at the age of thirty-nine, he took sick and died. His body was brought back to Fort Worth for burial in the Oakwood Cemetery, not far from Courtright's final resting place. Tombstone rubbings of both men hang on the wall above the bar, and the gunfight is reenacted yearly in front of the saloon.

In addition to the annual "shoot-out," the club features cowboy campfire concerts two to three times a year with troubadour Don Edwards, who has performed here ever since owner Joseph K. Dulle reopened the club. And an adjacent outdoor beer garden at 101 East Exchange Avenue is open from April to October.

The White Elephant is highly popular among tourists and Fort Worth businessmen, who stop in to hear live music 362 nights a year and to two-step or waltz on the raised 290-square-foot hardwood floor, which is small and crowded. The cover (charged only on Friday and Saturday nights) varies depending on which band performs.

By the way, eighteen-year-olds can patronize the White Elephant, but they must be accompanied by a parent or guardian and they cannot partake of any alcoholic beverages. And be sure to stop and admire the collections of white elephant figurines and cowboy hats (Chuck Moyer's is covered with lipstick kisses) in the back right corner of the saloon.

Utah

17

You might not expect to find a cowboy bar in Utah; after all, this is Brigham Young and Osmond territory. Yet the liquor flows here as freely as spring runoff on the Wasatch Mountains. Even though Mormons, who make up 70 percent of the state's population, frown on drinking, they cheerfully sell alcoholic beverages to nonbelievers. So if you are a disciple of the two-step rather than of Joseph Smith and have a hankering for a beer and some serious boot-scooting, Utah has plenty of private clubs (which are licensed to sell mixed drinks containing more than 3.2 percent alcohol) where both can be had. The main thing you need to know is that you have to be a member or a sponsored guest to gain entrance to one of these clubs. In most cases, you may purchase a temporary membership as long as somebody sponsors you; just ask one of the regular members at the door to do so.

To find a honky-tonk in Utah, I turned to Salt Lake native Bill Johnson, a fiddle player for singer Chris LeDoux, who recommended the oldest club in the state.

The Westerner Club
3360 South Redwood Road, Salt Lake City
801/972–5447

DIRECTIONS: From I-80/I-15 exit west on Route 171/3500 South Street and cross the Jordan River to Redwood Road, which runs parallel to the interstate. Turn left on Redwood. The Westerner is on the right.
DRESS CODE: Basic country attire–T-shirts are okay, but no tank tops.
DANCE DYNAMICS: Lots of line dancing, two-stepping, and western swing.
HOURS: Open Monday through Saturday 6 P.M. to 12:30 A.M. Closed Sunday.
MUSIC: Live music nightly.

The Westerner opened in 1965 when two country music lovers, Leon and Joy Krebs, leased an old chicken house in an agricultural area west of Salt Lake City, and transformed it into a passable dance hall with live music every night of the week. Leon, an ironworker by trade, had friends who specialized in all areas of construction and they worked together to get the building approved. As the years passed, they expanded the place as the business grew. The property owner noticed how successful the dance hall was and soon offered to let the couple buy the land, which included a furniture store and a large parking lot. By 1976, a twenty-thousand-square-foot facility was built to replace the old dance hall. At that time, the new and improved Westerner was the largest honky-tonk in the state and about the third largest in the country. A year later, the Krebs family moved to Colorado to raise horses and sold out to their bookkeeper, who has made the club a family enterprise.

Over the years, the Westerner has held its own against the competition, which has come and gone, and come again. The club draws close to nine hundred people on a good night compared with only two hundred or so at a neon cowboy bar twice the size, probably because it still offers live music every night it is open.

Before you enter the Westerner, however, you must follow a certain protocol. There are two lines at the door, one for members (on the right) and one for nonmembers (on the left). Remember, this is "a private club for members" and Utah law requires that this be made clear. Sponsored guests pay five dollars at the door for a two-week membership, in addition to a cover charge that varies nightly. Full-fledged members are required to pay fifteen dollars in yearly dues and any cover charges as well. Don't forget to take your identification with you because the doormen *will* check to see if you are over twenty-one. If you happen to have "forgotten" it, you may be turned away.

Tracy, a striking blond who holds the club's title of "Ultimate Cowgirl," will stroll by wearing black Earl Scheib pants and cowboy boots. Her cowboy hat dips low over eyes that roam the room looking for trouble. A huge walkie-talkie bounces on her butt and handcuffs jingle on her hip as she patrols the club. She is one of two female security guards employed by the Westerner because women, especially pretty ones, are quite effective at defusing explosive situations among the cowboys. Likewise, male guards are dispatched when the cowgirls go at it. Potential "situations" are controlled quickly and professionally here. So quickly, in fact, that I almost missed two perpetrators being helped out a side door after they exchanged words with Andy, the manager.

The Westerner looks out for its members and guests, though, especially the women, who are escorted to the parking lot when they are ready to go home for the night. So now that your fears have been allayed, you may as well stick around and dance. There are free dance lessons Monday through Saturday, dance etiquette is posted, and the disc jockey calls dances during band breaks–the Down and Dirty, the Electric Slide, the Cowboy Hip-Hop, ohmigod, even the Romeo!

As you may have guessed, folks love dancing solo here, which translates into fewer drink sales. Line dancing is a religious experience at the Westerner. So Mondays are their Sabbath and the Westerner is their church, with about three hundred line dancers congregating on what is notoriously the slowest night of the week for honky-tonks. It's a smart move on the part of management and the partner dancers know to stay home and watch *Monday Night Football* instead. The "professional" dancers, line and couples alike, come out during the week, and on weekends the street dancers take over.

The two-steppers pop a lot of windows here. A "window" in dance parlance is a two-step and waltz move where each partner's arms are joined to make a "frame," which they gaze through as they dance. The very slippery dance floor is a raised thirty-three-hundred-square-foot hardwood rectangle in the center of the club. The perimeter of the dance floor and behind the stage is a heavy traffic area, with people walking, ever so straight and tall and ever so slowly, searching for the perfect two-stepper. It gets a little obvious when you see the same person walk by over and over again. My advice to out-of-towners who want to dance with some of the regulars is to either grab them while they're trawling or move to the right of the dance floor.

Virginia

18

I know the honky-tonks in this state almost as well as I know myself, for it has been my home since 1982. Country singers and bands here are among the best. Many Virginia musicians have hit the country music big time and gone on to Nashville, including Roy Clark, the Statler Brothers, Mary Chapin Carpenter, Cleve Francis, Emmylou Harris, Juice Newton, and Ricky Van Shelton.

So, as logic would have it, a place with this much good music is bound to have good honky-tonks and dancers. You can find all three just about anywhere in Virginia, although some areas are better than others.

In the Tidewater region, Country Clubs and bands come and go so quickly it's hard to keep up with them. Only one boasts a real track record, the Banque in Norfolk, which is more than twenty years old. The only problem is that it has become "Line Dance City," which disqualifies it from Traditional status. The Rhinestone Cowboy in Newport News is also heavy on the line dances. All dances are called by the disc jockey, and Sunday is Family Day. The Rhinestone is home base for a group of wheelchair-bound dancers called the Dancing Wheels, and internationally known dance instructors Dick and Geneva Matteis. Although the Rhinestone may be the local hot spot, the D&D Corral, which offers live music, near Fort Eustis is more deserving of the honky-tonk moniker.

In Richmond, the oldest Country Club I've come across is Bronco's, whose biggest shortcoming is a poorly situated dance floor. Dakota's is a slick but safe yuppie-tonk with first-rate dancers. The Longhorn Saloon and Grille, somewhere in between, is always crowded on weekend nights. The Longhorn often books Mitch Snow, one of Virginia's best singers, so you may want to catch him before Nashville steals him away.

The place to go in Roanoke is Valley Country, which has three dance areas and a training pen for less experienced dancers.

Up in northern Virginia near Washington, D.C., you will find the best country dancers in the state. There are many fine new clubs: Houston's in Fredericksburg, the Red Moon Saloon in Fairfax, Blackie's in Springfield, and Chapps and Skinifatz in Woodbridge. I would have liked to have profiled Hillbilly Heaven, a legend in its time, where patrons joked about it being "the only place you could buy a beer, two-step, play pool, get a tattoo and a haircut, and hear good country music all at the same time." But, sadly, it closed a few years ago due to owner Earl Dixon's ill health. Earl is probably better known as actress Donna Dixon's father and comedian Dan Aykroyd's father-in-law. Hillbilly Heaven may be gone, but it's not forgotten. That leaves only one other club to write about–Zed.

Zed Restaurant & Public House
6151 Richmond Highway, Alexandria
703/768–5558

DIRECTIONS: From I-95/495 (the Capital Beltway) take Exit 1 south (the last exit before you cross the Woodrow Wilson Bridge) toward Mount Vernon. Zed is about one mile down Route 1 to your left.

DRESS CODE: Appropriate attire after 8 P.M. Men must wear shirts with collars.
DANCE DYNAMICS: Two-step, waltz, shuffle, polka, buckle-shiners, swing, minimal line dancing.
HOURS: Open daily 11 A.M. to 1:30 A.M.
MUSIC: Live music nightly.

When Tadeus Zubricki took over this honky-tonk in 1986 it suffered from an identity crisis, having been a pizza parlor, Irish pub, and sports bar, among other things. Even worse, it was located on a road with an identity crisis, the Jefferson Davis Highway, also known as the Jeff Davis Highway, Route 1, and the Richmond Highway. He couldn't do anything about the road, but Tadeus renamed the club "Zed" for the British pronunciation of the letter Z. The license plate on his Isuzu Rodeo reads: "Zedman."

"We never even thought about building a country and western place," says Tadeus. But from a business point of view, the country bars drew more customers than the Irish pubs the expat Brit was accustomed to running because, he says, "it's embarrassing for the cowboys to have a quarter of an empty glass."

Just a two-step away from the nation's capital, Zed is where many foreign visitors go to sample a real honky-tonk. Tadeus is proud that when Boris Yeltsin's Russian entourage wanted to see something American, the Heritage Foundation sent them to Zed. Here you can two-step, waltz, shuffle, and swing with bureaucrats and NASA engineers as well as construction workers and marines from Quantico. The well-worn dance floor is small (six hundred square feet), but that's only because local law requires so many seats per square foot of dance-floor space, something that affects all clubs in the area. Every so often on a band break, some daring souls will get up to do the Tush Push, Freeze, or Cowgirl Hustle (known as the Elvira out West) line dances, but that is about the extent of it. Folks here don't follow the fads, so don't expect to do any Four-Star Boogies or Watermelon Crawls.

One of those responsible for making Zed a favorite among dancers is Lloyd Thompson. He and partner Brenda Castle-Young, who have competed together since 1988, teach all levels of country dance to Zed patrons. By day, Lloyd is a process server in the District of Columbia and Brenda a clinical psychologist. They make a striking pair, she, a fragile blond, and he, a strapping African-American. For folks who find it ironic for a black man to teach two-step in a country bar, Lloyd is quick to point out that the majority of cowboys in days of old were freed slaves. He collects all manner of books and memorabilia on the culture and even spends summer vacations working on a cattle ranch outside Billings, Montana.

Concerts are another popular draw at Zed. Tadeus started booking national acts in 1989, in part to reward his regular customers. "It's such an expressive crowd here and country stars react so much better to an expressive crowd," he says.

Zed is a small but important venue in what music insiders say is one of the biggest country markets in the nation, the Washington-Baltimore corridor. Although Alexandria's Birchmere club traditionally garners national attention as the place to hear country music, locals know better. Unlike the Birchmere, there are no so-called acoustic nights at Zed. For a fraction of the Birchmere price, you can clap along to the music or even dance–that is, if the artist allows it and there is any room after seating is added for the show. Tadeus charges ten to fifteen dollars minimum, depending on the act, which is applied toward a food or drink purchase. "I never want to get in the position where I have to charge tickets," he says. "It's a business and you've got to be able to give somebody that something they can't get anywhere else."

And Tadeus delivers on that. In turn, he is rewarded with a loyal following of regulars. One by one, they come: "Animal," Barbara, Bertie, Dale, Dennis, Diana, Penny, Terry, Vickie, and the rest of the gang. When a national act is here, they are too, dressed in their finest. This is a close bunch, with hugs and kisses all around when they see each other. Sometimes there's even a birthday to celebrate, and Terry will buy drinks for the lot and Diana will make beaded key chains for everyone. Barbara's beads dangle gloriously from her back pocket as she scoots around the dance floor, whose hardwood boards, sanded smooth over the years by scores of suburban cowboys, rise and fall at every turn.

On a cold winter's night, this group typically bunches around the fireplace near the entrance, swapping stories with the doorman as he feeds logs into its hungry mouth. Then they'll stop over to say "hey" to the bartender and pick up a brew before heading to their spot against the west wall. As soon as the house lights dim and the stage lights shine, the place comes alive. Young dance with old and age knows no barriers.

Tadeus, an Englishman with a doctorate in ethics and psychology who studied at London, Cambridge, and Catholic universities and worked in the Ford and Reagan administrations, was determined to civilize this club, which had a long history of trouble. It took ten months, but he finally succeeded in turning its reputation around. Now whole families can patronize Zed and feel safe. "This is an apolitical, 'areligious' place where you can have a good time for free," he says. "We've got a lot of regulars, people who don't mind being themselves."

"I've got a guy who comes in here every day at lunchtime. He doesn't have any friends, he said all his friends are here. Life for him is being at a place where he feels comfortable and he can talk to people and call them friends. The people know him as soon as he walks through the door, but anywhere else he goes nobody knows him. He's just an alienated lonely guy. Here he feels he's one of the crowd."

It's not only the compassion of its owner that makes Zed one of the best-kept secrets in the Washington area, but also its unadvertised bargain prices and free dance lessons. Tadeus was the first club owner in the area to offer live entertainment seven nights a week without a cover charge. Other clubs followed suit to stay competitive. Drinks here are twice the size (but not any more expensive) as at other bars, and the food is outstanding and inexpensive, too. It's no wonder that readers of *Country Plus Magazine*, the bible of country music in these parts, consistently select Zed as their favorite local nightclub, favorite place to country-western dance, favorite place to dance, and favorite area concert venue, as well as having in its employ their favorite bartender, doormen, and waitresses.

Although Zed occasionally doesn't charge a minimum to see a national act, there was a time when one was never required. One night when Shelby Lynne was performing to a packed house, Tadeus noticed at least fifty people drinking water. After that he instituted the charge. His rationale? Patrons are seeing the show free, they're never farther than seventy feet from the stage, and they can talk to the stars between sets. As an added attraction on these nights, country singers who live in the area–most notably Mary Chapin Carpenter and Cleve Francis–are known to drop by unannounced to get an ear up on the up-and-coming competition.

Like many club owners, Tadeus books acts when their sound is big and their fee still small. The difference is, he doesn't profess to be an expert on country music and books acts only if he likes the way they sound and what they have accomplished.

Tadeus is the first to admit that his lack of fundamental knowledge about country music hurt him in the beginning. For example, "Dwight Yoakam was in here and I didn't know who the hell he was."

But that was nothing compared to the George Strait incident. It seems the singer asked Tadeus if he could do a video at Zed.

"I told him to send me a cassette and a song list," Tadeus recalls, "and if you're any good I'll call you. I went back to work and the guy said, 'I don't think you understand who I am.'

"'I'm sorry,' I said, 'but I've got a lot of people who want to play here.' Then he whispered, 'I'm George Strait.' I cut him short and said, 'Just send me a cassette and a song list.'

"The next day, I told a lot of people about it and they said, 'You've got to be kidding! That was the guy who did *All My Ex's Live in Texas!*' Unless the guy's name was Randy Travis or Dolly Parton, I didn't know who they were! I knew Narvel Felts more than I did these guys."

Autographed photos of "these guys" now line the soffits and walls of his establishment. Most of the inscriptions admonish Tadeus to "Keep it country." The most telling, however, is on former D.C. resident Ray Kennedy's poster: "To Zed–The greatest honky-tonk in D.C. with great food too! What a way to go!"

Washington

19

I thought finding a honky-tonk in Oregon was difficult until I ventured into the neighboring state of Washington. I started my search in Everett, where someone had told me about Gerry Andal's Ranch, which caters to families, but all three clubs in the chain were too new. Dance instructor Laurie Kral told me to check out the Riverside Inn in the Seattle suburb of Tukwila, which has been in business since 1963. I did, but I felt there must be something more historic elsewhere.

I decided to visit Roslyn, where the television show *Northern Exposure* is filmed. But while Roslyn boasts the oldest tavern in the state, that institution is devoted to rock and roll. Spokane had only one Country Club, Chili D's, that had been there for any length of time, and it was closed the Sunday I dropped by. So, I decided, the Riverside Inn could stand alone.

★

The Riverside Inn
14060 Interurban Avenue South, Seattle
206/244-5400

DIRECTIONS: From I-405 exit north on Interurban Avenue South. The Riverside Inn is on the right, bordering the Green River.
DRESS CODE: All manner of western dress, both city and country.
DANCE DYNAMICS: All types of country dances.
HOURS: Open twenty-four hours, 365 days a year.
MUSIC: Live music nightly.

At night the sign above the Riverside Inn is all lit up like a carnival, with wagon wheels at either end of the name spelled out in big block letters. The rustic, rambling building, which is almost as long as its name, looks like a block of storefronts out of the Old West rather than the New West.

"A lot of our customers still have horse crap on their boots here," says the club's marketing director Blake Dowen, vouching for the authenticity of its clientele–mainly ranchers from nearby Auburn.

A sign posted inside says: "If you look under 40, please have 'ID' ready." The fee to enter is $4.25, but the man collecting the money and stamping hands says there is only a cover charge on Friday and Saturday. And if you purchase a dinner of $7.95 or more before 9 P.M., the cover is waived.

Dancing accounts for 90 percent of the club's draw; in fact, a dancing duo from the Riverside placed third in the 1994 Black Velvet Smooth Steppin' Showdown. The eight-hundred-square-foot hardwood floor is often flooded with a sea of line dancers. This is the New West, but at least they do standards like the Sleazy Slide and the Tush Push. When they switch to partner dances, they tend to do the ten-step and a traveling Cowboy Cha-Cha. Then it's on to East Coast swing, the waltz, and the "washboard" two-step. Wait a minute, the washboard two-step? Yep. That's what I call it when a man clasps his left hand tightly around his partner's right and moves it back and forth in time to the music. A real rocking motion to the bodies goes along with this, something you would never see in Texas, where everything is straight and tall and real smooth.

"Washington state is probably about the most nontraditional of the western states," one of the locals explains. He should know; he has lived here all of his thirty-four years. Heck, he's only a little older than the Riverside itself. Greg is his name, he says, and Washington is "the Last Frontier." What about Alaska? "Well, of the forty-eight contiguous states," he concedes. Whatever. The point is, he continues, I can't really expect Washington to be like Texas or Oklahoma. He's right. States, like people and honky-tonks, are very different. At least I had found what a local newspaper called "the granddaddy of all country music clubs" in the Seattle area.

Energy is high here, with five hundred people, between twenty-one and sixty, talking, dancing, and listening to country music by the band Second Ride, which is good enough to be on the radio. And they will be Saturday night, when country radio station K106-FM, which is number five overall in the Seattle market, does its weekly live broadcast from a booth behind the stage.

"Saturday is our busiest night," says Blake, who is also the club's booking agent. The Riverside brings in a national act about once a month and often works out package deals with Kelly's Grand 'Ol Opry in State Line, Idaho, to guarantee a national act two dates instead of one.

Blake's dad, Steven, bought the Riverside in 1990, after having founded and run another restaurant in the area. Since he took over, the Riverside has been remodeled outside and major portions on the inside. A western wear store is one of the more recent additions.

The Riverside also operates a card room for poker and blackjack from 10 A.M. to 2 P.M. State law allows specially licensed clubs to have gaming, but the house can't win so the deal passes from one player to another.

By the way, children are permitted to join in the fun at the Riverside every night until 8 P.M. And there is also a full-service restaurant and a twenty-four-hour cafe for those 1:30 A.M. breakfasts after the dancing is done.

The best thing about the Riverside Inn, though, is management's commitment to keeping it country.

"Our philosophy is to do the things that made the Riverside," Dowen says, "which is to keep it live country 365 days–even on Christmas Eve and Christmas Day."

Wyoming

20

Wyoming is full of wide-open spaces, so its honky-tonks are scattered far and wide. It is also home to the Cheyenne Frontier Days, the rodeo that's touted as the "Daddy of 'em All." There are quite a few Country Clubs in Cheyenne, including the Cheyenne Club, Cowboy South, the Hitchen' Post Inn, and the Outlaw.

Pam Minick of Billy Bob's Texas, a fellow Las Vegan, told me about the Proud Cut up in Cody that's owned by Becky Crump, another refugee from southern Nevada. But I had planned to focus on Jackson Hole's Million Dollar Cowboy Bar, which was co-owned by yet another Las Vegan. The Stagecoach Bar in nearby Wilson also came highly recommended as the club where all the locals in the Jackson area go, especially on Sunday, which is the only night live music is offered there. You should definitely check it out.

Other options in the state for traveling boot-scooters include the Legal Tender in Evanston, Dad's Bar in Thayne, and the Saddle-Lite Saloon in Rock Springs. And, quite by accident, I stumbled upon the Cowboy Saloon and Dance Hall in Laramie.

Cowboy Saloon and Dance Hall
108 South Second Street, Laramie
307/721-3165

DIRECTIONS: From I-80 West take the Route 287 exit into Laramie. Turn left on Ivinson Street and right on Second Street; the Cowboy is in the first block on the left.
DRESS CODE: Anything goes, but don't dress too western if you want to fit in. Locals are more likely to be wearing Levis, ball caps, and tennis shoes.
DANCE DYNAMICS: Two-step, western swing, buckle-shiners, some line dancing.
HOURS: Monday through Saturday 11 A.M. to 2 A.M.; Sunday 4 P.M. to 10 P.M.
MUSIC: Jukebox; live music Wednesday through Saturday.

T-shirts at the Cowboy Saloon and Dance Hall boast "Laramie's largest dance floor." But your best bet to see any dance-floor action is to show up on a Thursday or Friday night when the University of Wyoming is in session. Mary, the bartender, says the Cowboy hops when the college crowd is back in town. Cowboys here wear Levis, tennis shoes, and baseball caps, like they do in Montana, and usually dance the two-step or western swing. In other words, any guy in a cowboy hat is probably of the drugstore variety.

At twenty-four, owner Jason Palumbo hardly looks old enough to be in a bar, let alone own one. He is, by far, one of the most unlikely honky-tonk owners I have met. Originally a Jersey boy raised in D.C., he is country at heart and knows that "country is where it's happening."

So how did he get the money to buy an old cowboy bar? He started working in fifth grade and saved his earnings along with his allowance. His father helped him invest in high-performing stocks and then, after a couple of big wins in Atlantic City, the Cowboy was his.

An English major at the university, Jason is a smart guy. He knows that if you take care of the ladies, the honky-tonk will take care of itself. So he put up a mirror in the ladies room where there was none and the women can't thank him enough, he says. He also buys them drinks occasionally because if they stick around, so will the cowboys.

The dynamics of Laramie and the Cowboy are fairly simple.

"In this town, there's basically three things to do," he continues. "Drink, have sex, and go to church. They do them all here–a lot."

Million Dollar Cowboy Bar
25 North Cache Street, Jackson Hole
307/733-2207

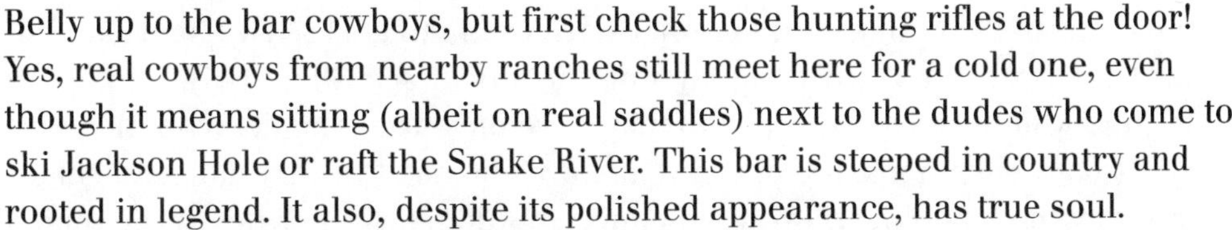

DIRECTIONS: Go north on Route 189/191, which becomes Broadway Avenue in Jackson Hole. Turn left on North Cache Street; the Cowboy is in the first block on the left.
DRESS CODE: Everything from boots to suits.
DANCE DYNAMICS: Buckle-shiners, two-step, waltz, four-count western swing.
HOURS: Daily 10 A.M. to 2 A.M. in summer and daily noon to 2 A.M. in winter.
MUSIC: Live bands nightly.

Belly up to the bar cowboys, but first check those hunting rifles at the door! Yes, real cowboys from nearby ranches still meet here for a cold one, even though it means sitting (albeit on real saddles) next to the dudes who come to ski Jackson Hole or raft the Snake River. This bar is steeped in country and rooted in legend. It also, despite its polished appearance, has true soul.

This is a honky-tonk of the first order. If you were to go up to co-owner and day manager Roger Dudley's office you would find out why. One of the first things you see is a cartoon on his bulletin board from the *Casper Star Tribune* that reads: "Welcome to Wyoming. Warning: Country music next 400 miles."

A fitting admonition as well to anyone who visits the Cowboy. Roger's father, a picker and singer in his own right, instilled a love for the old songs in his son, who in turn guarantees that the only music you will hear six nights a week at the Cowboy is live and pure country. You won't find any national country acts here, just touring bands such as the Nashville-based Dalton's Rain. The bands are not allowed to play higher than ninety decibels. He wants folks to be able to talk and enjoy themselves.

Roger says he was exposed to country music and cowboys as a boy. "Every morning I get up reminds me of when I used to rodeo," he says. His sister and he used to own the Silver Hondo Rodeo Company and they also planned the Nevada Centennial Rodeo in 1964.

It goes without saying that line dancing is banned here. As Roger says, "The floor's just not big enough." He's right. It is an odd-shaped slice of fifty-by-sixty-foot hardwood that curves in one spot to accommodate a seating area. Besides that, folks here are Traditionalists. Two-step, waltz, and western swing are the dances of choice among the regulars, who unlike the tourists don't have to pay a cover charge to gain entrance. Like most club owners, Roger has learned that dancers don't drink much and therefore don't contribute much to reducing the cost of overhead. So he tolerates them because they provide out-of-towners with a floor show. He rewards them with their own watercooler at the back bar. (That way they can get a drink without having to bother the bartenders, who are busy with the paying customers.) So if you are a visitor who knows how to country dance, go directly to the back bar, the one closest to the dance floor and the stage; this is where the locals congregate.

Tom, an instructor from the local Dancers Workshop that teaches free lessons here every Tuesday and Thursday, tells everyone to start with a slow-slow. He said he teaches this way to give beginners an extra beat rather than starting them with the quick-quick right off the bat. I would like to point out, however, that country dance councils are trying to get the two-step standardized so that the count always starts on the quick (see Chapter 3). And for any of you greenhorns out there who may have purchased books with incorrect two-step descriptions, the ones in here are correct. Country dancers feel quite strongly that people who want to dance should learn the rules of the road and that they have no excuse if free lessons are available. Tom explains dance etiquette at the start of each lesson so even novices can survive in a traveling line of dance. He says he'd like it just fine if dance rules were posted, something Roger won't do because he wants everyone to enjoy themselves.

Because Jackson Hole is located at the base of the Grand Tetons, near the Snow King and Jackson Hole ski areas and the National Elk Refuge, the Cowboy attracts a varied clientele. Many country greats, the likes of Merle Haggard, Willie Nelson, and Waylon Jennings among them, have had a good time or two here. The bar is also a favorite haunt of actress Heather Locklear, and banker Bob Whitaker. Whitaker, a native Kansan, always dreamed of spending his days in Jackson Hole–and he does. Now when friends come from back home to visit, they just go to the Cowboy and ask to see him. Then they are taken up the steep and narrow flight of stairs to Dudley's office, and Whitaker. There, high upon a shelf, sits a Jack Daniels bottle with a message written in feminine script on lined notebook paper taped above the black-and-white whiskey label. The note reads: "Cremains of Robert Irvin 'Bob' Whitaker–He died Oct. 16, 1991, of cancer. He was 46. Thanks to the Million Dollar Cowboy Bar for making part of his lifetime wish come true–to be in a bar in Jackson Hole, Wyoming."

Whitaker's widow, Betty, came all the way from Kansas to buy the fifth, which she poured out, and then filled half-full with the ashes of her dearly departed. She then sent it to Dudley along with a card that told of "an unusual request from usual folks." Dudley granted her request and vows that Bob "will stay as long as I'm here." The rest of Whitaker's cremains were sprinkled in the Pacific Ocean and in Oregon's Bobby Lake.

History buffs will appreciate the Cowboy's past. The bar has been on location since 1910, when it was a local watering hole. In 1934 Joe Ruby of Rock Springs put up a permanent structure, which was little more than a shed, and called it Joe Ruby's Cafe and Beer Garden. Ruby's became the town gathering place, with illegal gambling a big attraction. (Local legend has it that Ruby got into an argument during a card game, shot a man dead, and subsequently was run out of state.)

Then a onetime Jackson Hole rancher and moonshiner named Ben Goe stepped in and bought Ruby's place. He renamed it the Cowboy Bar and set about to improve the club. Ben hired Jack Kranenberg to help with the remodeling. They brought in knobbled pine on horse-drawn sleighs from the woods near Pinedale to trim the interior and to build chairs and the long fancy bar that is inlaid with 592 silver dollars. The wood is "knobbled" by a fungus that causes a bumpy cancerous growth only found in lodgepole pine. Ironically, Ben and Jack constructed the bar, the longest in Wyoming, in the basement of a Mormon church. That bar, one of five in the club today, is the main one to your right as you enter the club. When Ben sold the club to Casper resident Preston "Pres" Parkinson in the mid-1940s, Pres decided to turn the bar into a one-of-a-kind architectural landmark. He added on to the building and installed a sign with green neon pines and a neon cowboy chasing a calf. Charlie Peterson, who had managed the bar for Ben, went in as part owner. Charlie said that Pres, like Ben, teamed up with Jack and did even more creative renovations. Jack visualized embellishments and Pres gave him the go-ahead. Throughout the 1940s, Pres expanded the bar to the alley and had linoleum made with the cowboy design in it. Legend has it that a struggling artist painted a series of murals for the wall at this time in exchange for drinks.

In 1952 a gas explosion in the basement dealt a serious blow to the Cowboy. Apparently the pilot light on a heater went out. When Pres and a man named Lew Bartholomew went to check it out, Pres lit a match so they could see, and the ensuing explosion literally lifted the building up and set it back down. So forceful was the blast that a chair got stuck in the ceiling. One of the gamblers who was playing cards at a table near the front windows was blown clean out of the window and landed on a car outside, still looking at his hand of cards. He was not hurt, but both Pres and Lew were badly burned. Pres vowed from his hospital bed to rebuild. He was able to salvage nearly all the knobbled pine and restore the bar to its original glory. He also added the Cowboy Bar sign that still decorates the exterior. Renovations topped $1 million and, thus, Million Dollar was added to the Cowboy Bar's name in 1953.

In 1960 Pres sold the bar to a dozen Jackson residents and it began to change hands quite regularly. In 1973 the Cowboy was purchased by Ron Schultz, Bud Jensen, and Clifford Poindexter, who refurbished the interior and added the London-made red carpet that bears the Cowboy Bar name and insignia. It was Bud's idea to use saddles, which wear longer than seats, as bar stools. Locals squawked a bit because they felt they were catering to the tourists. The Cowboy's current owners, Roger Dudley and Art Anderson, came on board in 1988.

Roger says they have few problems at the Cowboy. About the biggest ones, he says, are tourists forgetting their purses, glasses, keys, and such, or people taking the silver conchos and leather strings off the saddles. "We have to replace about a hundred of the conchos each year," he said.

Clint Eastwood filmed a bar scene for *Any Which Way You Can* here back in 1980 and the club has been featured in *Vogue, USA Today,* and *Playboy,* among other publications. *Playboy* rated it "Number One Best Saloon" in ski country in 1982. More recently, the Cowboy hosted a gathering of cowboy poets. So visit the Million Dollar Cowboy Bar; it's definitely worth the experience. And while you're there, check out the full-service steakhouse restaurant in the basement.

And don't forget to offer up a toast to Bob!

★

PART THREE

The Best of the Rest

21 Where to Boot Scoot

It would be impossible for one person to track the hundreds of country music clubs scattered across the nation, but the ones in this directory are among those mentioned most. Some clubs may have more detailed information than others, depending on whether they received and responded to my survey. Generally you should assume there is a cover charge. Be sure to call ahead for hours and to check if a club is still in operation. And be forewarned, in 1995 thirteen states were in the process of adding new area codes; those numbers printed here may not reflect all of those changes.

Happy honky-tonking!

ALABAMA

Auburn

Silver Spur
3076 East University Drive
334/887-5383

Dadeville

Rodeo Club
10268 Highway 35
205/825-7503

Daphne

Judge Roy Bean
508 Main Street
205/626-9988

Decatur

Frontier Lounge
3838 Highway 31 South
205/350-4291

Dothan

Cowboys
4567 South Oates Street
205/793-6937

Huntsville

Wrangler
205/534-6401

Mobile

Wild Wild West
3679 Airport Boulevard
205/342-6219

Montgomery

Nashville Showcase
3560 Atlanta Highway
205/279-8001

Muscle Shoals

Desperado's
701 Davidson Avenue
205/383-7000

PJ's
2517 East Avalon Avenue
205/383-1438

ALASKA

Anchorage

Buckaroo Club
2811 Spenard Road
907/561-9251

GENRE: Traditional/Independent.
COVER CHARGE: Never.
CAPACITY: 100.
YEAR OPENED: 1961.
MUSIC: National touring bands nightly.
DANCE LESSONS: Free on Tuesday, Thursday, and Friday.
DANCE-FLOOR STATS: One 475-square-foot rectangular tile floor.
FOOD: Vending-machine snacks only.
MINIMUM AGE: 21.
FAMILY NIGHTS: Children must leave by 7 P.M.
SMOKE-FILTERING SYSTEM: Yes.
JUKEBOX WITH A COUNTRY SONG: Yes.
COMMENTS: Open 7 nights a week.

Last Frontier Bar
369 Muldoon Road
907/338-9922

Fairbanks

Silver Spur
285 Old Richardson Highway
907/456-6300

ARIZONA

Cave Creek

Harold's Cave Creek Corral
6875 Cave Creek Road
602/488-1906
GENRE: Traditional/Independent.
DANCE-FLOOR STATS: 1.

Chandler

The Corral
2020 North Arizona Avenue
602/814-8342

Flagstaff

Brandy's
1500 East Cedar Avenue
602/779-2187

Museum Club
3404 East Route 66
602/526-9434
GENRE: Traditional/Independent.
COVER CHARGE: Varies nightly.
CAPACITY: 250.
YEAR OPENED: 1936.
MUSIC: Live music Tuesday through Sunday by regional and national touring bands. Disc jockey on band breaks. Special concerts by national acts.
DANCE LESSONS: Free on Thursday.
DANCE-FLOOR STATS: One 900-square-foot hardwood floor.
MINIMUM AGE: 21.
SMOKE-FILTERING SYSTEM: Yes.
COMMENTS: Open 7 nights a week.

Redwood Bar & Grill
2136 North Fourth Street
602/526-0278
YEAR OPENED: 1965.
COMMENTS: Open 7 days a week.

Glendale

The Hayloft
4346 West Glendale Avenue
602/937-2520

Mesa

Country City
30 South Robson
602/644-1524

Payson

Winchester Saloon & Restaurant
236 East Highway 260
602/474-4510

Phoenix

Cheyenne Cattle Co.
455 North Third Street, Suite 284
602/253-6225
GENRE: New Breed/Chain.
COVER CHARGE: Varies nightly.
DRESS CODE: Casual but neat.
CAPACITY: 1,000.
YEAR OPENED: 1991.
MUSIC: Disc jockey. Live music for special concerts.
DANCE LESSONS: Free nightly except Monday and Friday.
DANCE ETIQUETTE: Rules are posted.
SPECIAL CLUB DANCES: Arizona two-step and West Coast swing.
DANCE-FLOOR STATS: One raised, 1,800-square-foot rectangular hardwood floor.
FOOD: Complimentary happy hour buffet.
MINIMUM AGE: 21.
SMOKE-FILTERING SYSTEM: Yes.
COMMENTS: Closed on Monday. Tuesday and Sunday are swing nights. Various promotions and specials nightly. Very little line dancing.

Denim & Diamonds
3905 East Thomas Road
602/225-0182
GENRE: New Breed/Chain.
COVER CHARGE: Varies nightly.

CAPACITY: 1,000.
YEAR OPENED: 1988.
MUSIC: Disc jockey. Special concerts by national acts.
DANCE-FLOOR STATS: One 1,100-square-foot rectangular raised hardwood floor.
MINIMUM AGE: 21.
COMMENTS: Owned by Graham Brothers.

Graham Central Station
4029 North 33rd Avenue
602/279–4226
GENRE: New Breed/Chain.
COVER CHARGE: Varies.
DRESS CODE: No T-shirts, work uniforms, or obscene clothes.
CAPACITY: 2,500.
YEAR OPENED: 1981.
MUSIC: Disc jockey. Special concerts by national acts.
DANCE LESSONS: Free on Sunday and Wednesday nights.
DANCE-FLOOR STATS: One raised 2,877-square-foot rectangular hardwood floor.
FOOD: Full-service restaurant.
MINIMUM AGE: 21.
FAMILY NIGHTS: Sunday from 5 to 9 P.M.
SMOKE-FILTERING SYSTEM: Yes.
MECHANICAL BULL: Yes.
COMMENTS: More stalls in the Cowgirls room than at the Kentucky Derby! West LA disco adjacent to club. Owned by Graham Brothers.

Mr. Lucky's
3660 Grand Avenue
602/246–0686
GENRE: Traditional/Independent.
CAPACITY: 600.
DANCE-FLOOR STATS: 2.

Toolies Country Saloon & Dance Hall
4231 West Thomas Road
602/272–3100
GENRE: Traditional/Independent.
COVER CHARGE: Varies nightly.
DRESS CODE: No tank tops or motorcycle apparel.
CAPACITY: 900.
YEAR OPENED: 1986.
MUSIC: Live music nightly by local, regional, and national touring bands. Special concerts by national acts.
DANCE LESSONS: Free on Sunday, Monday, and Wednesday.
DANCE-FLOOR STATS: One 2,000-square-foot square hardwood floor.
FOOD: Full-service restaurant.
MINIMUM AGE: 21.
FAMILY NIGHTS: Friday from 5 to 8 P.M. for a special barbecue dinner. The majority of concerts featuring national acts are for all ages.
SMOKE-FILTERING SYSTEM: Yes.
COMMENTS: 1994 ACM "Nightclub of the Year." Toolies consistently walks away with "Best Country Bar" awards in the Phoenix area. Food is first-rate; don't leave without trying a Toolies Burger! Open 7 nights a week. Sponsors a Christmas-in-July Party (with 10 tons of real snow), a customer-appreciation Christmas party, and St. Pat's Search for a $1,000 Pot of Gold. Toolies also conducts fund-raisers for liver-transplant patients and the National Cerebral Palsy Foundation. Many NASCAR events and off-track betting on greyhound races.

Scottsdale

Diamondback Steak House & Saloon
1601 North Pima Road
602/502–0815

Rockin' Horse
7000 East Indian School Road
602/949–0992

Stetson's Country Club
7316 East Stetson Drive
602/947–1000
GENRE: Traditional/Independent.
COVER CHARGE: $5 Thursday through Saturday.
DRESS CODE: No cutoffs or T-shirts with slogans.
CAPACITY: 297.
YEAR OPENED: 1994.
MUSIC: Live music 7 nights a week by local and regional touring bands. Disc jockey on band breaks.

DANCE LESSONS: Free every night except Saturday.
DANCE ETIQUETTE: Rules are posted.
DANCE-FLOOR STATS: One 900-square-foot rectangular oak floor.
FOOD: Full-service restaurant.
MINIMUM AGE: 21.
FAMILY NIGHTS: Children welcome in restaurant from 11 A.M. to 8:30 P.M.
SMOKE-FILTERING SYSTEM: Yes.
COMMENTS: Open 7 days a week.

Tempe

Rockin' Rodeo
7850 South Priest
602/496–4336
GENRE: New Breed/Chain.
YEAR OPENED: 1995.
MUSIC: Disc jockey.
MINIMUM AGE: 21.
COMMENTS: Owned by Graham Brothers.

Tucson

Cactus Moon
5470 East Broadway
602/748–0057
GENRE: New Breed/Chain.
COVER CHARGE: Varies nightly.
DRESS CODE: No tank tops or work uniforms.
CAPACITY: 1,000.
YEAR OPENED: 1994.
MUSIC: Disc jockey. Regional and national bands for special concerts.
DANCE-FLOOR STATS: One raised, 4,500-square-foot boomerang-shaped hardwood floor.
FOOD: Buffet on Friday nights.
MINIMUM AGE: 21.
SMOKE-FILTERING SYSTEM: Yes.
COMMENTS: Closed on Monday. Owned by Graham Brothers.

Maverick
4702 East 22nd Street
602/748–0456
GENRE: Traditional/Independent.
COVER CHARGE: Only on weekends.
DRESS CODE: No tank tops.
CAPACITY: 319.
YEAR OPENED: 1962.
MUSIC: National touring bands Monday through Saturday.
DANCE LESSONS: For a fee Tuesday, Wednesday, and Thursday.
DANCE-FLOOR STATS: One 1,200-square-foot polygon-shaped parquet floor.
FOOD: Appetizers only.
MINIMUM AGE: 21.
COMMENTS: Closed on Sunday. Diploma issued to anyone who survives 6 weeks of two-step lessons.

Wild Wild West
4385 West Ina Road
602/744–7744
GENRE: New Breed/Chain.
COVER CHARGE: Only on Friday and Saturday.
DRESS CODE: No tank tops, open-toed shoes, or ripped clothing.
CAPACITY: 2,305.
YEAR OPENED: 1991.
MUSIC: Disc jockey. Live music by national acts for special concerts only.
DANCE LESSONS: Free on Sunday, Tuesday, and Thursday.
DANCE-FLOOR STATS: One springboard 6,000-square-foot racetrack-shaped hardwood floor.
FOOD: Full-service restaurant.
MINIMUM AGE: 21 and up after 8 P.M.
FAMILY NIGHTS: Every holiday Sunday and every Thanksgiving children are allowed from 1 P.M. to 8 P.M.
COMMENTS: Closed on Monday. Adjacent rock and hip-hop club has 600-square-foot dance floor. Shops include a western wear store, general store, old-time photo shop, T-shirt store, hat shop, and hair salon.

ARKANSAS

Fayetteville

Club West
3615 West Sixth Street
501/442–7337

Fort Smith

Red Roper
501/648–0020

Little Rock

B. J.'s Star-Studded Honky-Tonk
9515 Interstate 30
501/562–6000
CAPACITY: 1,500.
DANCE-FLOOR STATS: One 3,000-square-foot racetrack floor.

Midnight Rodeo
5820 Asher Avenue
501/494–5348

Pine Bluff

Bad Bob's Country Nightclub
2204 East Harding
501/534–9515

CALIFORNIA

Alameda

Denim & Diamonds
2203 Mariner Square Loop
510/521–9200
GENRE: New Breed/Chain.
MUSIC: Disc jockey nightly. Special concerts by national acts.
COMMENTS: Owned by Graham Gilliam.

Anaheim

Cowboy Boogie Co.
1721 South Manchester Avenue
714/956–1410
GENRE: New Breed/Independent.
CAPACITY: 1,200.
MUSIC: Live 7 nights a week.
DANCE-FLOOR STATS: One medium-size floor; two small floors.

Bakersfield

Borrowed Money
10806 Rosedale Highway
805/588–2787

Cadillac Ranch
10701 Highway 178
805/366–2236

Grizzly's
Red Lion Inn
3100 Camino Del Rio Court
805/323–7111

Roxanne's
3501 California Avenue
805/323–5919

Canoga Park

Longhorn Saloon
21211 Sherman Way
818/340–4788

Chatsworth

Cowboy Palace Saloon
21635 Devonshire Street
818/341–0166
GENRE: Traditional/Independent.
COVER CHARGE: Never.
CAPACITY: 159.
YEAR OPENED: 1970.
MUSIC: Local and regional bands nightly.
DANCE LESSONS: Free nightly.
DANCE-FLOOR STATS: One 400-square-foot rectangular hardwood floor.
FOOD: Free barbecues on Sunday and Monday.
MINIMUM AGE: 21.
JUKEBOX WITH A COUNTRY SONG: Yes.
SPECIALTY BEVERAGES: A variety of non-alcoholic drinks and beers.
COMMENTS: Open 7 nights a week. Bills itself as "the last real honky-tonk." Talent contest every Wednesday with $100 first prize and $50 second prize; finals every quarter with $500 cash prizes.

Chico

Scotty's
12609 River Road
916/893–2020
GENRE: Traditional/Independent.
COVER CHARGE: Only on weekends.
CAPACITY: Varies.
YEAR OPENED: 1955.
MUSIC: Live country music on Friday and Saturday nights and outdoors during spring and summer, weather permitting, by local, regional, and national acts.
DANCE-FLOOR STATS: One 4,000-square-foot rectangular cement floor under covered outdoor patio.
LIQUOR: Low-octane beer and wine coolers only.
FOOD: Fast food such as burgers, hot dogs, chicken, fries, chili, etc.
MINIMUM AGE: All ages welcome.
FAMILY NIGHTS: Every night.
COMMENTS: Dance contests on Friday and Saturday. Various sports tournaments such as horseshoes, volleyball, and waterskiing.

Citrus Heights

Denim & Diamonds
6063 Sunrise Mall
916/961–5701
GENRE: New Breed/Chain.
CAPACITY: 500.
COMMENTS: Owned by Graham Gilliam.

Clovis

Inkahoots
446 Clovis Avenue
209/322–1444
GENRE: New Breed/Independent.

Jim's Place
430 Clovis Avenue
209/299–2597
GENRE: Traditional/Independent.
COVER CHARGE: Varies nightly.
DRESS CODE: No sleeveless shirts or tank tops.
CAPACITY: 450.
YEAR OPENED: 1934.
MUSIC: Local, regional, and national acts Wednesday through Sunday. Disc jockey during band breaks and all other nights.
DANCE LESSONS: Free Sunday through Wednesday nights.
DANCE-FLOOR STATS: One 904-square-foot rectangular parquet floor.
FOOD: Full-service restaurant.
MINIMUM AGE: 21.
JUKEBOX WITH A COUNTRY SONG: Yes.
COMMENTS: Club has offered live country music since 1964. Open 7 nights a week. Sponsors "Tight-Fittin' Jeans" contest, dance contests, and "Miss Rib" contest in conjunction with a rib cook-off, among other events.

Concord

Cadillac Ranch
1655-B Willow Pass Road
510/686–6809
GENRE: Traditional/Chain.
COVER CHARGE: Varies nightly.
DRESS CODE: Neat and clean appearance.
CAPACITY: 387.
YEAR OPENED: 1993.
MUSIC: Live music Wednesday through Sunday by local bands and national touring bands. Disc jockey on band breaks and all other nights.
DANCE LESSONS: For a fee.
DANCE ETIQUETTE: Rules are posted.
DANCE-FLOOR STATS: Two 1,500-square-foot rectangular hardwood floors.
FOOD: Appetizers and vending-machine snacks.
MINIMUM AGE: 21.
SMOKE-FILTERING SYSTEM: Yes.
COMMENTS: Open 7 days a week.

Cottonwood

OK Corral
3633 Main
916/347–9927

El Cajon

Zoo Country
1340 Broadway
619/593-6096

El Segundo

Hacienda Double H Club
525 North Sepulveda
310/615-0015

Escondido

Beaver Creek Saloon
1320-L East Valley Parkway
619/746-7408
GENRE: Traditional/Independent.
COVER CHARGE: Never.
CAPACITY: 375.
YEAR OPENED: 1989.
MUSIC: Local bands nightly.
DANCE LESSONS: Free Sunday through Thursday.
DANCE ETIQUETTE: Rules are posted.
DANCE-FLOOR STATS: One 1,300-square-foot rectangular parquet floor.
FOOD: Appetizers. Free homemade chili on Sunday and home-cooked barbecue every Wednesday.
MINIMUM AGE: 21.
SMOKE-FILTERING SYSTEM: Yes.
JUKEBOX WITH A COUNTRY SONG: Yes.
COMMENTS: Open 7 days a week.

Fairfield

Cadillac Ranch
364 Pittman Road, No. 8
707/864-8924
GENRE: New Breed/Chain.
COVER CHARGE: Varies nightly.
YEAR OPENED: 1993.
MUSIC: Disc jockey.
DANCE-FLOOR STATS: One 600-square-foot floor.

Fremont

South 40
46850 Warm Springs Boulevard
510/657-8935

Fullerton

InCahoots Dance Hall & Saloon
1401 South Lemon
714/441-1666
GENRE: New Breed/Chain.
COVER CHARGE: Yes.
DRESS CODE: Nice appearance required. Tank tops and open-toed shoes discouraged.
CAPACITY: 575.
YEAR OPENED: 1993.
MUSIC: Disc jockey nightly. Regional bands and national acts for special concerts.
DANCE LESSONS: Free, twice a day, 7 days a week.
DANCE ETIQUETTE: Rules are posted. DJ calls dances.
SPECIAL CLUB DANCE: InCahoot Scoot.
DANCE-FLOOR STATS: One 2,200-square-foot floating maple floor. Rectangular with added swing corner.
FOOD: Full-service restaurant, prices from $1.75 to $5.25.
MINIMUM AGE: 21.
FAMILY NIGHTS: Sunday noon to 6 P.M.
SMOKE-FILTERING SYSTEM: Yes.
COMMENTS: Open 7 days a week. No alcohol or smoking allowed on Family Day. Swing Sundays starting at 6 P.M. Various food and drink specials all week long. Happy hour nightly from 5 to 8 P.M. Hat steamer.

Glendale

InCahoots Dance Hall & Saloon
223 North Glendale Avenue
818/500-1669
GENRE: New Breed/Chain.
COVER CHARGE: Varies nightly.
DRESS CODE: No open-toed shoes or tank tops.

CAPACITY: 800.
YEAR OPENED: 1989.
MUSIC: Disc jockey nightly; local, regional and national acts for special concerts.
DANCE LESSONS: Free.
DANCE ETIQUETTE: Rules are posted.
DANCE-FLOOR STATS: One 2,000-square-foot rectangular floating hardwood floor.
FOOD: Full-service restaurant.
MINIMUM AGE: 21.
SMOKE-FILTERING SYSTEM: Yes.
COMMENTS: Open 7 days a week.

Hayward

Turf Club
22517 Mission Boulevard
510/881-9877
GENRE: New Breed/Gay/Independent.
COVER CHARGE: Never.
CAPACITY: 150.
YEAR OPENED: 1932.
MUSIC: Disc jockey most nights. Occasional live music. Special concerts by national acts.
DANCE LESSONS: Free every Saturday.
DANCE ETIQUETTE: DJ calls dances. Rules are posted.
DANCE-FLOOR STATS: One 300-square-foot square hardwood floor.
LIQUOR: Low-octane beer.
FOOD: Appetizers and vending-machine snacks.
MINIMUM AGE: 21.
JUKEBOX WITH A COUNTRY SONG: Yes.
COMMENTS: Open 365 days a year. Sponsors special events year-round, especially AIDS fund-raisers.

Huntington Beach

Denim & Diamonds
7979 Center Avenue
714/892-4666
GENRE: New Breed/Chain.
MUSIC: Disc jockey nightly. Special concerts by national acts.
COMMENTS: Owned by Graham Gilliam.

Lake Forest

Country Rock Cafe
23822 Mercury Road
714/455-1881
GENRE: New Breed/Independent.
COVER CHARGE: Varies nightly.
DRESS CODE: No tank tops.
CAPACITY: 535.
YEAR OPENED: 1993.
MUSIC: Disc jockey most nights. Live music on Monday and for special concerts only by local and national acts.
DANCE LESSONS: Free nightly.
DANCE ETIQUETTE: DJ calls dances.
SPECIAL CLUB DANCE: CRC Boogie.
DANCE-FLOOR STATS: One floating springboard 2,500-square-foot racetrack maple floor.
FOOD: Full-service restaurant.
MINIMUM AGE: 21 after 7 P.M. Monday through Friday.
FAMILY NIGHTS: Families 2 to 7 P.M. on Saturday and Sunday.
SMOKE-FILTERING SYSTEM: Yes.
COMMENTS: Open 365 days a year.

Long Beach

Floyd's
2913 East Anaheim Avenue
310/433-3708
GENRE: Gay/Independent.
CAPACITY: 300.
COMMENTS: Closed Monday.

Malibu

Borderline
30765 Pacific Coast Highway
310/457-5212

Mount Shasta

Wayside Inn
2217 South Mount Shasta Boulevard
916/926-2438

North Hollywood

The Palomino
6907 Lankershim Boulevard
818/764-4018
GENRE: Traditional/Independent.
COVER CHARGE: Varies nightly.
CAPACITY: 300.
YEAR OPENED: 1952.
MUSIC: Live music by local and regional acts nightly.
DANCE-FLOOR STATS: One small triangular-shaped tile area.
FOOD: Full-service restaurant.
MINIMUM AGE: 21.
COMMENTS: Won ACM "Nightclub of the Year" 15 times. Just about every known country singer of the past has played here.

Rawhide
10937 Burbank Boulevard
818/760-9798
GENRE: Gay/Independent.

Palm Springs

Cactus Corral
67-501 Highway 111
619/321-8558
GENRE: Traditional/Independent.
COVER CHARGE: $5 nightly.
CAPACITY: 600.
YEAR OPENED: 1988.
MUSIC: Live music nightly by local, regional, national acts. Disc jockey on band breaks.
DANCE LESSONS: Free on Wednesday, Thursday, Friday, and Saturday.
DANCE ETIQUETTE: Rules are posted and DJ calls dances.
DANCE-FLOOR STATS: Two 700-square-foot rectangular parquet floors.
FOOD: Full-service restaurant.
MINIMUM AGE: 21.
FAMILY NIGHTS: Children welcome only with parents; can stay until parents go home.
SMOKE-FILTERING SYSTEM: Yes.
COMMENTS: Open nightly except Monday and Tuesday.

Penngrove

Twin Oaks
5745 Old Redwood Highway
707/795-5118

Petaluma

Kodiak Jack's
256 Petaluma Boulevard North
707/765-5722
GENRE: New Breed/Independent.
COVER CHARGE: Varies nightly.
CAPACITY: 300.
YEAR OPENED: 1994.
MUSIC: Disc jockey; live music only on Saturday.
DANCE LESSONS: Free on weekends; for a fee weeknights.
DANCE ETIQUETTE: DJ calls dances.
DANCE-FLOOR STATS: One 1,600-square-foot rectangular springboard hardwood floor.
MINIMUM AGE: 21.
SMOKE-FILTERING SYSTEM: Yes.
MECHANICAL BULL: Yes.
COMMENTS: Open 7 nights a week. Club dances choreographed by owner Wayne Vieler.

Steamer Gold Country Cabaret
1 Water Street
707/763-1917

Pleasanton

Cadillac Ranch
GENRE: New Breed/Chain.
COVER CHARGE: Varies nightly.
YEAR OPENED: 1994.
MUSIC: Disc jockey.
COMMENTS: Still under construction at this writing. Check phone book for address and phone number.

Rancho Santa Fe

Rodeo Club
619/457-5590

Redding

The Saloon
3015 South Market
916/246-9120

Redondo Beach

Sweet Suzie Saloon
Redondo Horseshoe Pier
310/379-8831
GENRE: New Breed/Independent.
DANCE LESSONS: Free nightly from 8 to 9 P.M. and from 11 A.M. to noon on Saturday and Sunday.
COMMENTS: Karaoke sung here. Located where Torrance Boulevard meets the sea on the Redondo Horsehoe Pier. Open 7 days a week. Happy hour Monday through Friday from 5 to 7 P.M. and Saturday and Sunday from 10 A.M. to noon. Open for business Monday through Friday 2 P.M. to midnight and Saturday and Sunday 10 A.M. to midnight.

Riverside

Riverside Cowboy
3742 Park Sierra Drive
909/689-7281
GENRE: New Breed/Independent.
CAPACITY: 500.

Sacramento

Cotton Eyed Joe's
916/427-0469
LIQUOR: Nonalcoholic.

InCahoots Dance Hall & Saloon
1696 Arden Way
916/922-6446
GENRE: New Breed/Chain.
COVER CHARGE: Varies nightly.
DRESS CODE: No tank tops or backward baseball caps.
CAPACITY: 600.
YEAR OPENED: 1993.
MUSIC: Disc jockey nightly. Special concerts by national acts.
DANCE LESSONS: Free twice a night, 7 nights a week. Dance seminars offered on Saturdays for a fee.
DANCE ETIQUETTE: Rules are posted and DJ calls dances, but no dance-floor police!
SPECIAL CLUB DANCE: The Rip.
DANCE-FLOOR STATS: One 1,900-square-foot rectangular maple springboard floor.
FOOD: Various specials (see comments). Sandwiches available.
MINIMUM AGE: 21.
COMMENTS: Open 7 nights a week. Very promotion-oriented, with nightly food and drink specials, for example, prime rib dinners on Friday and Saturday for only $3.75.

San Bernardino

Branding Iron Saloon
320 South E Street
909/381-6172

InCahoots Dance Hall & Saloon
204 East Hospitality Lane
909/381-0377
GENRE: New Breed/Chain.
CAPACITY: 500.

Midnight Rodeo
295 East Caroline Street
909/824-5444
GENRE: New Breed/Chain.
COVER CHARGE: Varies nightly.
MUSIC: Disc jockey.

San Diego

Coyotes Live
8022 Claremont Mesa Boulevard
619/277-7326

InCahoots Dance Hall & Saloon
5373 Mission Center Road
619/291-1184
GENRE: New Breed/Chain.
COVER CHARGE: Varies nightly.
CAPACITY: 633.

Wrangler's Roost
6608 Mission Forge Road
619/280-6263

San Dimas

Western Connection
657 West Arrow Highway
909/592-2211

San Francisco

Rawhide
280 Seventh Street
415/621-1197
GENRE: Gay/Independent.

San Jose

The Saddle Rack
1310 Auzerais Avenue
408/286-3393
GENRE: Traditional/Independent.
COVER CHARGE: Never.
DRESS CODE: Yes.
CAPACITY: 1,400.
YEAR OPENED: 1976.
MUSIC: Live music Tuesday through Saturday by local and regional bands. Two bands on Friday and Saturday. National acts on Sunday or Monday.
DANCE LESSONS: Free on Tuesday, Wednesday, and Thursday.
DANCE ETIQUETTE: Rules are posted.
DANCE-FLOOR STATS: Three large and two small Terazel (smooth surface) floors.
MINIMUM AGE: 21.
MECHANICAL BULL: Yes.
COMMENTS: Tricycle barrel racing. Dance contests. Vocal contests. Open Tuesday through Saturday. Open Sunday or Monday for national acts.

San Juan Capistrano

Swallow's Inn
31786 Camino Capistrano
714/493-3188

San Leandro

Cadillac Ranch
150 West Juana
510/352-4111
GENRE: New Breed/Chain.
COVER CHARGE: Varies nightly.
YEAR OPENED: 1993.
MUSIC: Disc jockey nightly.
DANCE-FLOOR STATS: One 900-square-foot floor.

Santa Ana

Crazy Horse Steakhouse & Saloon
1580 Brookhollow Drive
714/549-1512
GENRE: Traditional/Independent.
COVER CHARGE: Varies nightly.
DRESS CODE: No tank tops or cutoffs.
CAPACITY: Concert area, 300; Dining area, 200.
YEAR OPENED: 1979.
MUSIC: Live music nightly by local, regional, and national acts.
DANCE LESSONS: Free.
DANCE-FLOOR STATS: One small rectangular hardwood floor.
FOOD: Full-service steakhouse.
MINIMUM AGE: No age restrictions in dining room; 21 and up in concert area after 9 P.M.
SMOKE-FILTERING SYSTEM: Yes.
COMMENTS: ACM "Nightclub of the Year," 1986 to 1990. Open 7 days a week for lunch, dinner, and dancing. Offers 80 to 100 concerts a year by major country artists. Many TV shows have been filmed here for TNN, ABC, and NBC. Also sponsors talent and dance contests.

Santa Barbara

Red Dog Steakhouse & Saloon
110 Santa Barbara
805/965-2231

Santa Monica

Denim & Diamonds
32000 Ocean Park
310/452-3446
GENRE: New Breed/Chain.
COVER CHARGE: Only on weekends.

DRESS CODE: Men–no sandals, shorts, sweats, sleeveless shirts, or ripped jeans. Ladies–anything goes.
CAPACITY: 500.
YEAR OPENED: 1991.
MUSIC: Disc jockey nightly. National acts and regional bands for special concerts only.
DANCE LESSONS: Free nightly.
DANCE ETIQUETTE: Rules are posted and DJ calls dances.
DANCE-FLOOR STATS: Two raised dance floors, one racetrack and one round. Total of 1,025 square feet of hardwood dance-floor space.
FOOD: Full-service restaurant.
MINIMUM AGE: 21 and up after 8 P.M.
FAMILY NIGHTS: Children welcome nightly until 8 P.M. Sunday is Family Day from 2 to 8 P.M.
SMOKE-FILTERING SYSTEM: Yes.
MECHANICAL BULL: Fridays only.
COMMENTS: A shot of country (80 percent) with a splash (20 percent) of rock and roll. Open 7 nights a week. Happy hour Monday through Friday from 5 to 8 P.M. with complimentary buffet and two-for-one drinks. Every Tuesday is Ladies Night. Owned by Graham Gilliam.

Sebastopol

Marty's Top of the Hill
8050 Bodega Avenue
707/823-5987
MUSIC: Live music on Friday and Saturday.

Stockton

Silverado Dance Hall
10480 North Highway 99
209/931-0275

Temecula

Midnight Round-Up
28721 Front Street
909/694-5686
GENRE: Traditional/Independent.
COVER CHARGE: Only on weekends.
CAPACITY: 987.
YEAR OPENED: 1993.
MUSIC: Live music Wednesday through Friday by local, regional, and national acts. Disc jockey during band breaks and on Sunday and Tuesday.
DANCE LESSONS: For a fee on Sunday, Tuesday, and Thursday.
DANCE ETIQUETTE: DJ calls dances.
DANCE-FLOOR STATS: One 4,000-square-foot hardwood floor. Dance floor has swing areas on either side of the stage, with a line dance area in the center separated by rails surrounded by a two-step track. Sports surface, both raised and spring-board.
FOOD: Vending-machine snacks only.
MINIMUM AGE: 21.
SMOKE-FILTERING SYSTEM: Yes.
MECHANICAL BULL: Yes.
COMMENTS: Closed Monday. Sponsors mechanical calf-roping contests, Midnight Round-Up Mechanical Rodeo Finals, and comedy shows.

Torrance

Alpine Village
833 Torrance Boulevard
310/327-4384

Tustin

The Barn
14982 Red Hill Avenue
714/259-0115

Vallejo

Josey Wales
11506 Marine World Parkway
707/554-0107

Victorville

Cocky Bull Rib House & Opry Hall
14180 Highway 395
619/241-2855
GENRE: Traditional/Independent.
COVER CHARGE: Varies.

CAPACITY: 400.
YEAR OPENED: 1978.
MUSIC: Live music nightly by local, regional, and national bands.
DANCE LESSONS: For a fee every night except Wednesday.
DANCE ETIQUETTE: DJ calls dances on band breaks.
DANCE-FLOOR STATS: One 1,000-square-foot rectangular parquet sunken floor.
FOOD: Full-service restaurant.
MINIMUM AGE: 21.
FAMILY NIGHTS: Sunday at 6 P.M.
SMOKE-FILTERING SYSTEM: Yes.
COMMENTS: Open 7 nights a week. National acts perform here on a regular basis. Western wear shop on premises.

Woodland Hills

Denim & Diamonds
21055 Ventura Boulevard
818/888-5134
GENRE: New Breed/Chain.
COVER CHARGE: Varies.
COMMENTS: Owned by Graham Gilliam.

COLORADO

Arvada

Urban Cowgirl
9575 West 57th Avenue
303/420-4444
GENRE: Traditional/Independent.
CAPACITY: 250.
MUSIC: Local bands Thursday through Saturday.
DANCE-FLOOR STATS: One 682-square-foot parquet floor.

Aurora

Stampede Mesquite Grill & Dance Emporium
2430 South Havana Street
303/696-7686
GENRE: New Breed/Independent.
COVER CHARGE: Varies nightly.
DRESS CODE: Yes.
CAPACITY: 999.
YEAR OPENED: 1992.
MUSIC: Disc jockey nightly; live music only for special concerts.
DANCE LESSONS: Free on some nights, for a fee on others.
DANCE ETIQUETTE: Taught in dance lessons; DJ calls dances.
DANCE-FLOOR STATS: One raised racetrack-style hardwood floor.
FOOD: Full-service restaurant.
MINIMUM AGE: 21.
SMOKE-FILTERING SYSTEM: Yes.
COMMENTS: Open 7 days a week. Special events include Annual Birthday Bash, Halloween Madness, New Year's Eve Bash, and a St. Patrick's Day Party. Founded by owner of Chi Chi's Mexican Restaurant chain.

Zanza Bar
10601 East Colfax Avenue
303/344-2510
GENRE: Traditional/Independent.
CAPACITY: 550.
MUSIC: Bands on Wednesday through Sunday.
DANCE-FLOOR STATS: One 1,008-square-foot rectangular hardwood floor.
COMMENTS: Scenes from *Every Which Way But Loose* filmed here.

Broomfield

Sweetwater Pub & Grill
9975 Wadsworth Parkway
303/420-1004
GENRE: Traditional/Independent.
CAPACITY: 299.
MUSIC: Bands on Thursday, Friday, and Saturday.
DANCE-FLOOR STATS: One 440-square-foot parquet floor.

Carbondale

Relay Station
14913 Highway 82
303/963-1334
GENRE: Traditional/Independent.

CAPACITY: 250.
MUSIC: Bands on Friday and Saturday.
DANCE-FLOOR STATS: One 440-square-foot floor.

Central City

Famous Bonanza Casino
107 Main Street
303/526-7568
GENRE: Traditional/Independent.
MUSIC: Bands on Friday and Saturday.
DANCE-FLOOR STATS: One expandable floor.

Glory Hole Saloon
129 Main Street
303/582-0749
GENRE: Traditional/Independent.
MUSIC: Live music nightly.
DANCE-FLOOR STATS: One expandable wood floor.

Colorado Springs

Cowboys Nightclub
3910 Palmer Park Boulevard
719/596-1212
GENRE: New Breed.
CAPACITY: 1,175.
MUSIC: Disc jockey nightly.
DANCE-FLOOR STATS: One 1,080-square-foot parquet floor.

Gambler Dance Hall & Saloon
3958 North Academy Boulevard
719/574-3369
GENRE: New Breed.
CAPACITY: 500.
MUSIC: Disc jockey nightly.
DANCE-FLOOR STATS: One 810-square-foot hardwood floor.

The Rodeo
3506 North Academy Boulevard
719/597-6121
GENRE: New Breed.
MUSIC: Disc jockey nightly.
DANCE-FLOOR STATS: One 1,800-square-foot hardwood floor.

Sundance Springs Saloon
2493 South Academy Boulevard
719/380-0542
GENRE: Traditional/Independent.
CAPACITY: 350.
MUSIC: Live music Tuesday through Sunday.
DANCE-FLOOR STATS: One 1,000-square-foot rectangular parquet floor.

Dacono

Tim Bob's
909 Carbondale Drive, No. 52
303/833-2633
GENRE: Traditional/Independent.
CAPACITY: 150.
MUSIC: Live music Friday and Saturday.
DANCE-FLOOR STATS: One 600-square-foot floor.

Denver

Club 70
2480 West Hampden
303/781-9408
GENRE: New Breed/Independent.
CAPACITY: 200.
MUSIC: Live music Thursday through Saturday; disc jockey all other nights.
DANCE-FLOOR STATS: One 1,850-square-foot hardwood floor.
COMMENTS: Formerly Pistol Pete's. Country 7 nights a week.

Cordial Lounge
1521 Pierce Street
303/233-9621
CAPACITY: 100.
MUSIC: Bands on Friday and Saturday.
DANCE-FLOOR STATS: One 126-square-foot floor.

Countryland
7600 Highway 2
303/288-9903
GENRE: Traditional/Independent.
CAPACITY: 275.
MUSIC: Live music Tuesday through Sunday.

DANCE-FLOOR STATS: One 665-square-foot hardwood floor.

Dance Country
I-25 at 38th Avenue
303/458-0808

Frontier Club
18881 East Colfax Avenue
303/367-8637
MUSIC: Live music Friday and Saturday.
DANCE-FLOOR STATS: One 476-square-foot parquet floor.

Grizzly Rose Saloon & Dance Emporium
5450 North Valley Highway
303/295-1330
COVER CHARGE: Varies.
CAPACITY: 1,200.
MUSIC: Live music by local and regional bands. Special concerts by national acts.
DANCE LESSONS: Free and for a fee.
SPECIAL CLUB DANCE: Colorado ten-step.
DANCE-FLOOR STATS: One 2,496-square-foot hardwood floor and one 432-square-foot parquet floor.
FOOD: Yes.
MINIMUM AGE: 21.
FAMILY NIGHTS: Sunday is Family Night starting at 5 P.M.
SMOKE-FILTERING SYSTEM: Yes.
COMMENTS: Arrive early for Family Night. Parking lot fills up by 5 P.M. and there is a line out the door waiting to get in.

Herman's Hideaway
1578 South Broadway
303/777-5840

Ollie's Roundup
5195 Morrison Road
303/935-8377
CAPACITY: 273.
MUSIC: Disc jockey nightly.
DANCE-FLOOR STATS: One 1,504-square-foot hardwood floor.

Rockin' West Caravan
11221 West 44th Avenue
303/467-3557
CAPACITY: 280.
MUSIC: Live music nightly.
DANCE-FLOOR STATS: One 464-square-foot hardwood floor.

Spurs
7301 North Federal Boulevard
303/426-4848
GENRE: New Breed.
MUSIC: Disc jockey Wednesday through Saturday.
DANCE-FLOOR STATS: One 3,200-square-foot hardwood floor and one 840-square-foot floor.

Durango

The Sundance Saloon
601 East Second Avenue
303/247-8821

Englewood

Mirage Night Club
9555 East Arapahoe
303/790-1386

Trail Dust Steak House
7101 South Clinton
303/709-2420
GENRE: Traditional/Chain.
COVER CHARGE: No cover charge, but dinner purchase is required Wednesday through Sunday.
DRESS CODE: No ties allowed. If you won't take it off, then they'll cut it off, hang it on the wall with a card, and give you a free beverage for it.
MUSIC: Local bands nightly starting at 7 P.M.
DANCE ETIQUETTE: Rules are posted.
DANCE-FLOOR STATS: One 665-square-foot hardwood floor.
FOOD: Full-service restaurant.
MINIMUM AGE: All ages allowed.
FAMILY NIGHTS: Every night is Family Night.
COMMENTS: Open 7 days a week.

Estes Park

Estes Park Event Center
470 Prospect Village Drive
303/586-5421
CAPACITY: 350.
MUSIC: Bands 7 nights a week.
DANCE-FLOOR STATS: One 1,100-square-foot hardwood floor.
COMMENTS: This is a nonsmoking club.

Evergreen

Little Bear Saloon
28075 Highway 74/Main Street
303/647-5355

Federal Heights

Ac'es Country
8980 Federal Boulevard
303/427-4757
GENRE: Traditional/Independent.
COVER CHARGE: Never.
CAPACITY: 175.
YEAR OPENED: 1987.
MUSIC: Local bands Thursday through Sunday.
DANCE LESSONS: Free on Thursday and Friday nights.
DANCE-FLOOR STATS: One 323-square-foot rectangular hardwood floor.
FOOD: Appetizers only.
MINIMUM AGE: 21.
SMOKE-FILTERING SYSTEM: Yes.
JUKEBOX WITH A COUNTRY SONG: Yes.
COMMENTS: Open 7 nights a week.

Fort Collins

Cow Palace
6520 South College Avenue
303/223-1968
GENRE: Traditional/Independent.
COVER CHARGE: Varies nightly.
CAPACITY: 450.
YEAR OPENED: 1980.
MUSIC: Live music Wednesday through Sunday by local bands. National acts for special concerts.
DANCE LESSONS: Free on Saturday, Sunday, and Wednesday.
DANCE ETIQUETTE: Rules are posted.
DANCE-FLOOR STATS: One 1,512-square-foot rectangular hardwood floor.
FOOD: Vending-machine snacks and appetizers.
MINIMUM AGE: 18.
FAMILY NIGHTS: On Wednesday 16 and up allowed from 6 to 10 P.M. Sunday is Family Night from 6 to 10 P.M.
SMOKE-FILTERING SYSTEM: Yes.
JUKEBOX WITH A COUNTRY SONG: Yes.
COMMENTS: Lounge is open 7 days a week; dance hall is open Wednesday through Sunday.

Lone Star Steakhouse & Saloon
100 West Troutman Parkway
303/225-6284

Sundance Steak House & Country Club
2716 East Mulberry
303/484-1600
GENRE: New Breed/Independent.
CAPACITY: 450.
YEAR OPENED: 1984.
MUSIC: Disc jockey and local bands.
DANCE LESSONS: Yes.
DANCE-FLOOR STATS: One 1,620-square-foot hardwood floor.
FOOD: Full-service restaurant.

Grand Junction

Rose Saloon & Dance Hall
2993 North Avenue
303/245-0606

Greeley

Diamond Spur
2961 West 29th Street
303/330-1309
CAPACITY: 400.
MUSIC: Live music Thursday through Saturday.
DANCE-FLOOR STATS: One 900-square-foot octagonal tile floor.

Lakewood

Smokehouse
1251 Wadsworth
303/232–2106
DANCE-FLOOR STATS: One 1,120-square-foot hardwood floor.
COMMENTS: Open Wednesday through Sunday.

Littleton

Tumbleweeds Tavern
11614 West Belleview Avenue
303/933–7761
CAPACITY: 177.
MUSIC: Bands on Friday and Saturday.

Longmont

Mustang Sally's
1515 Main Street
303/684–0850
CAPACITY: 500.
MUSIC: Bands Thursday through Saturday.
DANCE-FLOOR STATS: One 2,600-square-foot hardwood floor.

Loveland

Full Moon Saloon
3329 North Garfield
303/669–3727
CAPACITY: 266.
MUSIC: Bands Thursday through Sunday.
DANCE-FLOOR STATS: One 844-square-foot parquet floor.

Lucerne

Lucky Star Bar & Grill
33131 Highway 85
303/351–8000
CAPACITY: 248.
MUSIC: Bands Thursday through Saturday.
DANCE-FLOOR STATS: One 840-square-foot hardwood floor.

Parker

Main Street
19552 East Main Street
303/841–7179
CAPACITY: 250.
MUSIC: Bands on Friday and Saturday.
DANCE-FLOOR STATS: One 256-square-foot hardwood floor.

Pueblo

The Chief
611 North Main Street
719/546–1246

Rifle

Shabby's Shooting Star Saloon
2090 White River Avenue
303/625–5414

Severance

Bruce's Bar
345 First Street
303/686–2320
GENRE: Traditional/Independent.
COVER CHARGE: Never.
CAPACITY: 250.
YEAR OPENED: 1957.
MUSIC: House band Friday through Sunday. Jukebox all other nights.
DANCE-FLOOR STATS: One 1,500-square-foot L-shaped tile floor.
FOOD: Full-service restaurant.
MINIMUM AGE: 21.
FAMILY NIGHTS: Sunday from 6 to 9 P.M. Childen must leave club by 9 P.M. all other nights.
JUKEBOX WITH A COUNTRY SONG: Yes.
COMMENTS: Open 7 nights a week. Club sponsors all-you-can-eat Rocky Mountain oysters twice a week, fund-raisers, antique car rides, motorcycle rides. Tour buses like to stop here.

Thornton

Cactus Moon
Thornton Town Center
10001 Grant Street
303/451–5200
GENRE: New Breed/Independent.
CAPACITY: 2,195.
COVER CHARGE: Varies nightly.
YEAR OPENED: 1992.
MUSIC: Disc jockey nightly.
DANCE-FLOOR STATS: One 6,000-square-foot U-shaped hardwood floor.
MINIMUM AGE: 21.
SMOKE-FILTERING SYSTEM: Yes.
COMMENTS: Owned by GBI Management, a limited partnership, not the Graham Brothers.

Lake Avenue Inn
2181 Lake Avenue
303/452–9079
MUSIC: Bands on Friday and Saturday.
DANCE-FLOOR STATS: One 600-square-foot tile floor.

Trinidad

Chaps Lounge
Trinidad Motor Inn
303/846–2076

Vail

Garton's Saloon
143 East Meadow Drive
303/479–0607

Westminster

Trail Dust Steak House
9101 Benton Street
303/427–1446
GENRE: Traditional/Chain.
COVER CHARGE: No cover charge, but dinner purchase is required Wednesday through Sunday.
DRESS CODE: No ties allowed. If you won't take it off, then they'll cut it off, hang it on the wall with a card, and give you a free beverage for it.
CAPACITY: 564.
YEAR OPENED: 1980.
MUSIC: Local bands nightly starting at 7 P.M.
DANCE ETIQUETTE: Rules are posted.
DANCE-FLOOR STATS: One 408-square-foot rectangular hardwood floor.
FOOD: Full-service restaurant.
MINIMUM AGE: All ages allowed.
FAMILY NIGHTS: Every night is Family Night. Children must abide by rules about the slide and dance floor.
COMMENTS: Open 7 days a week.

Wheat Ridge

Club Corner
6651 West 44th Place
303/424–9996
GENRE: Traditional/Independent.
COVER CHARGE: Never.
CAPACITY: 195.
YEAR OPENED: Between 1930 and 1940. Current ownership since 1977.
MUSIC: Local bands Wednesday through Sunday.
DANCE LESSONS: Free on Thursday.
DANCE-FLOOR STATS: One 476-square-foot rectangular parquet floor.
FOOD: Snacks available.
MINIMUM AGE: 21 to drink.
FAMILY NIGHTS: Children are allowed until 9 P.M. nightly.
SMOKE-FILTERING SYSTEM: Well-ventilated.
JUKEBOX WITH A COUNTRY SONG: Yes.
COMMENTS: Open 7 days a week.

CONNECTICUT

Milford

Boot Scooters
141 Merwyn Avenue
203/878–8008

Plainville

Cadillac Ranch
32 Whiting Street
203/793–8805

Stamford

Terrace Club
1938 West Main Street
203/961-9770

DELAWARE

Bear

The Keg
Route 40
302/328-5945

New Castle

Cheryl's Sky Lounge
Route 273
302/322-3008

DISTRICT OF COLUMBIA

Remington's
639 Pennsylvania Avenue SE
202/543-3113
GENRE: Gay/Independent.
YEAR OPENED: 1992.

FLORIDA

Bradenton

Joyland IV
6424 14th Street West
813/756-6060

Village Barn
5520 14th Street West
813/751-4218

Cape Coral

Hired Hand Saloon
1017 47th Terrace East
813/542-4370

Clearwater

Joyland Country Music Nightclub
11225 U.S. Highway 19 North
813/573-1919

Davie

Davie Junction
6311 SW 45th Street
305/422-2434

Fort Lauderdale

Desperado's
2520 South Miami Road
305/463-7239

Fort Walton Beach

Texas Club
113 South Eglin Parkway
904/664-6255

Jacksonville

Crazy Horse Saloon of Jacksonville
5800 Phillips Highway
904/731-8891
GENRE: New Breed/Independent.
CAPACITY: 1,000.

Lakeland

Texan
300 Gary Road
813/683-4850

Lecanto

Cowboy Junction
3949 West Gulf
904/746-4754

Lighthouse Point

Smokin' Joe's Saloon
5360 Federal Highway (Route 1)
305/428-1404

Naples

Silver Dollar
2896 Tamiami Trail East
813/775-7011

Ocala

Painted Horse Saloon
2677 NW Tenth Street
904/629-1221

Orlando

Cheyenne Saloon & Opera House
129 West Church Street
407/422-2434
CAPACITY: 1,000.
DANCE-FLOOR STATS: Corral-shaped.
COMMENTS: TNN's *Church Street Station* is filmed here.

Crazy Horse Saloon
7050 South Kirkman Road
407/363-0071

Full Moon
500 Orange Blossom Trail
407/648-8725

Rodeo
12413 South Orange Blossom Trail
407/438-5456

Sullivan's Trailway Lounge
1108 South Orange Blossom Trail
407/843-2934

Ormond Beach

Rockin' Ranch
801 South Nova Road
904/673-0904

Sanford

The Barn
1200 South French Avenue
407/330-4978

Stuart

Rockin' Horse
1580 Federal Highway
407/286-1329

Tallahassee

The Moon
1105 East Lafayette Street
904/878-6900

Tampa

American Cowboy Company
3603 Waters
813/932-8823

Dallas Bull
8222 Highway 301 North
813/985-6877

Despaparados
9430 Lazy Lane
813/935-6863

Wild West Saloon
5305 North Armenia Avenue
813/873-2000

West Palm Beach

Country Nights
4833 Okeechobee Boulevard
407/689-7625

GEORGIA

Atlanta

KB's
2775 Clairmont Road NE
404/321-0303

Two Steps West
3535 Chamblee Tucker Road NE
404/458-9378

HONKY-TONKS

Augusta

Rascal's Country
1511 North Leg Road
706/737-6866

Buena Vista

Silver Moon Music Bar
912/649-2028

Columbus

Legendary Dallas Club
3433 North Lumpkin Road
706/689-8977

Roadhouse Honky Tonk
4817 Milen
706/561-1358

Conley

Charlie's
1326 Cedar Grove Road
404/363-8609

Conyers

TJ's Pure Country
2174 Salem Road
404/922-8650

Cumming

Cadillac Ranch
3885 Brown's Bridge Road
404/844-0304

Decatur

Mama's Country Showcase
3952 Covington Highway
404/288-6262
COMMENTS: Open Wednesday through Saturday at 7 P.M.

Silver Saddle
3889 Covington Highway
404/289-4955

Douglasville

Yellow Rose Saloon
7641 Hardrock Road
404/949-7706

Gainesville

Mule Camp Springs Saloon
311 Jesse Jewell Parkway
404/536-4880

Jonesboro

Sundance Saloon
335 Upper Riverdale Road
404/907-9164

Kennesaw

Crystal Chandelier
1750 North Roberts Road
404/426-5006

Lilburn

Country Club
4200 Stone Mountain Freeway
404/972-7545

Lithonia

Shooter's Restaurant and Lounge
6420 Hillandale Drive
404/482-1384

Macon

Nashville South
1015 Riverside Drive
912/745-7827

Whiskey River
4740 Pio Nona Avenue
912/788-3000

Marietta

Miss Kitty's Dance Hall & Saloon
1038 Franklin Road, Suite 11-304
404/426-9077

GENRE: Traditional/Independent.
CAPACITY: 900.
COVER CHARGE: Varies.
MUSIC: Local, regional, and national acts.
DANCE LESSONS: Free.
FAMILY NIGHTS: Sunday 4 to 10 P.M.

Norcross

Dodge City Dance Hall & Saloon
Jimmy Carter Boulevard and I-85
404/662-5904

Pooler

Randall's Nite Life
200 Governor Treutian Road
912/748-6850

Savannah

204 Lounge
I-95 at Route 204
912/352-7100

Smyrna

Buckboard Country Music Showcase
2080 Cobb Parkway SE
404/955-7340

HAWAII

Pearl City, Oahu

Pecos River Cafe
99-016 Kam Highway
808/487-7980

IDAHO

Boise

Rock 'N' Rodeo
1025 South Capitol Boulevard
208/344-7971
GENRE: New Breed/Chain.
COVER CHARGE: Varies nightly.
DRESS CODE: No cutoffs, tank tops on men, or T-shirts with obscene or derogatory statements printed on them.
CAPACITY: 295.
YEAR OPENED: 1992.
MUSIC: Disc jockey 7 nights a week.
DANCE LESSONS: Free lessons every night but Monday.
DANCE ETIQUETTE: Rules are posted. DJ calls dances.
DANCE-FLOOR STATS: One 1,200-square-foot rectangular hardwood floor.
LIQUOR: Law prohibits liquor sales on Election Day.
FOOD: Full-service restaurant.
MINIMUM AGE: 21.
SMOKE-FILTERING SYSTEM: Good ventilation.
COMMENTS: Club sponsors "Cowgirls Spoiled Rotten" Thursdays with 75¢ well drinks, wine, or draft beer for all. There is also a "Miss Rodeo" giveaway. Open 7 days a week.

Shorty's Country Western Saloon
5467 Glenwood
208/323-0555
GENRE: Traditional/Independent.
COVER CHARGE: Only on weekends.
DRESS CODE: Shoes and shirt required. Clean clothes and good personal hygiene.
YEAR OPENED: 1985.
MUSIC: Live music every night except Monday by local and regional acts. Occasional concerts by national acts.
DANCE LESSONS: Free on Sunday, Tuesday, and Thursday.
DANCE ETIQUETTE: "Rude dancers are informed of such soon enough by those near them."
DANCE-FLOOR STATS: Two parquet floors. Main (square), 440 square feet; upper (rectangular), 260 square feet.
FOOD: Free popcorn, snacks for sale at the bar. Free tacos, spaghetti, or chili for *Monday Night Football.*
MINIMUM AGE: 21.
SMOKE-FILTERING SYSTEM: Yes.
JUKEBOX WITH A COUNTRY SONG: Yes.

COMMENTS: Open 7 days a week. Sponsors "True Value Country Showdown" and "Wrangler Tight-Fittin' Jeans" contests, as well as dance contests, golf tournaments, etc.

Chubbock

Green Triangle Bar
4010 Yellowstone Avenue
208/237-0354

Lava Hot Springs

Wagon Wheel
208/776-5015

Lewiston

The Corral
1818 Main Street
208/746-5353

Meridian

127 Club
127 East Idaho Avenue
208/888-9603

Montpelier

Butch Cassidy's
260 North Fourth Street
208/847-3501

State Line

Kelly's Grand 'Ol Opry
6152 West Seltice Way
208/773-5002
GENRE: Traditional/Independent.
COVER CHARGE: Only on weekends.
CAPACITY: 622.
YEAR OPENED: 1984.
MUSIC: House band with special concerts by regional and national acts.
DANCE LESSONS: Free on Friday and Saturday.
SPECIAL CLUB DANCES: The Chicken Dance and the Snake Dance.
DANCE ETIQUETTE: Rules are posted.
DANCE-FLOOR STATS: One 3,264-square-foot rectangular tile floor.
MINIMUM AGE: 21.
COMMENTS: Only open Friday and Saturday nights. Indoor roping contests.

ILLINOIS

Bartlett

Cadillac Ranch Texas BBQ and Boot Bar
1175 West Lake Street
708/830-7200

Bensenville

Nashville North
101 East Irving Park Road
708/595-7878
COMMENTS: Oldest club in the Chicago area–opened in 1975.

Chicago

Silver Saddle
708/490-1666
MUSIC: Live music and disc jockey.

Whiskey River
1997 North Clybourn Avenue
312/528-3400

Fairview

Bobby's Goodtime Country
6000 Old Collinsville Road
618/632-6041

Mundelein

Sundance Saloon
2061 West Maple Avenue
708/949-0858

Rockford

Cactus Rose Saloon & Steakhouse
3911 Sandy Hollow
815/874-2765

Romeoville

Sidekick's Saloon
201 East Romeo Road
815/886-5600

South Chicago Heights

Dusty Trails
American Plaza Shopping Center
708/756-1590

Summit

Kickers Corral
7225 West 63rd
708/594-7788

INDIANA

Indianapolis

Cowboys
2440 Lafayette Road
317/638-1116
DANCE LESSONS: Free on Tuesday and Wednesday.
DANCE-FLOOR STATS: One 1,000-square-foot floor.

Little Bit of Texas
111 North Lynhurst Drive
317/487-9065
GENRE: New Breed/Chain.

Lafayette

The Dance
1174 South Creasy Lane
317/447-9101

South Bend

Heartland Texas BBQ Dance Hall & Theatre
222 South Michigan Street
219/234-5200

West Lafayette

Neon Cactus
360 Brown Street
317/743-6081

IOWA

Cedar Rapids

Country Club
3233 Sixth Street SW
319/366-2222

Country Connection
6909 Mount Vernon Road SE
319/363-7411

Kitty's Lounge
Best Western Longbranch
90 Twixt Town Road
319/377-6386

Nancy's Country Inn
6913 Mount Vernon Road SE
319/364-9342

Red Stallion
5101 16th Avenue SW
319/390-5500

Council Bluffs

Mosquito Creek Saloon
Interstate 80 and Madison Avenue
712/322-9621

Des Moines

Guitars & Cadillacs
4020 Merle Hay Road
515/270-6333

Waterloo

Wild E. Coyote's
53295 University Avenue
319/234-4333

KANSAS

Lawrence

Coyote's
1003 East 23rd
913/842-2380

Olathe

Guitars & Cadillacs
11950 South Strang Line Road
913/829-8200

Topeka

Remington's
1155 SW Wannamaker Road
913/271-8700

KENTUCKY

Bowling Green

Desperado's
551 Searcy Way
502/781-0628

Daysville

Libby's Steakhouse & Entertainment
Highway 6880
502/265-2630

Fort Mitchell

Coyote's Music & Dance Hall
I-75 at Buttermilk Park
606/341-5150

Lexington

Austin City Saloon
2350 Woodhill Drive
606/266-6891

Horseshoes Saloon
Days Inn
1987 North Broadway
606/299-1202

Louisville

Annie's
8009 Terry Lane
502/933-1049

Coyote's Music & Dance Hall
116 West Jefferson Street
502/589-3866
CAPACITY: 1,000.
DANCE-FLOOR STATS: One 2,500-square-foot floor.
FOOD: Full-service restaurant.
MINIMUM AGE: 21.
SMOKE-FILTERING SYSTEM: Yes.
COMMENTS: Serving greater Cincinnati and northern Kentucky. Country-western club is 20,000 square feet; 3 adjacent clubs include Hurricane O'Malley's, Rock-It Dance Club, and Backstage Cafe, featuring rhythm and blues.

Do-Drop Inn
1032 Story Avenue
502/582-9327
GENRE: Traditional/Independent.
COVER CHARGE: Always $1.50.
DRESS CODE: Casual.
YEAR OPENED: 1962.
MUSIC: Live music.
SPECIAL CLUB DANCE: Potato Dance.
DANCE-FLOOR STATS: One 1,250-square-foot hardwood floor.
MINIMUM AGE: 21.
COMMENTS: Take your own dance partner.

Jim Porter's Good Time Emporium
2345 Lexington Road
502/452-9531
COMMENTS: Country on Sunday from 6 P.M. to 2 A.M.

Rhinestone's
1211 Shelbyville Road
502/245-4614

Owensboro

Yellow Rose
3220 West Second Street
502/926-6104

Paducah

Silver Saddle
JR's Executive Inn
1 Executive Boulevard
502/443-8000

Richmond

Maverick Club
1507 East Main Street
606/623-0421

Silver Star
128 East Main Street
606/624-8340

Wilder

Bobby Mackey's
44 Licking Pike
606/431-5588
GENRE: Traditional/Independent.
COMMENTS: A slaughterhouse-turned-saloon–this place is haunted! Open only on Friday and Saturday 8 P.M. to 2:30 A.M.

LOUISIANA

Alexandria

Fool's Gold
1711 North McArthur Drive
318/487-1009

Baton Rouge

Texas Dance Hall
456 North Donmoor Avenue
504/928-4655

Gretna

Mudbugs Saloon
2024 Bell Chase Highway
504/392-0202
GENRE: New Breed/Chain.
COVER CHARGE: Varies.
MEMBERSHIP FEE: None.
CAPACITY: 2,500.
MUSIC: Disc jockey nightly.
DANCE-FLOOR STATS: One 6,000-square-foot hardwood floor.
MINIMUM AGE: 21.
SMOKE-FILTERING SYSTEM: Yes.
COMMENTS: Owned by Graham Brothers.

Houma

Crazy Horse Saloon & Dance Hall
201 Monarch Drive
504/872-3737

Lafayette

Yellow Rose Saloon
6880 Johnston Street
318/989-9702

Lake Charles

Cowboys
5329 Common Street
318/474-8010

Monroe

Honky Tonk
2003 Tower Drive
318/324-8805

Montpelier

Bear Creek Steakhouse & Club
Highway 16
504/777-4709
COMMENTS: Country music and dancing on Saturday night.

Shreveport

Denim & Diamonds
1251 Shreveport Boulevard/Barksdale Highway
318/869-0203
GENRE: New Breed/Chain.
COVER CHARGE: Varies.
MUSIC: Disc jockey nightly.
DANCE-FLOOR STATS: One 2,300-square-foot raised hardwood racetrack floor.
MINIMUM AGE: 21.
SMOKE-FILTERING SYSTEM: Yes.
COMMENTS: Closed Sunday and Monday. Owned by Graham Brothers.

MAINE

Brunswick

Sundance Corral
14 Main Street
207/798-4725

MARYLAND

Baltimore

County Line
7032 Elm Road
410/859-3300

Murphy's Country Palace
7916 Pulaski Highway
410/686-4432

Silverado
Best Western Travel Plaza
5625 O'Donnell Street
410/633-9500

Barstow

Country Docks
410/535-3989

Frederick

Silver Dollar Lounge
200 East Walser
301/662-0700
GENRE: Traditional/Independent.
MUSIC: Live music Thursday, Friday, and Saturday.
DANCE-FLOOR STATS: 1.

Glen Burnie

Cancun Cantina
7501 Old Telegraph Road
410/761-6188

Country Club at La Fontaine Bleu
7514 South Ritchie Highway
410/799-7110 or 800/345-2450

Greenbelt

Martin's Crosswinds
7400 Greenway Center Drive
301/474-8500

Jessup

Latela's Corral
Routes 175 and 295
410/799-7110
GENRE: Traditional/Independent.
CAPACITY: 365.
MUSIC: Local and regional bands.
DANCE LESSONS: Free.
DANCE-FLOOR STATS: 2.

Lanham

Country Club at La Fontaine Bleu
7963 Annapolis Road
301/535-1431 or 800/731-4333

Laurel

Randy's California Inn
Route 1 and Whiskey Bottom Road
410/792-4595
GENRE: Traditional/Independent.
MUSIC: Local and regional bands.

Timonium

Nashville's
Holiday Inn
2004 Greenspring Drive
410/252-7373

Waldorf

Spurs
2106 Crane Highway
301/843-9964

MASSACHUSETTS

Centerville

Steppin' With Style
29 Zeno Crocker Road
508/788-0737

Mansfield

Homestead/Sundown Saloon
Plain Street
508/339-9098

Marlboro

Lazy Armadillo Saloon
Routes 20 and 85
508/460-8895

Metheun

White Buffalo Saloon
Ayers Village Road (Route 97)
800/725-6661

Oxbridge

Jack's Saloon
Routes 16 and 122
508/278-7567

Raynham

Diamond Jack's
508/824-4850

MICHIGAN

Canton

Lucille's
43711 Michigan Avenue
313/397-1988

Flint

Cactus Moon
3187 North Genessee
810/736-9260

Grand Rapids

Howlin' Moon Saloon
141 28th Street SE
616/245-0472

Kalamazoo

Cheek to Cheek/Silver Bullet
3750 East Kilgore
616/345-1608

Lansing

Silver Dollar Saloon
3411 East Michigan Avenue
517/351-2451

Pontiac

Diamonds & Spurs
25 South Saginaw
313/334-4409

Quincy

Stampede
831 West Chicago Road
517/639-3390

DRESS CODE: No tank or tube tops.
DANCE-FLOOR STATS: One outer floor–3,300 square feet; one inner floor–1,100 square feet. Oak racetrack; fast and slow lanes marked; swing and line dance area in center.

Rochester Hills

Silver Spur Saloon
54 West Auburn Road
313/852-6460

MINNESOTA

Eagan

Stark's
3125 Dodd Road
612/454-8251

Eden Prairie

Cadillac Ranch
16397 Cadillac Drive
612/949-0393

Mahnomen

Shooting Star Casino
218/935-2701

Minneapolis

Billy Bob's Country Nights
1 Main Street SE
612/331-3589

Cowboy
400 Third Avenue North
612/333-1006

Moorhead

Pistol Pete's
3108 Ninth Street South
218/233-4010

MISSISSIPPI

Gulfport

Michael's Country Club
Highway 49 at I-10
601/867-6322

Jackson

DJ's Rodeo Club Inc
6101 Highway 18 South
601/922-3112

Rodeos/Stockyard Steaks
6107 Ridgewood Road
601/957-1400

MISSOURI

Branson

Crockey's
Highways 65 and 165
417/334-4995

Pure Country Cafe
Highways 65 and 248
417/335-7873

Columbia

New Silver Bullet
2508-B Paris Road
314/474-8884

Earth City

Little Bit of Texas
3590 Rider Trail South
314/298-7163

Hazelwood

Cactus Moon
41 Village Square Shopping Center
314/731-0120

Kansas City

Cheyenne Country Club
4207 Woodfield
816/767-0100

Guitars & Cadillacs
3954 Central
816/756-2221

Guitars & Cadillacs
5502 North Antioch
816/453-6767

Ropers
1725 Swift
816/221-7330
GENRE: New Breed/Independent.

Silkeston

Country Nites
Highway 60 East
314/471-6160

Springfield

Midnight Rodeo
3303 South Campbell
417/882-0309

MONTANA

Bainville

State Line Club
Highway 2
701/875-4353
GENRE: Traditional/Independent.
COVER CHARGE: Not since 1984.
DRESS CODE: Must be neat and presentable.
CAPACITY: 800.
YEAR OPENED: 1932.
MUSIC: Local bands once a month. National acts for special concerts.
DANCE-FLOOR STATS: One 625-square-foot square tile floor.
FOOD: Full-service restaurant. Specialty is $5.95 for 12-ounce prime rib. Appetizers and vending-machine snacks also available.
MINIMUM AGE: No one under 18 allowed after 10 P.M.
COMMENTS: "Open 365 days a year unless we're snowed under."

Billings

Drifters
3953 Montana Avenue
406/245-8346
GENRE: Traditional/Independent.
COVER CHARGE: Never.
CAPACITY: 300.
YEAR OPENED: 1979.
MUSIC: Live music by local and regional bands on Friday and Saturday. Disc jockey all other nights.
DANCE LESSONS: Free on Tuesday.
DANCE-FLOOR STATS: One sort of semicircular 500-square-foot parquet floor.
FOOD: Full-service restaurant.
MINIMUM AGE: 21.
SMOKE-FILTERING SYSTEM: Yes.
COMMENTS: Open 7 days a week.

Moose Breath
4242 State Avenue
406/252-5702

Columbia Falls

Blue Moon Nightclub
6105 Highway 2
406/892-9925
GENRE: Traditional/Independent.
YEAR OPENED: Late 1940s.
MUSIC: Live music on Thursday, Friday, and Saturday nights. Karaoke on Wednesday nights.
COMMENTS: Allegedly a strong contingent of country dancers here.

Harrison

Tobacco Root Tavern & Supper Club
Highway 287
406/685-3211

GENRE: Traditional/Independent.
COVER CHARGE: Never.
CAPACITY: 200.
YEAR OPENED: 1931. Original bar burned in 1971, rebuilt in 1972.
MUSIC: Local and regional touring bands on Saturday only.
DANCE LESSONS: For a fee, only on Saturday.
DANCE-FLOOR STATS: One 900-square-foot square springboard parquet floor.
FOOD: Cheap eats at bar, separate supper club with moderate prices.
MINIMUM AGE: Any age but must be 21 to drink.
JUKEBOX WITH A COUNTRY SONG: Yes.
COMMENTS: Open 7 nights a week.

Helena

Silver Spur
2000 North Montana Avenue
406/449-2512
GENRE: Traditional/Independent.
COVER CHARGE: Only on weekends.
CAPACITY: 395.
YEAR OPENED: 1952.
MUSIC: Local and regional bands on Friday and Saturday.
DANCE LESSONS: $2 per person on Tuesday nights.
DANCE-FLOOR STATS: One 810-square-foot rectangular hardwood floor.
FOOD: Snacks at the bar and in vending machines.
MINIMUM AGE: 21.
SMOKE-FILTERING SYSTEM: Yes.
JUKEBOX WITH A COUNTRY SONG: Yes.
COMMENTS: Open 7 nights a week. Offers reggae music 4 times a year.

Missoula

Limelight Nightclub
EconoLodge
1609 Broadway
406/543-7231

Norris

Norris Bar
Highway 287
406/685-3304
GENRE: Traditional/Independent.
COVER CHARGE: Never.
CAPACITY: 200.
YEAR OPENED: Established 1940s. Current owner since 1989.
MUSIC: Live music on Saturday and Sunday only by house or local bands.
DANCE-FLOOR STATS: One 625-square-foot square sunken hardwood floor.
FOOD: Burgers, pizza, and vending-machine snacks.
MINIMUM AGE: 18, but must be 21 to drink; 18-year-olds-must leave club by 11 P.M.
JUKEBOX WITH A COUNTRY SONG: Yes.
COMMENTS: Open 7 nights a week.

Stevensville

High Country Club
209 Main
406/777-9910

NEBRASKA

Lincoln

The Cactus Club
402/475-8007
CAPACITY: 200.
MUSIC: Live music Tuesday through Saturday.

Guitars & Cadillacs
5400 O Street
402/464-1100

Omaha

Guitars & Cadillacs
10865 West Dodge
402/333-5500
FAMILY NIGHTS: Sunday and Monday.

J. R.'s Lounge
3050 L Street
402/731-1446

Ralston

Bushwackers Saloon & Dance Hall
7401 Main Street
402/593-9037

NEVADA

Elko

Red Lion Inn & Casino
2065 Idaho Street
702/738-2111

Las Vegas

Cheyenne Saloon
3103 North Rancho Drive
702/645-4139

GENRE: New Breed/Independent.
COVER CHARGE: Varies nightly.
CAPACITY: 300.
YEAR OPENED: 1991.
MUSIC: Live music on Friday and Saturday by local and regional bands. Disc jockey all other nights.
DANCE LESSONS: Free every night but Monday.
DANCE ETIQUETTE: DJ calls dances.
DANCE-FLOOR STATS: One springboard 800-square-foot rectangular hardwood floor.
FOOD: Full-service restaurant.
MINIMUM AGE: 21.
FAMILY NIGHTS: Sunday 9 A.M. to 1 P.M. Children are welcome any day 9 A.M. to 1 P.M. and 6:30 to 10 P.M.
JUKEBOX WITH A COUNTRY SONG: Yes.
COMMENTS: Open 24 hours a day, 365 days a year. Local dancer Bill Ray says, "Don't eat before coming here because the food is great, drinks are honest, and the cocktail waitresses are friendly."

Dylan's Dance Hall & Saloon
4661 Boulder Highway
702/451-4006

MUSIC: Disc jockey.
DANCE LESSONS: Yes.
DANCE-FLOOR STATS: One hardwood floor.
MINIMUM AGE: 21.
COMMENTS: DJ "Kaz" was selected 1993 "Nightclub DeeJay for the West" by Country Club Enterprizes in Nashville.

Gold Coast Dance Hall
4000 West Flamingo Road
702/367-7111

GENRE: New Breed/Independent.
MUSIC: Live music every night except Tuesday.
DANCE LESSONS: From 6:30 to 8:30 P.M. Sunday, Monday, Wednesday, and Thursday.
DANCE-FLOOR STATS: One large floor.
COMMENTS: Gold Coast rotates its format every 3 weeks in cycles featuring country, big band, and rock and roll. Call to see what the format is before you go.

Rockabilly's
3785 Boulder Highway
702/641-5800

GENRE: New Breed/Independent.
MUSIC: Disc jockey.
DANCE LESSONS: Line dance lessons almost every night.
DANCE-FLOOR STATS: One 1,800-square-foot hardwood floor.
COMMENTS: Club may go out of business soon; owner is looking to sell. It was formerly known as the Country Club.

Saddles 'N' Spurs Saloon
2329 North Jones Boulevard
702/646-6292

GENRE: Traditional/Independent.
DRESS CODE: Yes.
CAPACITY: 299.
YEAR OPENED: 1984.
MUSIC: Live music Thursday through Saturday by local bands.
DANCE-FLOOR STATS: One 1,875-square-foot rectangular tile floor.

FOOD: Full-service restaurant with dirt-cheap prices.
MINIMUM AGE: 21.
SMOKE-FILTERING SYSTEM: Yes.
JUKEBOX WITH A COUNTRY SONG: Yes.
COMMENTS: Open 7 days a week.

Sam's Town Dance Hall
5111 Boulder Highway
702/456–7777
GENRE: Traditional/Independent.
COVER CHARGE: Never.
DRESS CODE: Shoes and shirts required.
CAPACITY: 250.
YEAR OPENED: 1981.
MUSIC: Local and regional bands Monday through Saturday. Disc jockey on band breaks.
DANCE LESSONS: Free dance lessons 7 nights a week.
DANCE ETIQUETTE: DJ calls dances.
DANCE-FLOOR STATS: One 600-square-foot raised rectangular hardwood floor.
FOOD: Full-service restaurant.
MINIMUM AGE: 21.
SMOKE-FILTERING SYSTEM: Yes.
COMMENTS: Open 24 hours a day, 7 days a week. Gambling in casino. Dance hall is scheduled for remodeling in connection with Sam's Town's $90 million expansion, which is currently underway.

Silver Dollar
2501 East Charleston Boulevard
702/382–6921
GENRE: Traditional/Independent.
COVER CHARGE: Never.
DRESS CODE: Yes, but not enforced.
YEAR OPENED: 1931.
MUSIC: Local and regional bands 7 nights a week.
DANCE LESSONS: Yes.
DANCE-FLOOR STATS: One 800-square-foot square hardwood floor.
FOOD: Vending-machine snacks.
MINIMUM AGE: 21.
JUKEBOX WITH A COUNTRY SONG: Yes.
COMMENTS: Open 24 hours a day, 365 days a year.

Laughlin

Western Lounge
Riverside Resort & Casino
1650 Casino Drive
702/298–2535
GENRE: New Breed/Independent.
COVER CHARGE: Never.
CAPACITY: 1,000.
MUSIC: Live music every night except Tuesday, which is Karaoke Night.
DANCE LESSONS: Thursday at 7:30 P.M.
DANCE-FLOOR STATS: One moderate-size hardwood floor.

Mill City

Mr. B's Casino
6000 East Frontage Road
702/538–7306
GENRE: Traditional/Truck Stop Chain.
COVER CHARGE: Never.
DRESS CODE: "Wear what you got."
CAPACITY: 150.
YEAR OPENED: 1983.
MUSIC: Live music 3 to 4 nights a week.
DANCE-FLOOR STATS: One 900-square-foot hardwood floor.
FOOD: Full-service restaurant.
MINIMUM AGE: 21.
SMOKE-FILTERING SYSTEM: Yes.
JUKEBOX WITH A COUNTRY SONG: Yes.
COMMENTS: Mill City, also known as Puckerbrush, is 142 miles east of Reno. A 50-room Super 8 Motel is nearby.

Reno

Rodeo Rock Cafe
1537 South Virginia Street
702/323–1600
GENRE: New Breed/Independent.
COVER CHARGE: Only on weekends.
DRESS CODE: Must be presentable.
CAPACITY: 900.
YEAR OPENED: 1989.
MUSIC: Disc jockey nightly. Live music only at special concerts.
DANCE LESSONS: Free Wednesday through Sunday.

DANCE ETIQUETTE: Rules are posted. DJ calls dances.
SPECIAL CLUB DANCE: Rodeo Rock Shuffle.
DANCE-FLOOR STATS: One 3,075-square-foot rectangular parquet floor.
FOOD: Full-service restaurant.
MINIMUM AGE: All ages until 9 P.M.
FAMILY NIGHTS: Sunday from 5 to 10 P.M.
SMOKE-FILTERING SYSTEM: Yes.
MECHANICAL BULL: Yes.
COMMENTS: Closed on Monday.

Zephyr Cove

Wild West
195 U.S. Highway 50
702/588-2175
GENRE: New Breed/Chain.
COVER CHARGE: Varies nightly.

NEW HAMPSHIRE

Belmont

Silver City Saloon
Route 106 North
603/524-4186
COMMENTS: 9½ miles north of the New Hampshire International Speedway.

Loudon

Loudon Country Hall
Route 106 South
603/783-0003
COMMENTS: 1 mile south of the New Hampshire International Speedway

NEW JERSEY

Buena

Country Palace
Route 54
609/697-1475

Carney's Point

Friendly's Tavern
State Highway 40 and Course's Landing
609/229-1222
COMMENTS: Near the Cowtown Rodeo grounds.

Deptford

Silver Rose Saloon
1102 Route 130
609/845-1010

Manville

Yellow Rose
South Main Street
908/526-4310
DANCE-FLOOR STATS: One 2,600-square-foot floor.
COMMENTS: Get there early because it fills up quickly.

Princeton

Oakley's
4355 U.S. Highway 1
609/452-2044

NEW MEXICO

Albuquerque

Boot Scoots
12000 Candelaria Road NE
505/299-2719
GENRE: New Breed/Independent.
CAPACITY: 1,000.
MUSIC: Disc jockey and bands; format varies nightly.
DANCE LESSONS: Free on Wednesday, Thursday, and Sunday.
DANCE-FLOOR STATS: One 1,000-square-foot floor.
COMMENTS: Formerly the Sundance Saloon.

Cadillac Ranch Nite Club
9800 Montgomery Boulevard NE
505/298-2113

Caravan East
7605 Central Avenue NE
505/265-7877
CAPACITY: 600.
MUSIC: Live bands nightly beginning at 5 P.M.
FOOD: Free buffet during happy hour, 4:30 P.M. to 7 P.M.

Midnight Rodeo
4901 McLeod NE
505/888-0100
GENRE: New Breed/Chain.
COVER CHARGE: Varies.
CAPACITY: 2,050.
MUSIC: Disc jockey.
DANCE-FLOOR STATS: One 5,000-square-foot racetrack floor.
FOOD: Cowboy Cafe.
COMMENTS: Old-time photo shop.

Clayton

Wagon Wheel Nightclub
501 North First Street
505/374-9975

Cliff

Cow Palace
505/535-9141

Flora Vista

Country Palace Nite Club
816 Highway 550 East
505/334-6298

Las Cruces

Cowboys of Las Cruces
2205 South Main Street
505/525-9050
GENRE: Traditional/Independent.
COVER CHARGE: Only on weekends.
DRESS CODE: Clean and casual.
CAPACITY: 574.
YEAR OPENED: Opened in 1986 as RRR Bar, became Cowboys in 1990.
MUSIC: Live music nightly by local, regional, and national acts. Disc jockey on band breaks.
DANCE LESSONS: Free on Tuesday.
DANCE-FLOOR STATS: One raised 1,600-square-foot square hardwood floor.
FOOD: Free hamburger fry on Thursday and Friday.
MINIMUM AGE: 21.
JUKEBOX WITH A COUNTRY SONG: Yes.
COMMENTS: Club plays some rock and roll. Open Monday through Friday 10 A.M. to 1:30 A.M., Saturday 4 P.M. to 1:30 A.M., Sunday 4 P.M. to midnight.

The Desert Sun
1390 North Main Street
505/523-5705
GENRE: Traditional/Independent.
COVER CHARGE: Only on weekends.
CAPACITY: 350.
YEAR OPENED: 1968.
MUSIC: Live music Tuesday through Sunday by local, regional, and national acts.
DANCE LESSONS: Free.
DANCE-FLOOR STATS: One 900-square-foot rectangular hardwood floor.
FOOD: Appetizers and vending-machine snacks.
MINIMUM AGE: 21.
SMOKE-FILTERING SYSTEM: Yes.
JUKEBOX WITH A COUNTRY SONG: Yes, 2 of them.
COMMENTS: Open 7 days a week.

Las Vegas

Byron T's Saloon
230 Old Town Plaza
505/425-3591

Raton

Schwede's Saloon
1466 South Second Street
505/445-9985
GENRE: Traditional/Independent.

Santa Fe

Luna
519 Cerillos
505/489-4888

NEW YORK

Deer Park

Matty T's Nashville USA
356 Commack Road
516/667-6868
GENRE: Traditional/Independent.
CAPACITY: 250.
YEAR OPENED: 1974.
MUSIC: Live.
DANCE LESSONS: Yes.

Henrietta

Rustler's Roost
4853 West Henrietta Road
716/334-0360

Herkimer

Silverado
136 Marginal Road
315/866-8835

Loudonville

Desperados
471 Albany Shaker Road
518/453-2557

Manhattan

Denim & Diamonds
511 Lexington Avenue
212/371-1600
GENRE: New Breed/Chain.
MUSIC: Disc jockey.
COMMENTS: Formerly the Playboy Club. Owned by Graham Gilliam.

New York City

Do-Da's
20 West 20th Street
212/727-8840

Vernon

Nothin' Fancy Country Addition
Ruth Street
315/829-4503

West Seneca

Golden Nugget
2464 Seneca Street
716/825-9013

Williamsville

How-Dee's
8166 Main Street
716/623-5043

NORTH CAROLINA

Asheville

Cowboy's Nightlife
1329 Tunnel Road East
704/298-7182

Burlington

The Palomino
2125 North Church Street
919/227-3848

Charlotte

Carol's Country Jamboree
3819 South Tyron
704/523-5023

Country City U.S.A.
4809 Wilkinson Boulevard
704/393-1149
GENRE: Traditional/Independent.

COVER CHARGE: Varies.
MEMBERSHIP FEE: Yes.
DRESS CODE: Casual.
CAPACITY: 500.
MUSIC: Chrome Elvis house band.
DANCE-FLOOR STATS: One 750-square-foot horseshoe-shaped hardwood floor. Outdoor patio for summer dancing.
COMMENTS: Birthplace of singer Randy Travis's musical career. Closed Monday and Tuesday.

Coyote Joe's
4621 Wilkinson Boulevard
704/399-4946
GENRE: New Breed/Independent.

The Palomino
9607 Albemarle Road
704/568-6104

Fayetteville

Midnight Rodeo
210 Owen Drive
910/323-8877

Gastonia

Frontier
2549 West Franklin Boulevard
704/867-1117

Greensboro

The Palomino
4514 High Point Road
910/547-7002

Santa Fe Rose
3222 High Point Road
910/292-0024

Hickory

Clement Center
2010 Clement Boulevard NW
MUSIC: Band from 8 to 11 P.M. Saturday.
DANCE LESSONS: Free from 7 to 8 P.M.
LIQUOR: Nonalcoholic.
COMMENTS: Club is open the first week of September through the last week of May on Saturdays only. Closed in summer.

New Country Music Bar
1822 Tenth Avenue SW
704/322-2471

Jacksonville

Austin's
701 Marine Boulevard
910/347-6111

Kannapolis

Desperado's
1910 North Main Street
704/933-9909

Raleigh

Longbranch Saloon
608 Creekside Drive
919/829-1125

Wilmington

Country Music U.S.A.
5523 Oleander Drive
910/392-2075

Yellow Rose Saloon & Dance Hall
5025 Market Street
910/791-2001

NORTH DAKOTA

Fargo

Windbreak Saloon
3150 39th Street SW
701/282-5507

OHIO

Cleveland

Silver Spurs
Marriott Hotel
216/252-5333

Columbus

Club Dance
1921 Channingway Center Drive
614/866-5920

InCahoots Dance Hall & Saloon
6252 Busch Boulevard
614/848-5020
GENRE: New Breed/Chain.
CAPACITY: 650.

Cuyahoga Falls

Boot Scoot'n Saloon
4193 State Road
216/929-7123

Dayton

Yellow Rose
111 East Fourth Street
513/461-3241

Geneva

Yucatan
216/992-3737

Independence

Diamond Armadillo
6901 Rockside Road
216/573-7583

Lancaster

Desert Rose
1941 West Fair Avenue
614/653-1968

Portsmouth

White Stallion
924 Gallia Street
614/353-6209

Reynoldsburg

Chaps
6332 East Livingston Avenue
614/860-9992

Rootstown

Bronco's
3116 State Route 14
216/947-1711

Toledo

Country Connection
419/241-1580
GENRE: Traditional/Independent.
MUSIC: Live music Tuesday through Saturday.
COMMENTS: Open 7 days a week.

Country Palace
725 Jefferson Avenue
419/248-9237

Wapokoneta

Cowboy's Country Lounge
Route 33 A
419/738-2383

OKLAHOMA

Ada

Ken Lance Sports Arena and Dance Pavilion
Ken Lance Road (off Route 3, halfway between Ada and Stonewall)
405/265-4423
GENRE: Traditional/Independent.
COVER CHARGE: $5.

CAPACITY: 1,500.
MUSIC: Live music Saturday night by local and regional bands. National acts perform at yearly rodeo.
DANCE-FLOOR STATS: One 5,600-square-foot square hardwood floor (floating).
LIQUOR: Beer and wine coolers only.
FOOD: Snacks.
MINIMUM AGE: 18.
MECHANICAL BULL: Yes.
ROPING PEN: Yes.
COMMENTS: Open only on Saturday night. Sponsors yearly Ada Pro Rodeo. Call ahead to make sure club is open.

Ardmore

P. J. & Company
6 miles south of Ardmore
405/223-9193
GENRE: Traditional/Independent.
COVER CHARGE: Varies nightly.
CAPACITY: 635.
YEAR OPENED: 1992.
MUSIC: Live music by local, regional, and national acts Thursday through Saturday. Disc jockey during band breaks.
DANCE LESSONS: For a fee on Thursday.
SPECIAL CLUB DANCE: P. J. Boogie line dance.
DANCE-FLOOR STATS: One 1,800-square-foot square tile floor.
FOOD: Appetizers only.
MINIMUM AGE: 21.
SMOKE-FILTERING SYSTEM: Yes.
COMMENTS: Open Thursday through Saturday only. Locals swear by this club.

Bartlesville

Boondocks
3104 Minnesota Street
918/336-0123
GENRE: New Breed/Independent.
COVER CHARGE: Varies nightly.
DRESS CODE: Shoes and shirts required.
CAPACITY: 350.
YEAR OPENED: 1993.
MUSIC: Local bands on Friday and Saturday nights, disc jockey all other nights. National acts for special concerts.
SPECIAL CLUB DANCE: Boot-Scootin' Boogie.
DANCE-FLOOR STATS: One 965-square-foot square tile floor.
MINIMUM AGE: 21.
SMOKE-FILTERING SYSTEM: Yes.
COMMENTS: X-rated at times. Club has special events featuring sumo, oil, and mud wrestling and male and female strippers on occasion.

Comanche

County Line Corral
Jefferson-Stephens County Line, Highway 81
405/439-6368

Davis

Arbuckle Ballroom
I-35 and Highway 7
405/369-3870
GENRE: Traditional/Independent.
COVER CHARGE: Yes.
CAPACITY: 999.
YEAR OPENED: 1981.
MUSIC: House band. Disc jockey. National acts.
DANCE LESSONS: Periodically.
DANCE-FLOOR STATS: One 7,500-square-foot rectangular floor with epoxy finish.
LIQUOR: Low-octane beer and wine coolers.
FOOD: Concession stand.
MINIMUM AGE: 18.
SMOKE-FILTERING SYSTEM: Exhaust fans that kick on at various intervals.
COMMENTS: Open on Saturday nights. Occasionally Nashville acts will perform on Friday nights.

Enid

City Boots
800 West Broadway
405/242-3663
CAPACITY: 1,200.
YEAR OPENED: 1991.

Lawton

Brander's
1924 SW Highway 277
405/353-7876
GENRE: Traditional/Independent.
COVER CHARGE: Only on weekends.
CAPACITY: 500.
YEAR OPENED: 1991.
MUSIC: Live music by local, regional, and national acts on Friday and Saturday. Disc jockey on Wednesday and Thursday and during band breaks.
DANCE LESSONS: Free.
DANCE-FLOOR STATS: One 900-square-foot rectangular tile floor.
FOOD: Vending-machine snacks only.
MINIMUM AGE: 21.
SMOKE-FILTERING SYSTEM: Yes.
JUKEBOX WITH A COUNTRY SONG: Yes.
COMMENTS: Open Wednesday through Saturday.

McAlester

Cowboys
Highway 69 Bypass
918/456-5168

Oklahoma City

Chastain's Club
2616 South I-35 Service Road
405/677-1613
GENRE: Traditional/Independent.
COVER CHARGE: Varies.
MUSIC: Local bands.
DANCE-FLOOR STATS: One moderate-size square tile floor.
MINIMUM AGE: 21.
COMMENTS: Singer Toby Keith's old stomping grounds. Dance floor is very slippery.

Chisholm's Club
Radisson Inn
401 South Meridian
405/947-7681
GENRE: New Breed/Independent.
COVER CHARGE: Never.
DRESS CODE: Proper dress required. No bathing suits, etc.
CAPACITY: 160.
YEAR OPENED: 1984.
MUSIC: Disc jockey 7 nights a week.
DANCE LESSONS: Free on Sunday and Tuesday.
DANCE ETIQUETTE: No spurs. Rules are posted.
SPECIAL CLUB DANCE: Southside Shuffle.
DANCE-FLOOR STATS: One 768-square-foot rectangular hardwood floor.
LIQUOR: Law prohibits serving 2 drinks of hard liquor to one person.
FOOD: Free popcorn. Can order room service from hotel.
MINIMUM AGE: 21.
SMOKE-FILTERING SYSTEM: Yes.
COMMENTS: Owned by 5 partners in a hotel franchise. Line dances by request. Favorite hangout of participants for nearly all the national horse shows and rodeos that are held 2 miles away at the fairgrounds. Open 7 days a week.

Cimarron Steak House
201 North Meridian
405/948-7778
GENRE: New Breed/Independent.
DANCE ETIQUETTE: Children must abide by posted rules.
DANCE-FLOOR STATS: One large square hardwood floor.
FOOD: Full-service restaurant. The food is very good, but it takes a long time because most everything is grilled.
MINIMUM AGE: All ages.
FAMILY NIGHTS: Every night.
SMOKE-FILTERING SYSTEM: Yes.
COMMENTS: Sunday is Karaoke Night.

Cowboys Entertainment Center
2300 North MacArthur Boulevard
405/942-6721
MINIMUM AGE: 18.

Diamond Ballroom
8001 Southeastern (off I-240)
405/677-9169
COMMENTS: Family-oriented. Open Thursday through Saturday. Very old.

Graham Country Dancing
3700 West Reno
405/362–0401
GENRE: New Breed/Chain.
CAPACITY: 2,000.
COVER CHARGE: Varies nightly.
YEAR OPENED: 1980.
MUSIC: Disc jockey.
DANCE-FLOOR STATS: One raised 1,870-square-foot rectangular oak floor.
MINIMUM AGE: 21.
SMOKE-FILTERING SYSTEM: Yes.
COMMENTS: Closed on Monday and Tuesday. Owned by Graham Brothers.

InCahoots Dance Hall & Saloon
2301 South Meridian
405/686–1131
GENRE: New Breed/Chain.
COVER CHARGE: Varies nightly.
CAPACITY: 1,500.
YEAR OPENED: 1993.
MUSIC: Disc jockey, national acts at special concerts.
DANCE LESSONS: Free.
DANCE-FLOOR STATS: One large racetrack hardwood floor.
FOOD: Specials at bargain prices on various nights.
MINIMUM AGE: 21.
SMOKE-FILTERING SYSTEM: Yes.
COMMENTS: Not far from Will Rogers Airport.

Midnight Rodeo
2208 NW 19th
405/943–8604
GENRE: New Breed/Chain.
COVER CHARGE: Varies.
MUSIC: Disc jockey.

Rhinestone Cowboy
900 SE 59th
405/634–5545
GENRE: Traditional/Independent.
YEAR OPENED: 1974.

Rodeo's
3705 West Memorial
405/752–8400
COVER CHARGE: Varies nightly.
YEAR OPENED: 1994.
DANCE LESSONS: Sunday from 6 to 8 P.M.
COMMENTS: Open Wednesday through Sunday.

Sugar Baker's
2506 North Harrison
405/275–8611

Seminole

Ropers Country Connection
Highway 99 North
405/382–6906
GENRE: Traditional/Independent.
COVER CHARGE: Varies nightly.
DRESS CODE: Shoes and shirt required.
CAPACITY: 1,300.
YEAR OPENED: Was Circle W in 1970; became Ropers in 1991.
MUSIC: Live music Thursday through Saturday by local, regional, and national acts; DJ all other nights and on band breaks.
DANCE LESSONS: Free Thursday through Saturday.
DANCE-FLOOR STATS: Two rectangular floors; country-western parquet floor is 5,500 square feet; rock-and-roll cement floor is small.
LIQUOR: Not allowed to serve hard liquor on Sunday.
FOOD: Appetizers only.
MINIMUM AGE: 21.
SMOKE-FILTERING SYSTEM: Yes.
COMMENTS: National dance competition held here the last week of every April. Concerts by national acts periodically. Open Wednesday through Sunday.

Stillwater

Tumbleweed Dance Halls & Concert Arena
Lakeview and Country Club Roads
405/377–0076
GENRE: New Breed/Independent.
COVER CHARGE: Varies nightly.
CAPACITY: 1,500 inside; 7,500 outside.
YEAR OPENED: 1981.
MUSIC: Disc jockey. Live music for special concerts by local, regional, and national acts.

DANCE ETIQUETTE: DJ calls dances.
DANCE-FLOOR STATS: Two floating rectangular hardwood floors; main club's is 3,200 square feet; Diamondback's is 1,200 square feet.
FOOD: Vending-machine snacks. Food at special events such as the Annual Calf Fry (every April) and picnics.
MINIMUM AGE: 18 to enter; 21 to consume beer or mixed drinks.
FAMILY NIGHTS: Children allowed only on concert dates.
MECHANICAL BULL: Occasionally.
COMMENTS: This is Garth Brooks's old stomping ground. He sang in the house band and worked as a bouncer here. Open Wednesday through Saturday. Picnic and concert every July. Anniversary party every September. Periodic indoor and outdoor concerts by national recording artists.

Tecumseh

Cowtown, U.S.A.
Highway 177 and Benson Park Road
405/275-0108
GENRE: Traditional/Independent.
COVER CHARGE: Varies. Price includes snacks.
CAPACITY: 800.
YEAR OPENED: 1979.
MUSIC: Live music Thursday through Saturday.
DANCE-FLOOR STATS: One large square hardwood floor.
FOOD: Snacks available at bar.
MECHANICAL BULL: Yes.
COMMENTS: Sports bar adjacent to country-western club has occasional exotic dance acts for both men and women.

Tulsa

Cain's Ballroom
423 North Main Street
918/584-2306
GENRE: Traditional/Independent.
COVER CHARGE: Varies nightly.
CAPACITY: 1,210.
YEAR OPENED: 1924.
MUSIC: Live music by national acts only for special concerts.
DANCE-FLOOR STATS: One springboard 8,000-square-foot rectangular curly maple floor.
LIQUOR: Low-octane beer and wine coolers.
MINIMUM AGE: All ages.
FAMILY NIGHTS: All nights.
COMMENTS: Cain's is a national landmark. Formerly owned by Bob Wills, it was home to Bob Wills and the Texas Playboys from 1934 to 1958. The club is open only on Friday and Saturday September through June. It is closed June 24th through the end of August because there is no air-conditioning. Facilities are rented out to various groups for dances or special concerts. All genres of music are now played here–not just country. Waltzing is the dance of choice when there are dances.

Caravan Cattle Club
7901 East 41st Street
918/663-5632
CAPACITY: 1,200.
COMMENTS: Place for kids of all ages. Open only on Friday and Saturday nights.

Chisholm's
Ramada Hotel
5000 East Skelly Drive
918/622-7000

Hall of Fame
19011 East Admiral Place
918/266-3049
GENRE: Traditional/Independent.
COVER CHARGE: Only on weekends.
DRESS CODE: Shirts and shoes required.
CAPACITY: 400.
YEAR OPENED: 1968.
MUSIC: Live music Thursday through Saturday by local and regional bands. Disc jockey on band breaks and all other nights.
DANCE LESSONS: Free.
DANCE-FLOOR STATS: One 1,500-square-foot rectangular parquet floor.
FOOD: Snacks available.

MINIMUM AGE: 21.
SMOKE-FILTERING SYSTEM: Yes.
JUKEBOX WITH A COUNTRY SONG: Yes.
COMMENTS: Popular with the truckers. This is a real family operation. Ray and Lynda Adams own and operate it; Lynda and son tend bar; Lynda's mother handles the door; Lynda's sister washes dishes; Lynda's nephew is the disc jockey. Open 7 days a week.

Lonesome Dove
11907 North Garnett Street
918/371-9107

Midnight Rodeo
9379 East 46th Street
918/664-0325
GENRE: New Breed/Chain.
COVER CHARGE: Varies.
MUSIC: Disc jockey.

Tulsa City Limits
2117 South Garnett
918/438-7411

Yukon

Ernie's Country Palace
Southwest of Oklahoma City
405/354-9327

OREGON

Aloha

Chaps & Spurs Restaurant and Lounge
18641 SW Tualatin Valley Highway
503/649-1006
GENRE: New Breed/Independent.
COVER CHARGE: Only on weekends.
CAPACITY: 275.
YEAR OPENED: 1993.
MUSIC: Vocalist who sings to soundtracks.
DANCE LESSONS: Free.
DANCE ETIQUETTE: Rules are announced by dance instructors.
DANCE-FLOOR STATS: Two 620-square-foot rectangular parquet floors.
FOOD: Full-service restaurant.
MINIMUM AGE: 21.
SMOKE-FILTERING SYSTEM: Yes.
COMMENTS: Open 7 nights a week.

Beaverton

BeBop U.S.A.
Beaverton Towne Square
11573 SW Beaverton Hillsdale Highway
503/644-4433

Central Point

Triple Tree Restaurant
4999 Highway 234
503/830-8992

Eugene

Cadillac Ranch
1045 Willamette
503/485-2893

Rock 'N' Rodeo
44 East Seventh Avenue
503/683-5160
GENRE: New Breed/Chain.
COVER CHARGE: Varies.
MUSIC: Disc jockey.

Gresham

The Roadhouse
2370 East Burnside Avenue
503/666-2624

Hillsboro

Old Hich'en Post The Lounge
10565 SW Glencoe Road
503/647-5080
MUSIC: Live music only on weekends.

Medford

Rock 'N' Rodeo
Holiday Inn
2300 Crater Lake Highway
503/779-3141
GENRE: New Breed/Chain.
COVER CHARGE: Only on weekends.

DRESS CODE: No ripped or torn clothes.
CAPACITY: 550.
YEAR OPENED: 1992.
MUSIC: Disc jockey.
DANCE LESSONS: $1 per person Monday through Saturday.
DANCE ETIQUETTE: Rules are posted and DJ calls dances.
DANCE-FLOOR STATS: Two square parquet floors–875 square feet on the lower level; 100 square feet on the upper level.
FOOD: Coyote Grill and Steakhouse.
MINIMUM AGE: 21.
FAMILY NIGHTS: Sunday is Family Day from 2 to 6 P.M.
SMOKE-FILTERING SYSTEM: Yes.
COMMENTS: Open 7 nights a week. Various promotions that "change with the weather."

Shenandoah Restaurant & Lounge
4635 Crater Lake Highway
503/779–6281

Milwaukie

Oasis Country Night Club
12300 SE Mallard Way
503/654–8126

Pendleton

Happy Canyon Dance Hall
800/524–2984
COMMENTS: Only open during the Pendleton Round-Up in mid-September. Call for more information and directions.

Let 'er Buck Room
800/524–2984
COMMENTS: Only open during the Pendleton Round-Up in mid-September. Call for more information and directions.

Portland

C. C. Slaughter's Restaurant & Lounge
1014 SW Stark
503/248–9135
GENRE: Gay/Independent.
COMMENTS: Home of "The Rose City Ramblers" gay men's country dance club.

The Drum
14601 SE Division Street
503/760–1400
GENRE: Traditional/Independent.
COVER CHARGE: Only on weekends.
DRESS CODE: Shoes and shirts required. No offensive or vulgar clothing allowed.
CAPACITY: 600.
YEAR OPENED: 1963.
MUSIC: Live music 7 nights a week by local bands. Concerts by national acts.
DANCE LESSONS: For a fee Sunday through Thursday.
DANCE ETIQUETTE: Rules are posted.
SPECIAL CLUB DANCE: Dee's Around and Sweet Pea.
DANCE-FLOOR STATS: One raised springboard 990-square-foot square hardwood floor.
FOOD: Full-service Mexican restaurant adjacent to club.
MINIMUM AGE: 21.
SMOKE-FILTERING SYSTEM: Yes.
SPECIALTY BEVERAGE(S): Local microbrews.
COMMENTS: Home of the "B-52," a 52-ounce burrito that serves 16 people. Club also offers dance workshops, private dance lessons, pool leagues and tournaments, parties, and wedding receptions.

Jubitz Truck Stop
10310 North Vancouver Way
503/283–1111
GENRE: Traditional/Independent.

Red Steer
2514 North Marine Drive
503/289–8725
GENRE: New Breed/Independent.
COVER CHARGE: Never. Special events by outside groups may charge.
CAPACITY: 299.
YEAR OPENED: 1909.
MUSIC: Live music on Tuesday for ballroom dancing from 7 to 11 P.M. Disc jockey Friday and Saturday for country dancing. Special events always on Sunday.
DANCE LESSONS: Teachers charge $2.50 per person on Monday, Wednesday, and Thursday.

DANCE ETIQUETTE: Rules are posted and DJ calls dances.
DANCE-FLOOR STATS: One raised 1,000-square-foot rectangular hardwood floor.
FOOD: Full-service restaurant.
MINIMUM AGE: 21 in bar.
FAMILY NIGHTS: Any age allowed in restaurant.
SMOKE-FILTERING SYSTEM: Yes.
COMMENTS: Closed only on Christmas and New Year's Day. Open all other nights from 6 A.M. until closing. Club is available on Sunday for those who want to practice their dance steps; has more than 900 CDs in its music library and more than 900 country music videos.

Rock 'N' Rodeo
220 SE Spokane
503/235-2417
GENRE: New Breed/Chain.
COVER CHARGE: Varies.
MUSIC: Disc jockey 7 nights a week.
DANCE-FLOOR STATS: One 2,200-square-foot floor.
FOOD: Full-service restaurant.
FAMILY NIGHTS: Sunday is Teen and Family Day from 2 to 6 P.M.
COMMENTS: Open from 4 P.M. to 2 A.M. Thirty-foot ceiling reduces smog level. Eighteen speakers and 13 big-screen TVs.

Salem

Neon Cactus
503/371-6339
COMMENTS: Formerly the Spinning Wheel.

Troutdale

Mr. B's Lounge/Burns Brothers Truck Stop
790 NW Frontage Road
503/661-0575
GENRE: Traditional/Chain.
COVER CHARGE: Never.
DRESS CODE: No thongs, bare chests, or bare feet.
CAPACITY: 301.
YEAR OPENED: 1988.
MUSIC: Live music nightly by local and regional bands.
DANCE LESSONS: Tuesday through Friday for $1 token.
DANCE ETIQUETTE: Rules are posted.
DANCE-FLOOR STATS: One 1,200-square-foot square hardwood floor with adjoining floor.
FOOD: Full-service restaurant.
MINIMUM AGE: Must be 21 unless performing in the band.
SMOKE-FILTERING SYSTEM: Yes.
JUKEBOX WITH A COUNTRY SONG: Yes.
COMMENTS: Open 7 nights a week. Home of the Country Fun Dancers. Club sponsors a "Dancers Nite Out" every Wednesday, a "Mystery Trip," and a "New Year's in August" party. Band starts at 8 P.M. Western wear store next door. Lounge is part of a truck-stop chain.

Yamhill

Flying "M"
23029 Flying "M" Road
503/662-3222
GENRE: Traditional/Independent.
MUSIC: Live music Friday and Saturday nights and Sunday afternoons.
COMMENTS: This is up in the mountains and hard to find, so call ahead for directions and accommodations.

PENNSYLVANIA

Grantville

Winner's Circle Saloon
Holiday Inn
717/469-0661

Philadelphia

Bronko Bill's
Grant Avenue and Bluegrass Road
215/677-8700

KP Corral
160 North Gulph Road
215/265–7226

Tin Angel
20 South Second Street
215/928–0978

Pittsburgh

Nashville North
7824 Saltsburg Road
412/795–8000

Rodeo Dance Hall & Saloon
1165 McKinney Lane
412/921–5695

Stetson's
1226 Herron Avenue
412/363–2670

Plains

Western Corral
Foxhill Road
717/823–7202

RHODE ISLAND

Providence

Desperado's
180 Pine Street
401/751–4263

SOUTH CAROLINA

Charleston

Lazy-B
6401 Dorchester Road
803/552–3599

Greenville

Cowboys Nightlife
1117 Cedar Lane Road
803/294–7041

The Palomino
COMMENTS: Opening in 1995.

Lancaster

Country Countdown
Route 6
803/286–8028

SOUTH DAKOTA

Sioux Falls

Borrowed Bucks
3609 South Western Avenue
605/331–2448
GENRE: New Breed.
MUSIC: Disc jockey.

Grain Bin
5013 North Cliff Avenue
605/339–1264
GENRE: Traditional/Independent.
MUSIC: Local and regional bands.

TENNESSEE

Chattanooga

Denim & Diamonds
5600 Brainerd Road
Eastgate Mall
615/899–8337
GENRE: New Breed/Chain.
COVER CHARGE: Varies.
MUSIC: Disc jockey nightly.
DANCE-FLOOR STATS: One raised 3,000-square-foot horseshoe-shaped hardwood floor.
MINIMUM AGE: 21.
SMOKE-FILTERING SYSTEM: Yes.
COMMENTS: Closed Monday and Tuesday. Owned by Graham Brothers.

Governor's Lounge
4251 Bonny Oaks Drive
615/624–2239

Shirley's Country
8133 East Brainerd Road
615/855-1368

Wrangler's Live Country
3617 Brainerd Road
615/698-5982

Concord

Cotton-Eyed Joe's
11220 Outlet Drive
615/675-4563

Knoxville

Wild Horse Saloon
7355 Kingston Pike
615/588-6459

Madison

Denim & Diamonds
Madison Square Shopping Center
950 Gallatin Pike
615/868-1459
GENRE: New Breed/Chain.
COVER CHARGE: Varies.
MUSIC: Disc jockey nightly.
MINIMUM AGE: 21.
SMOKE-FILTERING SYSTEM: Yes.
COMMENTS: Owned by Graham Brothers.

Memphis

Denim & Diamonds
5353 Mendenhall Mall
901/365-3633
GENRE: New Breed/Chain.
CAPACITY: 2,200.
COVER CHARGE: Varies.
MUSIC: Disc jockey nightly.
DANCE-FLOOR STATS: One raised 3,000-square-foot horseshoe-shaped hardwood floor.
MINIMUM AGE: 21.
SMOKE-FILTERING SYSTEM: Yes.
COMMENTS: Closed on Monday. Owned by Graham Brothers.

Desperado's
2080 Brooks Road East
901/345-0563

Midnight Rodeo
4069 Lamair
901/794-9111
GENRE: New Breed/Chain.
COVER CHARGE: Varies.
MUSIC: Disc jockey nightly.

Spurs
3588 Ridgeway
901/360-1222

Murfreesboro

City Limits
2146 Thompson Lane
615/893-3999

Nashville

Broken Spoke
1412 Brick Church Pike
615/226-3230

Bull Pen Lounge
Stockyard Restaurant
901 Second Avenue North
615/255-6464
GENRE: Traditional/Independent.
CAPACITY: 500.
MUSIC: Live music.
DANCE LESSONS: Yes.
DANCE-FLOOR STATS: One zigzagged hardwood floor.
FOOD: Full-service restaurant.
MINIMUM AGE: 21.

Nashville Palace
2400 Music Valley Drive
615/885-1540
GENRE: Traditional/Independent.
COVER CHARGE: Varies.
CAPACITY: 300.
MUSIC: Live music nightly.
MINIMUM AGE: 21.
CAPACITY: 300.

Rodeo's
1031 Murfreesboro Road
615/399-2666
GENRE: New Breed.
MUSIC: Disc jockey nightly.

Rose Room
579 Stewart's Ferry Pike
615/889-8631
GENRE: Traditional/Independent.
COVER CHARGE: Varies.
MUSIC: Live music.
DANCE-FLOOR STATS: One medium-sized tile square floor.
MINIMUM AGE: 21.
COMMENTS: Sunday night is jam night for musicians.

South Fork Saloon
2275 Murfreesboro Road
615/361-9777

Wildhorse Saloon
120 Second Avenue North
615/251-1000
GENRE: New Breed/Independent.
CAPACITY: 1,500.
YEAR OPENED: 1994.
COMMENTS: TNN's *Wildhorse Saloon* is filmed here.

Wrangler
1204 Murfreesboro Pike
615/361-4440
GENRE: New Breed/Independent.
COVER CHARGE: Varies.
MUSIC: Disc jockey alternates country and rock music every half hour.
SPECIAL CLUB DANCE: Tennessee Schottische.
DANCE-FLOOR STATS: One medium-sized hardwood racetrack floor with trees in the middle.

TEXAS

Abilene

Cactus Moon
1850 South Clack
915/695-0781
GENRE: New Breed/Chain.
COVER CHARGE: Varies.
CAPACITY: 781.
MUSIC: Disc jockey. National acts for special concerts.
DANCE-FLOOR STATS: One raised 1,816-square-foot racetrack-style hardwood floor.
MINIMUM AGE: 21.
SMOKE-FILTERING SYSTEM: Yes.
COMMENTS: Closed on Monday. Owned by Graham Brothers.

The Corral
2895 East Highway 80
915/677-0645

Cutter's Club
4125 South Danville Drive
915/698-2902
GENRE: New Breed/Chain.
COVER CHARGE: Varies nightly.
CAPACITY: 320.
YEAR OPENED: 1993.
MUSIC: Disc jockey Monday through Friday. Live music on Saturday night only. Special concerts by national acts.
DANCE-FLOOR STATS: One 680-square-foot octagonal hardwood floor.
FOOD: Snack bar on premises.
MINIMUM AGE: 19.
FAMILY NIGHTS: Children under 12 allowed with parent but must leave at 7 P.M.
SMOKE-FILTERING SYSTEM: Yes.
COMMENTS: Closed on Sundays.

Ponderosa Ballroom
3881 Vine Street
915/698-2102
GENRE: Traditional/Independent.
COVER CHARGE: Varies nightly.

DRESS CODE: No tank tops or muscle shirts.
CAPACITY: 665.
YEAR OPENED: 1975.
MUSIC: Local bands, disc jockey, and national acts.
DANCE-FLOOR STATS: One square 2,500-square-foot smooth-finish concrete floor.
FOOD: Appetizers and vending-machine snacks.
MINIMUM AGE: 18.
SMOKE-FILTERING SYSTEM: Yes.
COMMENTS: Open 7 nights a week; drink specials 7 to 9 P.M. Monday through Thursday.

Alvin

Dark Horse Dance Hall & Saloon
17009 County Road 143
713/331-0179

R & I Country Saloon
4448 Highway 35
713/585-9903

Texas Rose Dance Hall
801 Wheeler
713/331-9193

Amarillo

Cadillac Ranch
2523 Britain Drive
806/359-6111

Caravan
3601 Olson Boulevard
806/359-5436
GENRE: Traditional/Independent.
COVER CHARGE: Varies nightly.
YEAR OPENED: 1975.
MUSIC: Local and regional touring bands nightly.
DANCE-FLOOR STATS: One large rectangular hardwood floor.
MINIMUM AGE: 21.
COMMENTS: This place looks more like a bank than a honky-tonk, but you'll have a boot-scooting good time, especially if you're lucky enough to get Bobby Burrell for a partner.

Midnight Rodeo
4400 South Georgia
806/358-7083
GENRE: New Breed/Chain.
COVER CHARGE: Varies.
MUSIC: Disc jockey.

Arlington

Cowboys
2540 East Abrams Street
817/265-1535
GENRE: New Breed/Chain.
COVER CHARGE: Varies nightly.
CAPACITY: 4,000.
YEAR OPENED: 1994.
MUSIC: Disc jockey, house band.
DANCE LESSONS: Free.
DANCE-FLOOR STATS: One raised 3,500-square-foot rectangular hardwood floor.
FOOD: Vending-machine snacks only.
MINIMUM AGE: 21.
SMOKE-FILTERING SYSTEM: Yes.
COMMENTS: Open Wednesday through Sunday.

Cutter's Live
1621 East Lamar Boulevard
817/469-6070
GENRE: New Breed/Chain.
COVER CHARGE: Varies.
COMMENTS: Caters to a younger crowd.

Denim & Diamonds
2188 South Cooper
817/261-4409
GENRE: New Breed/Chain.
CAPACITY: 1,017.
COVER CHARGE: Varies nightly.
MUSIC: Disc jockey.
DANCE-FLOOR STATS: One raised 4,000-square-foot racetrack hardwood floor.
MINIMUM AGE: 21.
SMOKE-FILTERING SYSTEM: Yes.
COMMENTS: Closed on Monday. Owned by Graham Brothers.

Neon Moon
309 North Great Southwest Parkway
817/633-5771

Austin

81 Club
8402 South Congress Avenue
512/282-9133

Broken Spoke
3201 South Lamar Boulevard
512/442-6189
GENRE: Traditional/Independent.
COVER CHARGE: Varies nightly.
DRESS CODE: Shirts and shoes required; nothing too revealing.
CAPACITY: 661.
YEAR OPENED: 1964.
MUSIC: Mostly Austin bands Tuesday through Saturday. Special concerts by national acts.
DANCE LESSONS: When requested.
DANCE ETIQUETTE: Rules are posted.
DANCE-FLOOR STATS: One sunken rectangular 1,400-square-foot smooth-finish concrete floor.
FOOD: Full-service restaurant noted for its chicken-fried steak.
MINIMUM AGE: All ages welcome.
FAMILY NIGHTS: Every night. Austin curfew law states no one under 18 allowed after 12:30 A.M.
JUKEBOX WITH A COUNTRY SONG: Yes.
COMMENTS: The Spoke was rated best honky-tonk in Texas by *Texas Highways* magazine and is one of *National Geographic's* favorite nightspots. Many movies and videos have been filmed here. Country greats such as Bob Wills, Ernest Tubb, Willie Nelson, and Roy Acuff have performed here. Closed Sunday and Monday.

City Slickers
7601 North Lamar, Suite A
512/453-6616

Continental Club
1315 South Congress Avenue
512/441-2444
GENRE: Traditional/Independent.
COVER CHARGE: Varies nightly.
DRESS CODE: Shoes and shirts required.
CAPACITY: 200.
YEAR OPENED: 1957.
MUSIC: Live music nightly by local, regional, and national acts.
DANCE-FLOOR STATS: One 500-square-foot rectangular tile floor.
LIQUOR: High octane. Liquor and beer served until 2 A.M. Monday through Sunday.
MINIMUM AGE: 21.
SMOKE-FILTERING SYSTEM: Yes.
JUKEBOX WITH A COUNTRY SONG: Yes.
COMMENTS: Open 7 days a week.

Country Music Showplace
11940 Manchaca Road
512/282-9804
GENRE: Traditional/Independent.
COVER CHARGE: Currently only on Teen Night; subject to change.
YEAR OPENED: Circa 1984.
MUSIC: Live music on Wednesday, Friday, and Saturday. Disc jockey on Tejano Night and jukebox all other nights.
DANCE-FLOOR STATS: One 2,000-square-foot semicircular tile and cement floor.
LIQUOR: Beer and wine and setups. Bring your own bottle.
MINIMUM AGE: 21 on weekends.
FAMILY NIGHT: Wednesday night teens are allowed in from 8 P.M. to 12 A.M.
JUKEBOX WITH A COUNTRY SONG: Yes.
COMMENTS: Open 4 P.M. to 2 A.M., 365 days a year. Club also has darts and shuffleboard.

Country Palace
16511 Bratton Lane
512/255-9622

Dallas Night Club
7113 Burnet Road
512/452-2801

Dance Across Texas
2201 East Ben White Boulevard
512/441-9101

Dessau Hall
13422 Dessau Road
512/251-4421

Donn's Depot
1600 West Fifth Street
512/478-0336

GENRE: Traditional/Independent.
COVER CHARGE: Only on weekends.
DRESS CODE: No shirts, no shoes, no service. Anything from casual to formal attire.
CAPACITY: 200.
YEAR OPENED: 1972.
MUSIC: Local bands Monday through Saturday.
DANCE-FLOOR STATS: Two square parquet floors, one 1,396 square feet and the other 140 square feet.
FOOD: Appetizers during happy hour.
MINIMUM AGE: 21.
SMOKE-FILTERING SYSTEM: Yes.
JUKEBOX WITH A COUNTRY SONG: Yes.
COMMENTS: Closed on Sunday.

Drugstore Cowboy
11800 North Lamar Boulevard
512/834–1858

Lumberyard Nightclub
16511 Bratton Lane
512/255–9622
GENRE: Traditional/Independent.
COVER CHARGE: Varies nightly.
DRESS CODE: No muscle shirts, sandals, or T-shirts with lewd, rude, or crude slogans.
CAPACITY: 1,080.
YEAR OPENED: 1984.
MUSIC: Live music by local, regional, and national acts. Disc jockey on breaks.
DANCE LESSONS: Free.
DANCE-FLOOR STATS: One 1,512-square-foot rectangular parquet floor.
FOOD: Appetizers only.
MINIMUM AGE: 18.
FAMILY NIGHTS: Children allowed only at private functions.
SMOKE-FILTERING SYSTEM: Yes.
COMMENTS: Club's claim to fame is bringing national recording artists in an intimate setting at an affordable price. Many of these artists, which include Tim McGraw, Garth Brooks, and Alan Jackson, are represented on the "Wall of Fame." Free pool on Tuesday nights. Wednesday night is "Young Guns Band Showcase," featuring up-and-coming bands from the Austin area. Thursday night, the oldest running nickel-beer night in the city, caters to the college crowd. Cajun Fest Friday mixes country, cajun, and zydeco music and features blackened catfish cooked on an outdoor grill. Closed on Sunday and Monday nights.

New West
7934 Great Northern Boulevard
512/467–6134

Peggy's Two-Stepper
1115½ Bastrop Highway
512/385–6042

Post Oak Ranch
1101 Reinly Street
512/467–2624
GENRE: Traditional/Chain.
COVER CHARGE: Varies.
YEAR OPENED: 1994.
MUSIC: Local and regional bands nightly.
DANCE-FLOOR STATS: One large square hardwood floor.
FOOD: Buffet.
MINIMUM AGE: 21.
SMOKE-FILTERING SYSTEM: Yes.
COMMENTS: This is a slick fern bar of a honky-tonk with its share of West Coast swingers, but the dance-floor surface and music are first-rate.

Scoot Inn
1308 East Fourth Street
512/472–0023

South Forty
29 West Ben White Boulevard
512/444–9329

Texas Bar & Grill
14611 Burnet Road
512/255–1300

Threadgill's
6416 North Lamar Boulevard
512/451–5440
COMMENTS: This is a Pickers club. No dancing.

Y'all Come Back Saloon
10542 Manchaca Road
512/282–2931

Bandera

Arkey Blue's Silver Dollar Night Club
308 Main Street
210/796-8826
GENRE: Traditional/Independent.
COVER CHARGE: Only on Wednesday and weekends.
CAPACITY: 150.
YEAR OPENED: 1968.
MUSIC: Live music by local and house bands. Arkey Blue and the Blue Cowboys perform on Saturday.
DANCE-FLOOR STATS: One rectangular 2,400-square-foot concrete floor, sawdust, and all.
LIQUOR: Beer, wine coolers, and setups, BYOB.
MINIMUM AGE: 21, unless accompanied by parent or legal guardian.
FAMILY NIGHTS: Families welcome every night.
JUKEBOX WITH A COUNTRY SONG: Yes.
COMMENTS: Don't miss this place. Arkey is a Texas institution. Open 7 nights a week.

Bella Union Dance Hall and Saloon
210/796-4046

Cabaret Dance Hall
801 Main Street
210/460-3095

Baytown

Silverado Dance Hall
700 Interstate 10 East
409/421-1588

Beaumont

Cutter's
4120 College
409/842-3840
GENRE: Traditional/Chain.
COMMENTS: Mark Chesnutt and Clint Black cut their honky-tonk teeth here.

Beeville

City Limits
301 FM 351 South
512/358-9447

Brenham

Silver Wings Ballroom
Route 7
409/836-4836

Bryan

The Cowboy
2820 Finfeather Road
409/775-0494
GENRE: New Breed/Independent.
COVER CHARGE: Never.
DRESS CODE: No T-shirts or tank tops; shirts must have collars. No motorcycle apparel. Must be clean and neat.
CAPACITY: 200.
YEAR OPENED: 1979.
MUSIC: Disc jockey nightly.
DANCE-FLOOR STATS: One raised 600-square-foot rectangular hardwood floor.
MINIMUM AGE: 21.
SMOKE-FILTERING SYSTEM: Yes.
COMMENTS: Club claims it has the best boot-shiner around, Bobby Graham. Open Monday through Saturday.

Denim & Diamonds
1600-B South College Avenue
409/823-2726
GENRE: New Breed/Chain.
COVER CHARGE: Varies.
CAPACITY: 1,800.
MUSIC: Disc jockey.
DANCE-FLOOR STATS: One raised 2,800-square-foot rectangular oak floor.
MINIMUM AGE: 21.
SMOKE-FILTERING SYSTEM: Yes.
COMMENTS: Closed on Monday. Owned by the Graham Brothers.

Texas Hall of Fame
409/822-2222

Third Floor Cantina
201-B West 26th Street
409/822-3743

Cleburne

Red Horse Tavern
3121 North Main
817/556-9922

Colleyville

Nine Acres Entertainment Complex
811 McDonwell School
817/498-1465

Conroe

League Line Ballroom
4201 North Frazier
409/856-2962

Corpus Christi

Midnight Rodeo
24 Parkdale Plaza
512/857-8088
GENRE: New Breed/Chain.
MUSIC: Disc jockey.

Stetson's
5831 Webber Street
512/855-4886

Crosby

Betty's Hard Times
3615 FM 1492
713/421-7180

Cypress

Tin Hall
14800 Huffmeister Road
713/373-4555
GENRE: Traditional/Independent.
COVER CHARGE: Only on weekends.
DRESS CODE: Shirts must have collars. No baseball caps or shorts.
CAPACITY: 1,200.
YEAR OPENED: 1890.
MUSIC: Live music by local, regional, and national acts on Friday and Saturday. Disc jockey on band breaks.
DANCE-FLOOR STATS: Two square floors made of Tennessee Red Oak. Upstairs, 4,300 square feet; downstairs, 300-square-foot practice floor.
MINIMUM AGE: 21.
FAMILY NIGHTS: Children allowed on specified Family Days and for some concerts and special events.
SMOKE-FILTERING SYSTEM: Yes.
COMMENTS: Second-oldest operating dance hall in Texas. Open only on Friday and Saturday. It is located on 40 acres and has two fenced areas for outdoor events. Trail rides, outdoor cook-offs, shrimp boils, charity benefits, concerts, banquets, Family Days, weddings, and receptions are some of the many functions sponsored by Tin Hall. There is also a hat shaping and cleaning service.

Dallas

Adair's Saloon
2624 Commerce
214/939-9900
GENRE: Traditional/Independent.
COVER CHARGE: Never.
DRESS CODE: Clothes must be clean.
CAPACITY: 244.
YEAR OPENED: 1963.
MUSIC: Live music by local bands Tuesday through Thursday.
DANCE ETIQUETTE: "You daince with the one who brung you or no damn daincing!"
DANCE-FLOOR STATS: Building is 2,000 square feet and floor is concrete. You can dance anywhere you want except on the tables.
FOOD: Dirt-cheap half-pound burgers, the only thing on the menu.
MINIMUM AGE: 21.
JUKEBOX WITH A COUNTRY SONG: Best in the state!
COMMENTS: Adair's has been featured in many regional publications. Its jukebox is legendary, one that all others should emulate; selections include "Cold, Cold Heart" and "Walking the Floor Over You." Closed on Sunday.

Bandera
10815 Ferguson Road
214/279-3774

Big "D" Jamboree
216 Corinth Street
214/428-3128

Billy's
441 Bruton Terrace Shopping Center
214/381-9261

Chances
9840 North Central Expressway, No. 340
214/696-0110

Charlie's III Club
2900 Walnut Hill
214/358-3164

Collateral Club
11407 Emerald
214/241-1969

Country Connection
2052 West Northwest Highway
214/869-9923

Country Roks
2051 West Northwest Highway
214/869-9922

Cowboys
7331 Gaston Avenue
214/321-0115
GENRE: New Breed/Chain.
COVER CHARGE: Varies nightly.
CAPACITY: 3,000.
YEAR OPENED: 1989.
MUSIC: Live music nightly. House band, disc jockey, national acts.
DANCE LESSONS: Free.
SPECIAL CLUB DANCE: LeDoux Shuffle.
DANCE-FLOOR STATS: One sunken 3,500-square-foot rectangular hardwood floor.
LIQUOR: Cannot serve liquor until after noon on Sunday.
FOOD: Vending-machine snacks.
MINIMUM AGE: 21.
SMOKE-FILTERING SYSTEM: Yes.
COMMENTS: Closed on Monday and Tuesday. DJ plays rock and rap during band breaks.

Crystal Chandelier
9400 North Central, Suite 1212
214/223-5881

Cutter's Western Club
4107 West Camp Wisdom Road
214/709-9080
GENRE: New Breed/Chain.

Dallas Alley
603 Munger
214/988-0581
GENRE: New Breed/Chain.
COVER CHARGE: Varies.
COMMENTS: Owned by Graham Brothers.

Dallas Cheers
10569 Denton Drive
214/350-9748

Debonair Danceland
2810 Samuell Boulevard
214/826-5890
DANCE LESSONS: Free on Tuesday.

Denim & Diamonds
8872 North Central Expressway
214/265-8295
GENRE: New Breed/Chain.
COVER CHARGE: Varies nightly.
DRESS CODE: No tank tops or work uniforms.
CAPACITY: 1,000.
YEAR OPENED: 1993.
MUSIC: Disc jockey. Regional and national bands for special concerts only.
DANCE-FLOOR STATS: One raised L-shaped hardwood floor.
FOOD: Buffet on Friday nights.
MINIMUM AGE: 21.
SMOKE-FILTERING SYSTEM: Yes
COMMENTS: Closed 2 days a week. Owned by Graham Brothers.

Let's Dance Country
6522 "B" East Northeast Highway
214/368-5675

Roadhouse Saloon
2019 North Lamar, Suite 200
214/720-0170

Stampede
5818 LBJ Freeway
214/701-8081
GENRE: New Breed.
CAPACITY: 1,200.
MUSIC: Disc jockey.
DANCE LESSONS: For a fee on Sunday; free on Monday and Tuesday.
COMMENTS: Free dance contests every Sunday and Monday.

Texas Star
10260 Ferguson Road
214/327-9944

Top Rail Ballroom
2110 West Northwest Highway
214/556-9099
GENRE: Traditional/Independent.
COVER CHARGE: Varies nightly.
DRESS CODE: No caps, T-shirts, cutoffs; must have clean, neat appearance. Dress code applies every day but Sunday, which is come-as-you-are day.
CAPACITY: 500.
YEAR OPENED: 1932.
MUSIC: Live music nightly by local, regional, and national acts. Disc jockey on band breaks.
DANCE LESSONS: Both free and for a fee.
DANCE ETIQUETTE: Rules are posted.
DANCE-FLOOR STATS: One 1,700-square-foot round parquet floor.
FOOD: Free buffet Tuesday through Friday, 4 to 7 P.M.
MINIMUM AGE: 21.
SMOKE-FILTERING SYSTEM: Yes.
COMMENTS: Primarily a dance hall. Dirt-cheap prices. Wednesday is dance clubs practice night.

Wild West Club
6532 East Northwest Highway
214/361-6083
GENRE: New Breed/Chain.
COVER CHARGE: Varies.
MUSIC: Disc jockey.

Dennison

Calhoun's
4801 Highway 75 South
903/463-3561

Outlaws
2300 West Morton
903/465-4440

The Junction
7311 Highway 691 West
214/463-7522

Denton

Benchmark
200 West Congress
817/382-9700

Eldorado

Cactus Cafe
318 SW Main
915/853-2809

El Paso

Cheers
6901 Montana
915/778-6752
GENRE: New Breed/Chain.
COVER CHARGE: Varies.
DANCE-FLOOR STATS: One 300-square-foot rectangular dance floor.
MINIMUM AGE: 21.
SMOKE-FILTERING SYSTEM: Yes.
COMMENTS: Owned by Graham Brothers.

Denim & Diamonds
9505 Viscount
915/595-3334
GENRE: New Breed/Chain.
COVER CHARGE: Varies.
MUSIC: Disc jockey.
DANCE-FLOOR STATS: One 1,728-square-foot horseshoe-shaped hardwood floor.
MINIMUM AGE: 21.
SMOKE-FILTERING SYSTEM: Yes.
COMMENTS: Owned by Graham Brothers.

Rodeo Nite Club
6930 Alameda Avenue
915/778-2266

San Antonio Mining Co.
800 East San Antonio Avenue
915/533-9516

Flower Mound

Circle R Ranch
5901 Cross Timber Road
817/430-1561

Fort Worth

Billy Bob's Texas
2520 Rodeo Plaza at the Stockyards
817/624-7117
GENRE: New Breed/Independent.
COVER CHARGE: Varies nightly.
DRESS CODE: Almost anything goes.
CAPACITY: 6,000.
YEAR OPENED: 1981.
MUSIC: Disc jockey, local bands, regional touring, national acts, house band. Live music 7 nights a week.
DANCE LESSONS: Free on Thursdays. For a fee on Saturdays and Sundays.
DANCE-FLOOR STATS: One 2,000-square-foot rectangular parquet floor and one 4,000-square-foot square hardwood floor.
FOOD: Full-service restaurant. Snacks available in gift shop.
MINIMUM AGE: Anyone under 17 can enter with a parent. Must be 21 to drink.
FAMILY NIGHTS: Every day is Family Day.
SMOKE-FILTERING SYSTEM: Several. Very low smoke factor.
JUKEBOX WITH A COUNTRY SONG: Yes.
COMMENTS: Billy Bob's is a breed apart from other honky-tonks. A fun center for the whole family.

Boot Scootin'
7400 Rendon-Bloodworth Road
817/561-2668

Cattle Baron Country
4750 Cattle Baron Drive
817/448-9790

Cheyenne Cattle Co.
Bryant Irvin Road
817/370-2662
GENRE: New Breed/Chain.
COVER CHARGE: Varies.

Country Palace
13325 Highway 287
817/439-2310

Cowboy City
11601 Jacksboro Highway
817/237-8121

Cowtown Opry
The Stockyards
817/626-5329

Crazy Horse Saloon
2411 North Main Street
817/626-6969

Katie Lynn's
3101 Joyce
817/244-7399
GENRE: Traditional/Independent.
COVER CHARGE: Only on New Year's Eve.
DRESS CODE: No tank tops on Friday and Saturday.
CAPACITY: 200.
YEAR OPENED: 1986.
MUSIC: Local and regional bands Wednesday through Sunday nights. Disc jockey on other nights. Mix of country and old rock and roll.
DANCE LESSONS: A customer teaches at the club.
DANCE ETIQUETTE: DJ calls only line dances.
SPECIAL CLUB DANCE: Mostly two-stepping and some line dancing.
DANCE-FLOOR STATS: Two square parquet floors (the one upstairs is 180 square feet, the one downstairs 625 square feet).
LIQUOR: Law prohibits serving one person more than 2 alcoholic beverages at a time.
FOOD: Free popcorn. Buffets provided for special holiday parties and sporting events.
MINIMUM AGE: 21.
SMOKE-FILTERING SYSTEM: Ceiling fans and high ceilings only.

JUKEBOX WITH A COUNTRY SONG: Yes.
COMMENTS: Open 7 days a week from noon until 2 A.M. Holiday and special events almost every month of the year, such as October's Scavenger Hunt and Meat Loaf and Potato Salad Cook-Off. Club also has 2 big-screen TVs for sporting events.

Longhorn Saloon
121 West Exchange Avenue
817/624–4242

GENRE: Traditional/Independent.
COVER CHARGE: Varies nightly.
CAPACITY: 450.
YEAR OPENED: 1919.
MUSIC: National acts. Live music Wednesday through Sunday.
DANCE LESSONS: "If they're good looking and want to learn."
DANCE-FLOOR STATS: One rectangular parquet floor.
FOOD: Vending-machine snacks only.
MINIMUM AGE: 18.
FAMILY NIGHTS: Families welcome any night.
SMOKE-FILTERING SYSTEM: Yes.
LIVE-BULL RIDING: Yes.
COMMENTS: No line dancing! Western Swing Sunday is the first Sunday of every month. Closed on Monday and Tuesday.

Rockin' Rodeo
4200 South Freeway D-2
817/922–0325

GENRE: New Breed/Chain.
COVER CHARGE: Varies nightly.
DRESS CODE: No tank tops or work uniforms.
CAPACITY: 3,500.
YEAR OPENED: 1993.
MUSIC: Disc jockey. Regional and national touring bands only for special concerts.
DANCE-FLOOR STATS: One 3,200-square-foot racetrack parquet floor.
FOOD: Buffet on Friday nights.
MINIMUM AGE: 21.
SMOKE-FILTERING SYSTEM: Yes.
COMMENTS: Closed Monday and Tuesday.

Rodeo Exchange
221 West Exchange Avenue
817/626–0181

GENRE: Traditional/Independent.
COVER CHARGE: Varies nightly.
DRESS CODE: No tank tops, T-shirts, or dirty or torn clothing. Ball caps only permitted on Tuesday, Wednesday, and Thursday.
CAPACITY: 350.
YEAR OPENED: 1986.
MUSIC: Regional touring bands, disc jockey nightly.
DANCE LESSONS: Free on Tuesday and Wednesday nights.
DANCE-FLOOR STATS: One raised 1,200-square-foot rectangular hardwood floor.
MINIMUM AGE: 21.
SMOKE-FILTERING SYSTEM: Yes.
COMMENTS: Open Tuesday through Saturday.

Stagecoach Ballroom
2516 East Belknap
817/831–2261

Texasville
3900 Highway 3775
817/560–7632

White Elephant Saloon
106 East Exchange Avenue
817/624–1887

GENRE: Traditional/Independent.
COVER CHARGE: Only on weekends.
DRESS CODE: Nudity is discouraged.
CAPACITY: 175.
YEAR OPENED: 1976.
MUSIC: Local and regional bands nightly.
DANCE-FLOOR STATS: One raised 290-square-foot rectangular hardwood floor.
FOOD: Peanuts only.
MINIMUM AGE: 18 with parent or guardian. Must be 21 to be served alcohol.
JUKEBOX WITH A COUNTRY SONG: Yes—"nothing but country songs."
COMMENTS: Open 7 days a week. Special events include annual reenactment of 1887 shoot-out between the saloon's owner, Luke Short, and former lawman T. I. "Longhaired Jim" Courtright. Cowboy campfire concerts by Don Edwards 2 or 3 times a year.

Frisco

Broken Spoke Saloon
FM 720 and FM 423
214/335-3444
GENRE: Traditional/Independent.
COVER CHARGE: Only on weekends.
MEMBERSHIP FEE: $2 per year.
DRESS CODE: Collared shirts and dress shorts in summer, collared shirts and jeans–no shorts–in winter.
CAPACITY: 800.
YEAR OPENED: 1992.
MUSIC: Live music nightly by local and regional bands.
DANCE LESSONS: Free on Sunday and Thursday.
DANCE-FLOOR STATS: One 1,300-plus-square-foot racetrack-style epoxy floor.
FOOD: Light service.
MINIMUM AGE: 21.
FAMILY NIGHTS: Children welcome on Sunday only with parent.
SMOKE-FILTERING SYSTEM: Yes.
JUKEBOX WITH A COUNTRY SONG: Yes.
COMMENTS: Closed Monday through Wednesday.

Garland

Big "G" Jamboree
610 West State Street
214/530-5185

Red Onion Club
3211½ Forest Lane
214/487-0819
GENRE: Traditional/Independent.
COVER CHARGE: Only on weekends.
MEMBERSHIP FEE: $5 a year.
CAPACITY: 275.
YEAR OPENED: 1965.
MUSIC: Local bands on Friday and Saturday nights.
DANCE-FLOOR STATS: One 400-square-foot square tile floor.
MINIMUM AGE: 21.
JUKEBOX WITH A COUNTRY SONG: Yes.
COMMENTS: Red Onion was featured as one of the best honky-tonks in "*D*" magazine in 1992. Club sponsors dart and shuffleboard leagues. Wednesday is Karaoke Night. Bring your own dance partner.

Gladewater

Country Showcase
108 East Commerce
214/845-2059

Grand Prairie

Mary's Outpost
1002 South Great Southwest Parkway
214/660-6844

Stepper's Shuffle City
2155 South Great Southwest Parkway
214/988-8249
DANCE LESSONS: Free on Sunday and Monday.

Grapevine

Grapevine Opry
308 South Main Street
817/481-8733

Harlingen

Shooters
3811 West Business 83
210/421-2101

Helotes

John T. Floore's Country Store
14464 Old Bandera Road
210/695-8827
GENRE: Traditional/Independent.

Houston

Black Jack's Ice House
13903 Muscatine
713/453-0288

Blanco's Bar & Grill
3406 West Alabama
713/439-0072
GENRE: Traditional/Independent.
COVER CHARGE: Only on Friday.
DRESS CODE: No nudity.
CAPACITY: 200.
YEAR OPENED: 1981.
MUSIC: Live music on Thursday and Friday by local, regional, and national acts.
DANCE LESSONS: Thursday night.
DANCE-FLOOR STATS: One 850-square-foot rectangular tile floor.
FOOD: Full-service restaurant.
MINIMUM AGE: 21 after 8 P.M.
FAMILY NIGHTS: Monday through Friday. Children may stay after 8 P.M. if accompanied by parent over age 21.
SMOKE-FILTERING SYSTEM: Yes.
JUKEBOX WITH A COUNTRY SONG: Yes.
COMMENTS: Open Monday through Friday. Special promotions such as barbecue, chili, and wild game cook-offs take place throughout the year to benefit various charities.

Cattle Kings Grill
5430 Westheimer
713/623-6000

Cheyenne Club
17460 Northwest Freeway
713/937-6900

Dance Town U.S.A.
7214 Airline Boulevard
713/697-2083

Larkin's Last Frontier
16602 El Camino Real
713/286-1191

Post Oak Ranch
1625 West Loop South
713/627-2624

Rockefeller's
3620 Washington Avenue
713/861-4977

Texas Longhorn #1
1216 Beaumont Highway
713/458-7674

Texas Longhorn Saloon
800 NW Mall
713/683-0386

Wild West
10086 Longpoint
713/465-7121
GENRE: New Breed/Chain.
MUSIC: Disc jockey.

Willie Nelson's Nightlife
921 FM 1960 West #109
713/580-5638

Humble

Back Door
5840 FM 1960 East
713/852-4511

Katy

Mo's Place
21940 Kingsland Boulevard
713/392-3499
GENRE: Traditional/Independent.
COMMENTS: Mo's comes highly recommended.

Killeen

Sam's Station
3310 South Highway 195
817/526-7376

Lancaster

Crystal Chandelier
2520 South Beckley Street
214/223-5898

La Porte

Blondie's Club on the Bayou
1026 South Eighth
713/354-1039

Leon Springs

Leon Springs Dance Hall
24135 Interstate 10 West
210/698-7070

Lewisville

Cadillac Ranch
542 East Highway 121
214/436-0631
COMMENTS: Attracts a younger crowd.

Longview

Reo Palm Isle
903/753-4440

Lubbock

Cowboys
7301 University
806/745-4629

Lonesome Dove
2216 Interstate 27
806/762-3683

Midnight Rodeo
7301 South University
806/745-2813
GENRE: New Breed/Chain.

Luckenbach

Luckenbach Dance Hall
Luckenbach General Store
210/997-3224
GENRE: Traditional/Independent.

Magnolia

Dry Creek Dance Hall
910 FM 1488
713/259-9022

Manvel

Eddie's Country Ballroom
835 Chocolate Mustang Road
713/489-8181

Merkel

Shady Creek Ranch
Route 3
915/846-3012

Mexia

Cowboy Club
South Highway 14
817/562-5307

Midland

Cactus Moon
1008 South Midkiff Road
915/520-0056
GENRE: New Breed/Chain.
COVER CHARGE: Varies.
YEAR OPENED: 1978.
MUSIC: Disc jockey.
DANCE-FLOOR STATS: One 1,700-square-foot rectangular hardwood floor.
MINIMUM AGE: 21.
SMOKE-FILTERING SYSTEM: Yes.
COMMENTS: Closed Sunday and Monday. Owned by Graham Brothers.

Mingus

Trio Club
I-20, 3 miles north of Thurber
817/672-5664
GENRE: Traditional/Independent.
YEAR OPENED: 1960.
MUSIC: Live music on Saturday nights and Sunday afternoons.

Mount Pleasant

Orange Blossom
903/572-3532

Nacogdoches

Jitterbugs
3009-A NW Stallings Drive
409/560-2779
GENRE: New Breed/Independent.
COVER CHARGE: Varies nightly.

MEMBERSHIP FEE: $1 a year. Private club has 32,597 adult members.
DRESS CODE: Men not allowed to wear sleeveless shirts.
CAPACITY: 2,000.
YEAR OPENED: 1993.
MUSIC: Live music by local, regional, and national acts on Friday and Saturday. Disc jockey on Wednesday and Thursday.
DANCE LESSONS: Free on Wednesday.
DANCE-FLOOR STATS: One sunken 4,200-square-foot rectangular hardwood floor.
LIQUOR: Only members can be served alcohol.
FOOD: Vending-machine snacks.
MINIMUM AGE: 18.
FAMILY NIGHTS: Children of any age welcome when accompanied by a parent.
SMOKE-FILTERING SYSTEM: Yes.
COMMENTS: Open Wednesday through Saturday. Music format varies nightly: 80 percent country and 20 percent Top 40 and dance on Wednesday; 70 percent country and 30 percent Top 40 and dance on Thursday; 90 percent country and 10 percent Top 40 and dance on Friday and Saturday. Top five club dances are two-step, polka, waltz, jitterbug, and Tush Push. Jitterbugs has indoor fireworks nightly. Although it is a new club, it received recognition by the William Morris Agency as "Club of the Quarter" in the summer of 1994.

New Braunfels

Gruene Hall
1281 Gruene Road
210/606-1281
GENRE: Traditional/Independent.
COVER CHARGE: Varies nightly, but usually only on Saturday.
CAPACITY: 500.
YEAR OPENED: 1878; under current ownership since 1975.
MUSIC: Local, regional, and national acts nightly, except Mondays from Memorial Day through Labor Day, then Thursday through Sunday the rest of the year.
DANCE-FLOOR STATS: One 1,600-square-foot rectangular hardwood floor.
LIQUOR: Only beer and wine are served here. No alcohol may be brought in. Law prohibits serving alcohol after midnight Monday through Friday and Sunday, after 1 A.M. on Saturday, and before noon on Sunday.
FOOD: Vending-machine snacks. Grist Mill restaurant located 50 feet behind Gruene Hall on the Guadalupe River.
MINIMUM AGE: All ages.
FAMILY NIGHTS: Every night.
COMMENTS: Texas's oldest continually operating dance hall. Many special events throughout the year.

Odessa

Cheers
815 North Grandview
915/334-9941
GENRE: New Breed/Chain.
COVER CHARGE: Varies.
YEAR OPENED: 1972.
MUSIC: Disc jockey. Special concerts by national acts.
DANCE-FLOOR STATS: One very slippery square hardwood floor.
MINIMUM AGE: 21.
SMOKE-FILTERING SYSTEM: Yes.
MECHANICAL BULL: On occasion.
COMMENTS: Wednesday is rock-and-roll night.

Pasadena

BJ's Beer Garden
5329 Spencer Highway
713/487-7219

Bushwacker's
1001 East Southmore Avenue, #509
713/473-4410

Texas Saloon
7337 Spencer Highway
713/476-9213

Plano

Country Fair
3312 North Central Expressway
214/424-7224

Porter

Glenda's Lounge
2304 Ford Road
713/354-1039

Richardson

W. W. Fairfield's
147 North Plano Road
214/231-3844
DANCE LESSONS: Free on Sunday.

Richmond

Big Steve's County Line Market/ Ice House
19412 FM 1093
713/492-7500

Brazos Bottom Bar & Grill
7010 FM 762
713/341-5210

Rockwall

Southern Junction Nightclub & Steakhouse
Highway 276, 5 miles east of FM 205
214/771-2418
GENRE: Traditional/Independent.
COVER CHARGE: Varies nightly.
MEMBERSHIP FEE: Yes. It's a "dry" county so memberships are required. Unicard memberships accepted.
DRESS CODE: No cutoffs or tank tops.
CAPACITY: 1,200.
YEAR OPENED: 1986.
MUSIC: Live music by local bands. Disc jockey on band breaks. Special concerts by national acts.
DANCE LESSONS: Free on Thursday.
DANCE ETIQUETTE: Rules are posted.
DANCE-FLOOR STATS: One 2,000-square-foot square parquet floor.
FOOD: Steak and chicken, separate snack bar.
MINIMUM AGE: 18.
FAMILY NIGHTS: Children are welcome any day, but if under 18 and not accompanied by their own parent they must leave by 10:30 P.M. Wednesday, Thursday, and Friday it is Family Night until closing.
SMOKE-FILTERING SYSTEM: Yes.
COMMENTS: Open Wednesday through Saturday.

San Angelo

Old Coach Inn
4205 South Bryant
915/653-6966
COMMENTS: Older clientele.

Santa Fe Junction
1524 South Bryant
915/658-5068
COMMENTS: Younger clientele.

San Antonio

Cibolo Creek Country Club
8640 East Evans Road
210/651-6652
GENRE: Traditional/Independent.

Country Gold
7405 Pearsall Road
210/623-1760

Coyote's
8759 Grissom
210/647-4695

Dallas
2335 NW Military Highway
210/349-9469
GENRE: New Breed/Chain.

Farmer's Daughter
542 White
210/333-7391

Midnight Rodeo
12260 Nacogdoches
210/655-0040
GENRE: New Breed/Chain.

COVER CHARGE: Varies nightly depending on drink specials.
DRESS CODE: No ball caps; all men must wear collared shirts.
CAPACITY: 2,000.
YEAR OPENED: 1982.
MUSIC: Disc jockey plays 80 percent country western, 20 percent Top 40. Live acts twice a month.
DANCE LESSONS: $2 a person on Thursday nights.
DANCE-FLOOR STATS: One raised racetrack hardwood floor. One-eighth mile in length.
FOOD: Complimentary supper buffet until 8 P.M. 6 nights a week.
MINIMUM AGE: 21; 18 and up on Sundays only.
SMOKE-FILTERING SYSTEM: Yes.
COMMENTS: Closed Monday and Tuesday. Club sponsors a yearly Christmas toy drive for children with a giant stocking that is listed in *Ripley's Believe It or Not* as "the largest in the world." It also sponsors an annual chili cook-off benefiting the National Kidney Foundation.

Texas Country Down Under
258 Central Park Mall
210/340-8811

Selma

Blue Bonnet Palace
16847 Interstate 35 North
210/651-6702

Southlake

The Ranch of Lonesome Dove
2299 Lonesome Dove
817/329-1100
LIQUOR: BYOB.
COMMENTS: A younger clientele.

Spring

Midnight Rodeo
19959 Holzwarth
713/353-8898
GENRE: New Breed/Chain.
CAPACITY: 900.
MUSIC: Disc jockey.

Stephenville

City Limits
1802 East Washington
817/968-5222

Sunnyvale

Cripple Creek County Line
774 East Highway 80
214/226-6236

Temple

Cactus Canyon
4501 South General Bruce Drive
817/778-2727

Terrell

Lee's Silver Fox
1708 Highway 34 South
214/563-7644
GENRE: New Breed/Independent.
COVER CHARGE: Varies nightly.
DRESS CODE: No ball caps, cutoffs, or shorts for men.
CAPACITY: 1,850.
YEAR OPENED: 1982.
MUSIC: Live music by local bands on Friday and Saturday. Disc jockey plays mix of Top 40, dance, and country on band breaks. Major label national acts for special concerts.
DANCE-FLOOR STATS: One floating 5,000-square-foot rectangular hardwood floor.
FOOD: Popcorn and hot dogs available at the bar.
MINIMUM AGE: 18.
SMOKE-FILTERING SYSTEM: Yes.
COMMENTS: Only open on Friday and Saturday. On Amateur Nights anyone can sing with the band during the midnight set.

Uvalde

Purple Sage
210/278-1006

Waco

Cody's
6512 Woodway
817/776-6134

Melody Ranch
2315 Robinson Drive
817/662-0842

Wichita Falls

Cheyenne Cattle Co.
3711-C Callfield
817/696-0055

GENRE: New Breed/Chain.
COVER CHARGE: Varies nightly.
DRESS CODE: On Western Nights (Wednesday, Friday, and Saturday) guests must have collars on shirts, no ball caps, soiled or worn clothing. Alternative Nights (Tuesday, Thursday, and Sunday) are very casual.
CAPACITY: 820.
YEAR OPENED: 1985.
MUSIC: Primarily disc jockey with local, regional, and national bands for special concerts.
DANCE LESSONS: Free.
DANCE ETIQUETTE: Disc jockey calls dances.
DANCE-FLOOR STATS: One raised 1,200-square-foot rectangular hardwood floor.
MINIMUM AGE: 16 and up allowed in with parent or guardian any night; 18 and up on Tuesday, Thursday, Friday, and Sunday nights; 21 and up on Wednesday and Saturday nights.
SMOKE-FILTERING SYSTEM: Yes.
MECHANICAL BULL: On occasion.
COMMENTS: Sponsors many special promotions throughout the year such as the Golden Boots Dance Contest, the Cowboy Cadillac Contest, and the "Cheyenne Chute Out" mechanical bull contest. Official sponsor of the Texas Ranch Round-Up, the largest ranch roundup rodeo competition in the United States.

Yoakum

Country Music U.S.A.
1226 East Gonzales
512/293-5426

UTAH

Salt Lake City

The Bay
404 SW Temple
801/363-2623

COMMENTS: Two country nights for teens.

Charley's Club
2827 South State
801/483-9167

Country Christi's
3793 South State
801/261-9111

Upper Country
3500 South Main Street
801/466-6664

The Westerner Private Club
3360 South Redwood Road
801/972-5447

GENRE: Traditional/Independent.
COVER CHARGE: Varies nightly.
MEMBERSHIP FEE: $15 annual fee; $5 two-week guest membership.
DRESS CODE: Basic country attire. Jeans and T-shirts okay, but no tank tops.
CAPACITY: 850.
YEAR OPENED: 1965.
MUSIC: Live music nightly by local bands, regional and national touring bands. Disc jockey on band breaks. Special concerts by national acts.
DANCE LESSONS: Free.
DANCE ETIQUETTE: Rules are posted and DJ calls dances.
DANCE-FLOOR STATS: One raised 3,300-square-foot rectangular hardwood floor.

FOOD: Full-service restaurant with dirt-cheap prices.
MINIMUM AGE: 21.
SMOKE-FILTERING SYSTEM: Yes.
COMMENTS: Memberships are required and sponsored guests must be over 21. Closed only on Sunday nights. Sponsors pre-concert and pre-rodeo events with local radio stations and an annual Deer Hunter Widows' Ball.

Sandy

Sandy's Station
8925 South 255 West
801/255-2289
GENRE: Traditional/Independent.
COVER CHARGE: Only on weekends.
MEMBERSHIP FEE: $29 a year. No cover charge for members. Guests may purchase a two-week temporary membership for $6.
DRESS CODE: No tank tops or soiled or torn clothes.
CAPACITY: 750.
YEAR OPENED: 1990.
MUSIC: Local, regional, and national acts perform Wednesday through Sunday.
DANCE LESSONS: Saturday night line dance lesson is free. All other lessons Sunday through Wednesday for a fee.
DANCE ETIQUETTE: Rules are posted.
DANCE-FLOOR STATS: One springboard 1,200-square-foot rectangular parquet floor.
FOOD: Full-service restaurant.
MINIMUM AGE: 21.
SMOKE-FILTERING SYSTEM: Yes.
COMMENTS: This is a private club for members only that is open 7 days a week. Temporary guest memberships are available if sponsored by a member.

VERMONT

Barre

Billy Bob's
Main Street
802/479-5664

Ludlow

Coyote Crossing
802/228-7400

Rutland

Broomsticks
802/775-6789

White River Junction

Cactus Jack's
3 Bowling Lane
802/296-5853

VIRGINIA

Alexandria

The Birchmere
3901 Mount Vernon Avenue
703/549-5919
COMMENTS: This is a Pickers club–no dancing allowed. Tickets required for entry.

Cowboys
8501 Richmond Highway
703/360-8322

GW's
1319 King Street
703/739-2274
GENRE: Traditional/Independent.
MUSIC: Local and regional bands every night but Monday.
DANCE LESSONS: Free.
DANCE-FLOOR STATS: Small hardwood floor.
MINIMUM AGE: 21.

Zed Restaurant & Public House
6151 Richmond Highway
703/768-5558
GENRE: Traditional/Independent.
COVER CHARGE: Never. A $10 or $15 minimum for special concerts is applied to food or drink purchase.
DRESS CODE: Proper attire after 8 P.M. Collared shirts for men; no tank tops for men.
CAPACITY: 250.
MUSIC: Live music nightly; national acts for special concerts.
DANCE LESSONS: Free.
DANCE-FLOOR STATS: One 600-square-foot hardwood floor.
FOOD: Full-service restaurant.
MINIMUM AGE: 21 to drink.
FAMILY NIGHTS: Families welcome any time.
JUKEBOX WITH A COUNTRY SONG: Yes.
COMMENTS: Open from 11 A.M. to 1:30 A.M.

Fairfax

Red Moon Saloon
Holiday Inn
11787 Lee Jackson Highway
703/352-2525

Fredericksburg

Houston's Steakhouse & Saloon
1917 Princess Anne Street
703/371-0300

Harrisonburg

The Round-Up
Route 42 South
703/344-6510

Herndon

Cactus Cowboy Grill
724 Tine Street
703/435-3800

Newport News

D&D Corral
16912 Warwick Boulevard
804/887-0424
GENRE: Traditional/Independent.

Rhinestone Cowboy
Heartbreak Alley
100 Newmarket Square West
804/245-3313
GENRE: New Breed/Independent.
COVER CHARGE: Varies nightly.
DRESS CODE: No ball caps or torn jeans.
YEAR OPENED: 1992.
MUSIC: Disc jockey. National acts for special concerts.
DANCE LESSONS: Free.
DANCE ETIQUETTE: DJ calls dances.
SPECIAL CLUB DANCE: RC Stomp.
DANCE-FLOOR STATS: One oblong tile floor.
FOOD: Full-service restaurant (buffet from 4 to 7 P.M.).
MINIMUM AGE: 21.
FAMILY NIGHTS: Sunday.
SMOKE-FILTERING SYSTEM: Yes.
COMMENTS: Rock-and-roll club adjacent.

Norfolk

The Banque
1849 East Little Creek Road
804/480-3600

Richmond

Bronco's
11001 Midlothian Turnpike
804/379-0242
GENRE: Traditional/Independent.
COVER CHARGE: $2 before 8 P.M.; $3 after 9 P.M.
CAPACITY: 640.
MUSIC: Local and regional bands; national acts for special concerts.
DANCE-FLOOR STATS: 1.
COMMENTS: Dance floor is poorly situated.

Dakota's
Innsbrook Plaza
4036 Cox Road
804/346-2100

GENRE: Traditional/Independent.
COVER CHARGE: Varies.
MUSIC: Local and regional bands.
MINIMUM AGE: 21.
SMOKE-FILTERING SYSTEM: Yes.
FOOD: Full-service restaurant.

Longhorn Saloon & Grille
804/262–0075
GENRE: Traditional/Independent.
COVER CHARGE: Varies.

Roanoke

Valley Country
3348 Salem Turnpike NW
804/344–6510
DANCE-FLOOR STATS: Three floors, one is a "training pen."

Springfield

Blackie's
6710 Commerce Street
703/971–4200
GENRE: Traditional/Independent.
COVER CHARGE: Varies.
MUSIC: Local and regional bands.
DANCE-FLOOR STATS: One moderate-sized square hardwood floor.
FAMILY NIGHTS: Sunday.

Woodbridge

Chapps
1309 Jefferson Plaza
703/551–4408

Skinifatz
703/550–9252

WASHINGTON

Auburn

Gerry Andal's Ranch
635 "C" Street SW
206/833–5251
GENRE: New Breed/Chain.
COVER CHARGE: Only on weekends.
CAPACITY: 500.
YEAR OPENED: 1993.
MUSIC: Bands alternate with disc jockeys every 30 minutes. No bands on Monday and Tuesday nights.
DANCE LESSONS: $2 per person nightly.
DANCE ETIQUETTE: Rules are posted.
DANCE-FLOOR STATS: One 840-square-foot rectangular hardwood floor.
FOOD: Full-service restaurant.
MINIMUM AGE: 21 after 10 P.M.
FAMILY NIGHTS: 7 to 10 P.M. nightly.
SMOKE-FILTERING SYSTEM: Yes.
COMMENTS: Open 7 nights a week.

Everett

Gerry Andal's Ranch
620 SE Everett Mall Way
206/355–7999
GENRE: New Breed/Chain.
COVER CHARGE: Only on weekends.
CAPACITY: 600.
YEAR OPENED: 1986.
MUSIC: Bands alternate with disc jockeys every 30 minutes. No bands on Monday and Tuesday nights.
DANCE LESSONS: $2 per person nightly.
DANCE ETIQUETTE: Rules are posted.
DANCE-FLOOR STATS: One 896-square-foot rectangular parquet floor.
FOOD: Full-service restaurant.
MINIMUM AGE: 21 after 10 P.M.
FAMILY NIGHTS: 7 to 10 P.M. nightly.
SMOKE-FILTERING SYSTEM: Yes.
COMMENTS: Open 7 nights a week.

Marysville

Billy Bob's
1352 State Avenue
206/653–3333

Olympia

Gerry Andal's Ranch
7842 Trails End Drive SE
206/943–6330
GENRE: New Breed/Chain.
COVER CHARGE: Only on weekends.

CAPACITY: 400.
YEAR OPENED: 1994.
MUSIC: Bands alternate with disc jockeys every 30 minutes. No bands on Monday and Tuesday nights.
DANCE LESSONS: $2 per person nightly.
DANCE ETIQUETTE: Rules are posted.
DANCE-FLOOR STATS: Two 534-square-foot rectangular parquet floors.
FOOD: Full-service restaurant.
MINIMUM AGE: 21 after 10 P.M.
FAMILY NIGHTS: 7 to 10 P.M. nightly.
SMOKE-FILTERING SYSTEM: Yes.
COMMENTS: Open 7 nights a week. Olympia bar and restaurant is part of a horse show arena.

Rochester

The Red Barn
6222 197th SW
206/273-5439

Seattle

The Riverside Inn
14060 Interurban Avenue South
206/244-5400
GENRE: Traditional/Independent.
COVER CHARGE: Only on weekends.
CAPACITY: 500.
YEAR OPENED: 1963.
MUSIC: Local, regional, national touring bands 7 nights a week. National acts about once every 6 weeks.
DANCE LESSONS: Free 7 nights a week.
DANCE ETIQUETTE: Yes. Rules are posted.
DANCE-FLOOR STATS: One square 800-square-foot hardwood floor.
FOOD: Full-service restaurant open 24 hours; vending-machine snacks.
MINIMUM AGE: 21.
JUKEBOX WITH A COUNTRY SONG: Yes.
COMMENTS: Open for business 24 hours a day, 365 days a year. Yes, even on Christmas.

Timberline Tavern
2015 Boren
206/622-6220
GENRE: Gay/Independent.

Soap Lake

Soap Lake Businessmen's Club
GENRE: Traditional/Private Club.
MEMBERSHIP FEE: Yes.
COMMENTS: Honky-tonk home of Bonnie Guitar. Guest passes available.

Spokane

Chili D's
152 South Browne Street
509/455-9210

Sunset Junction
West 1801 Sunset
509/455-9131
GENRE: New Breed/Independent.
CAPACITY: 194.
YEAR OPENED: 1993.
MUSIC: Disc jockey during week and local bands on Friday and Saturday.
DANCE-FLOOR STATS: One moderate-size rectangular tile floor.
FOOD: Full-service restaurant.
MINIMUM AGE: 21 to drink; children must leave by 9 P.M.
SMOKE-FILTERING SYSTEM: Yes.
JUKEBOX WITH A COUNTRY SONG: Yes.
COMMENTS: Open 7 nights a week.

Tacoma

Denim & Diamonds
GENRE: New Breed/Chain.
YEAR OPENED: Opening slated for 1995.
MUSIC: Disc jockey.
COMMENTS: Owned by Graham Brothers. Still under construction at time of publication. Call information for address and phone number.

Vancouver

Dodge City Bar & Grill
7201 NE 18th Street
206/253-6603

Wenatchee

T. J. Cooper's
27 South Chelan
509/663-1227

WEST VIRGINIA

Huntington

Mill Runn
Ramada Inn
5600 U.S. Route 60 East
304/736-3451

WISCONSIN

Green Bay

Grizzly Rose Saloon
1905 North Irwin Avenue
414/433-9521

Lake Geneva

Longhorn Ranch
West 2565 Kruger Road
414/248-3344

Milwaukee

Bronco Billy's
3555 South 27th Street
414/643-9440

Kicker Corral
11400 West Silver Springs Road
414/463-1347

WYOMING

Cheyenne

Cheyenne Club
1617 Capitol Avenue
307/635-7777

Cowboy South
312 South Greeley Highway
307/637-3800

Hitchen' Post Inn
1700 West Lincolnway
307/638-3301

Little Bear Inn
Take Interstate 25 North, Exit 16, Little Bear Road North
307/634-3684

GENRE: Traditional/Independent.
COVER CHARGE: Never.
CAPACITY: 250.
YEAR OPENED: 1958.
MUSIC: Live country music Tuesday through Saturday by local bands.
DANCE-FLOOR STATS: One racetrack tile floor.
FOOD: Full-service restaurant.
MINIMUM AGE: All ages.
FAMILY NIGHTS: Children welcome any time.
SMOKE-FILTERING SYSTEM: Yes.
COMMENTS: Cheyenne's original steakhouse. Open 7 days a week.

The Outlaw
Knight's Inn
3839 East Lincolnway
307/635-7552

Cody

Proud Cut
1227 Sheridan Avenue
307/527-6905

Evanston

Legal Tender
Dunmar Inn
1601 Harrison Drive
307/789-3770

Jackson Hole

Million Dollar Cowboy Bar
25 North Cache Street
307/733-2207

GENRE: Traditional/Independent.

COVER CHARGE: Varies nightly.
DRESS CODE: Shirts and shoes required.
CAPACITY: 350.
YEAR OPENED: 1910.
MUSIC: Local, regional, and national acts nightly.
DANCE LESSONS: Free on Thursdays.
DANCE-FLOOR STATS: One 120-square-foot hardwood floor.
FOOD: Full-service steakhouse in basement.
MINIMUM AGE: 21.
SMOKE-FILTERING SYSTEM: Yes.
COMMENTS: Open 7 days a week.

Rancher Spirits & Billiards
20 East Broadway
307/733-3886

Laramie

Cowboy Saloon & Dance Hall
108 South Second Street
307/721-3165
GENRE: Traditional/Independent.

Rock Springs

Saddle-Lite Saloon
1704 Elk Street
307/362-8704

Thayne

Dad's Bar
383 North Main Street
307/883-2300
GENRE: Traditional/Independent.
COVER CHARGE: Never.
CAPACITY: 240.
YEAR OPENED: 1933.
MUSIC: Local and regional bands on Friday and Saturday.
DANCE LESSONS: Free lessons for one 4-week period during the year.
DANCE-FLOOR STATS: 1.
FOOD: Steaks and chicken on weekends only. Vending-machine snacks all other times.
MINIMUM AGE: 21.
JUKEBOX WITH A COUNTRY SONG: Yes.
COMMENTS: Open 7 days a week. Dad's pulls four "all-nighters" a year: New Year's Eve, Memorial Day, Pioneer Day (July 24th), and October 3rd weekend for the Hunter's Ball.

Wilson

Stagecoach Bar
Highway 22
307/733-4407
GENRE: Traditional/Independent.
COVER CHARGE: Never.
CAPACITY: 185.
YEAR OPENED: 1939
MUSIC: Same house band since 1968 on Sunday nights, disc jockey now and then, CD jukebox during the week.
DANCE-FLOOR STATS: One 450-square-foot rectangular tile floor.
FOOD: Full-service restaurant and free popcorn.
MINIMUM AGE: 21.
FAMILY NIGHTS: Children allowed in cafe only.
SMOKE-FILTERING SYSTEM: Yes.
JUKEBOX WITH A COUNTRY SONG: Yes.
COMMENTS: Open 7 nights a week, but state law requires that bar close at 10 P.M. on Sundays.

Bibliography

Abramovitch, Ingrid, and Chodan, Lucinda. "Honky-Tonk Holiday: Two Gals on a Tear in Texas," *The Wall Street Journal,* September 1, 1994.

Appleford, Steve. "Pumping Life Back Into the Old Pal," *Los Angeles Times,* August 2, 1994.

Atkinson, Jim. "The Bar Bar," *Texas Monthly,* May 1983.

———. "The 89 Greatest Texas Bars," *Texas Monthly,* May 1983.

Baird, Robert. "The Arizona Roadhouse," *New Times,* February 26–March 3, 1992.

Brinkhoff, Peg. "Dressed in the West," *Country America,* October 1993.

———. "The King of Clubs," *Country America,* February 1994.

Bruce, Bob. "Honky-Tonk Heavens," *Texas Highways.* Austin: Texas State Highway Department, February 1990.

Country Music Foundation, et al. *Country: The Music and the Musicians.* New York: Abbeville Press, 1994.

Dary, David. *Cowboy Culture: A Saga of Five Centuries.* Kansas: Univ. of Kansas Press, 1989.

Davis, John T. "Broken Spoke's 30th Anniversary," *Austin American-Statesman,* November 10, 1994.

DeWeese, Daniel. "Mo'Betta: Riding on Garth's Shirttails," *That's Country,* September 1993.

Dooley, Kirk. *The Book of Texas Bests.* Dallas: Taylor Publishing Co., 1988.

Flodin, Mickey and Carol. *The Country Western Guide to Life.* Chicago: Contemporary Books, 1993.

Garcia, Guy. "Scoot Your Booty," *Time,* March 15, 1993.

Gilchriest, Gail. *The Cowgirl Companion.* New York: Hyperion, 1993.

Goettsch, Curt. "50 Country Hot Spots," *Country America,* April 1993.

Harris, Pat. "Heel, Toe, Do-Si-Do," *Music City News,* 1992.

Henderson, S. D. "The Ultimate Honky-Tonk Tour," *D Magazine,* November 1992.

BIBLIOGRAPHY

Jennings, William Dale. *The Cowboys.* New York: Bantam, 1972.

McEntire, Reba with Tom Carter. *Reba: My Story.* New York: Bantam, 1994.

Manning, Anita. "Life in '94 Will Offer Glimpse Into Next Century," *USA Today,* December 22, 1993.

Marrin, Albert. *Cowboys, Indians and Gunfighters.* New York: Atheneum, 1993.

Mather, Andrea. "Wild Strides," *Western Styles,* August 1994.

Nash, Alanna. "This Ain't No Honky-Tonk!" *Entertainment Weekly,* April 23, 1993.

Painton, Priscilla. "Country Rocks the Boomers," *Time,* March 30, 1992.

Riley, Rene E. "Hats Off!," *Western Styles,* August 1994.

———. "Kick & Pivot," *Western Styles,* February 1994.

Savage, William W. Jr. *The Cowboy Hero.* Norman: Univ. of Oklahoma Press, 1979.

Seo, Diane. "In Los Angeles, Tough Guys Do Dance," *Los Angeles Times,* 1994.

Stambler, Irwin and Grelun Landon. *The Encyclopedia of Folk, Country & Western Music.* New York: St. Martin's Press, 1984.

Tetreault, Eileen. "Squares Dance: Why We're a Country Capital," *The Washington Post,* October 7, 1990.

———. "Praising Arizona: Honky-Tonk Nights in Phoenix," *The Washington Post,* September 1, 1991.

Tichi, Cecilia. *High Lonesome: The American Culture of Country Music.* Chapel Hill: Univ. of North Carolina Press, 1994.

Unknown author. "Broken Spoke a Country Music Landmark," *Austin American-Statesman,* December 17, 1988.

Unknown author. "Ten Best Roadhouses," *Car and Driver,* January 1992.

Unknown author. "The City," *Daily Ardmoreite.* Ardmore, Chickasaw Nation, Indian Territory, February 27, 1894.

Woolley, Bryan. *The Edge of the West.* El Paso: Texas Western Press UTEP, 1990.

———. Kay Cattarulla, ed. "Beer, Burgers and Patsy Cline," *Texas Bound.* Dallas: Southern Methodist Univ. Press, 1986.

Zimmerman, David. "Foreign Video Channel Improves Singers Reception," *USA Today,* March 29, 1994.